THROUGH A GLASS DARKLY

BERNARD LONERGAN & RICHARD RORTY ON KNOWING WITHOUT A GOD'S-EYE VIEW

THROUGH A GLASS DARKLY

BERNARD LONERGAN & RICHARD RORTY ON KNOWING WITHOUT A GOD'S-EYE VIEW

by

R. J. SNELL

MARQUETTE
UNIVERSITY
PRESS

MARQUETTE STUDIES IN PHILOSOPHY
NO. 45
ANDREW TALLON, SERIES EDITOR

Library of Congress Cataloging-in-Publication Data

Snell, R. J., 1975-
Through a glass darkly : Bernard Lonergan and Richard Rorty on knowing without a God's-eye view / by R. J. Snell.
    p. cm. — (Marquette studies in philosophy ; No. 45)
Includes bibliographical references and index.
ISBN-13: 978-0-87462-668-1 (pbk. : alk. paper)
ISBN-10: 0-87462-668-4 (pbk. : alk. paper)
1. Knowledge, Theory of. 2. Lonergan, Bernard J. F. 3. Rorty, Richard. I. Title.
BD161.S62 2006
121—dc22
                                                              2006026574

© 2006 Marquette University Press
Milwaukee, Wisconsin 53201-3141
www.marquette.edu/mupress/
Second printing 2010

♾ The paper used in this publication meets the minimum requirements of the American National Standard for Information Sciences— Permanence of Paper for Printed Library Materials, ANSI Z39.48-1992.

Cover photo from the Basilica of Saint Denis by Andrew J. Tallon

MARQUETTE UNIVERSITY PRESS
MILWAUKEE

The Association of Jesuit University Presses

TABLE OF CONTENTS

ABBREVIATIONS

AOC   *Achieving Our Country*. Cambridge, MA: Harvard University Press, 1998.

C   *Collection: Papers by Bernard Lonergan, SJ*. Edited by F. E. Crowe. New York: Herder and Herder, 1966.

CIS   *Contingency, irony and solidarity*. New York: Cambridge University Press, 1989.

COP   *Consequences of Pragmatism*. Minneapolis: University of Minnesota Press, 1982.

EHO   *Philosophical Papers*. Vol. 2, *Essays on Heidegger and Others*. New York: Cambridge University Press, 1991.

I   *Collected Works of Bernard Lonergan*. Edited by Frederick E. Crowe and Robert M. Doran. Vol. 3, *Insight: A Study of Human Understanding*. Toronto: University of Toronto Press, 1997.

LR   *The Lonergan Reader*, eds. Mark D. Morelli and Elizabeth A. Morelli. Toronto: University of Toronto Press, 1997.

M   *Method in Theology*. New York: Seabury Press, 1972.

ORT   *Philosophical Papers*. Vol. 1, *Objectivism, Relativism, and Truth*. New York: Cambridge University Press, 1991.

PMN   *Philosophy and the Mirror of Nature*. Princeton: Princeton University Press, 1979.

PSH   *Philosophy and Social Hope*. New York: Penguin, 1999.

SC   *A Second Collection*. Edited by William F.J. Ryan and Bernard J. Tyrrell. Toronto: University of Toronto Press, 1974.

TP   *Philosophical Papers*. Vol. 3. *Truth and Progress*. New York: Cambridge University Press, 1998.

UB   *Collected Works of Bernard Lonergan*. Edited by Elizabeth A. Morelli and Mark D. Morelli. Vol. 5, *Understanding and Being: The Halifax Lectures on INSIGHT*. Toronto: University of Toronto Press, 1990.

V   *Collected Works of Bernard Lonergan*. Edited by Frederick E. Crowe and Robert M. Doran. Vol. 2, *Verbum: Word and Idea in Aquinas*. Toronto: University of Toronto Press, 1997.

ACKNOWLEDGEMENTS

While philosophical work is often performed in solitude, it is never done in isolation. I have had the good fortune of friends, teachers, and mentors to assist me in this work. To them I owe much gratitude.

Dr. Andrew Tallon, has graciously formed my mind and work, both in classes and through the completion of this project. His kindness and good-will in providing an independent study of Lonergan and in encouraging this research allowed not only this work but also provides the roots of my ongoing questions and concerns. He has shown me much patience and care throughout and remains a model of the Transcendental Precepts in act.

Additionally, Dr. Stanley Harrison, Fr. Walter Stohrer, and Fr. Thomas Krettek read the manuscript. I thank each of them for their close readings and corrections which allowed me to avoid errors and improve my writing and research substantially. I was struck by their concern for the research and their respect for me as a young scholar. I can repay my debt only by acknowledging my own respect for them.

In addition, I thank the Department of Philosophy and the Graduate School at Marquette University for their generous financial support during my time of study and writing, first as a teaching assistant and then through a Rev. J.P. Raynor, S.J. Fellowship.

My parents have provided many prayers and encouragement. I am humbled by their support. And there are no words sufficient to express my gratitude to Amy, who puts up with the odd hours and habits of an academic, and whose love seems inexhaustible. Thank you.

Finally, I am honored to have received so much of my education at Jesuit institutions. In the spirit of the rigorous and robust tradition of the Society of Jesus I offer this work: *Ad Majorem Dei Gloriam.*

CHAPTER I
INTUITIONISM & THE END OF PHILOSOPHY

Recent times have seen the rise to prominence of various doctrines
which tend to devalue even the truths which had been judged certain. A legitimate plurality of positions has yielded to an undifferentiated pluralism, based upon the assumption that all positions are
equally valid, which is one of today's most widespread symptoms of
the lack of confidence in truth... On this understanding, everything
is reduced to opinion; and there is a sense of being adrift... With
a false modesty, people rest content with partial and provisional
truths, no longer seeking to ask radical questions about the meaning and ultimate foundation of human, personal and social existence. In short, the hope that philosophy might be able to provide
definitive answers to these questions has dwindled.

(John Paul II, *Fides et Ratio*, §5)

1.1 THE END OF PHILOSOPHY

Philosophy began as inquiry into the best way to live, but from
its advent philosophy has only with difficulty justified its existence. To ask questions about the best manner of living implies
that the norms of the culture are potentially inadequate and revisable.
Conventional wisdom—the opinions, laws, myths and narratives of
the culture—which the vast majority of people assume to be normative or natural, are relegated to mere custom in the face of the philosopher's questions. Consequently, philosophy threatens to disrupt
the preservation of order within the culture. Potential enemies of order, philosophers are subsequently charged with hubris for examining
things on earth and in heaven, for making the weaker argument appear stronger and for displacing the gods of the city with their questions. Philosophy is thought to be useless or dangerous and eventually
the philosopher is rejected or killed.

Of course, the lives of most philosophers are hardly as dramatic as
that of Socrates, but the Platonic need to differentiate philosophy from
sophistry and to defend the functions of philosophy continues. Thomas Aquinas felt compelled to defend the functions of reason against

fideistic rejections of Greek paganism. Kant suffered through the seeming irrelevance of philosophy in the face of the natural sciences, and subsequent centuries unveiled the shrinking glory of the queen of the sciences to the continual advances of natural science, social science and psychology. The decreasing domain of philosophy and doubts of its supremacy have good precedence, but unique to late modernity is the attack on philosophy from within its own ranks.

Since Nietzsche's attack on Socrates, it is not uncommon for philosophers to hold that philosophy held wrong assumptions since the beginning, and just as a small miscalculation made early in a math equation results in a grossly incorrect answer or as an imperceptible variance in initial trajectory results in missing the target by a huge margin, so these early assumptions perverted the course of philosophy. Thus philosophy's attempt to maintain some relevance for itself by downplaying its task from the study of Being to a theory of knowledge is insufficient, since it is still plagued by logocentrism, onto-theology, the metaphysics of presence and so on.

The editors of the influential anthology *After Philosophy: End or Transformation?* note four common themes in the contemporary call to abandon philosophy (Baynes, Bohman and McCarthy 1987, 3-7):

> 1. *Against the claims that reason involves universality and necessity, stress is placed on the "contingency and conventionality of the rules, criteria, and products of what counts as rational speech and action at any given time and place"* (3). Logic and the canons of reason are not universal but local, the language games within which thought occurs are incommensurable, and items of belief are tangled within a web of other beliefs which are themselves entangled and impossible to justify in any immediacy of self-evidence. In short, any and all foundations are impossible (4). The impossibility of foundations does away with any Archimedean point, any god's-eye view from which to arbitrate competing claims, and all systems of rationality become contextual and perspectival—pure reason has become impure.
>
> 2. *The assumption of the sovereign rational subject is nullified* (4). No longer is it possible to accept the Cartesian subject—disembodied, autonomous, atomistic—or any transcendental subjectivity fleeing the finitude of the body, the enculturation of a tradition, the biases and passions of the unconscious or the emotions. Dispelling with the myth of the pure presence of self, the subject is no longer ca-

pable of providing absolute objectivity and autonomy and is itself disclosed only within the linguistic world (4).

3. *No longer is knowledge considered as representation or mirroring of reality* (4). Previously, the subject was considered to stand "here" over against the world of objects "over there". In addition to rejecting this image and the problem of bridging the subject/object gap, the notion of an objective and independent world is now called into question. There is no independent world of given facts and "the object of knowledge is always already pre-interpreted, situated in a scheme, part of a text, outside of which there are only other texts" (5). Consequently, there is no method, no process, by which to "get it right" or know the world as it is in and of itself, at best there is interpretation or even just "coping" with the world.

4. *Philosophy is not an exalted science but merely another genre of literature* (5). Reason is not somehow purer than rhetoric, poetry or literature, but is just another style or tradition of persuasion. Only by ignoring rhetorical devices and strategies within philosophy has the tradition succumbed to the illusion that philosophy engages in pure thought. Plato utilized rhetoric to attack the rhetoricians, and philosophy does so still.

Of course, there is disagreement on what task remains for philosophy given these critiques, but there is wide agreement that philosophy in the Platonic-Cartesian-Kantian tradition is to be abandoned.

I contend that a major cause of the disillusionment with philosophy is the fall from grace of *intuitionism*. By intuitionism I mean *the position holding that knowing is somehow like looking*. Giovanni Sala (1994) explains:

> For intuitionism, the essence of knowledge in general lies in a kind of looking or intuition…it is obvious that seeing, in the primary and genuine sense of the word, is an act that is capable of achieving transcendence. My eyes are in my head, seeing is something I do with my eyes, and yet I reach with my seeing something that lies outside of me…Thus intuitionism rests upon the following principle: an intuitive act is the transcendental condition of the possibility of the objectivity (in the sense of transcendence) of knowledge. (81)

As I attempt to demonstrate later in this chapter, the principle of intuitionism has operated in philosophic systems from Plato to Kant. Although largely unsuccessful in establishing its claims, intuitionism has held the tradition captive because it promises, in the last analysis, a *god's-eye view*. I define a gods'-eye-view as *universal and necessary knowledge of the world as it actually is without any mediating factors that skew or slant the perception of reality*—knowledge a god has, a divine look. If the story I tell in later sections of this chapter is correct, then the disillusionment to which contemporary philosophy has fallen prey is the inevitable outcome of the failure of intuitionism and the promised god's-eye view. The diagnosis of philosophy outlined in *After Philosophy* merely spells out the implications of rejecting intuitionism without offering a better and more rational account of knowledge.

Unfortunately, this is not merely an academic exercise or thought experiment. Just as Socrates warns in the *Phaedo*, naïve trust in flawed arguments too easily results in misology or the hatred of reason itself. Disillusionment with intuitionism has resulted in a reason impure, weak, doubtful. After the promises of the tradition falter, reason seems incapable of disclosing the truth of human existence; humanity is left alone and floundering in the cosmos, incapable of distinguishing the true from the false, the beautiful from the ugly and the good from the bad. We have lost the truth of being and inherited a flirtation with nihilism bordering on antihumanism:

> …*nihilism* is a denial of the humanity and of the very identity of the human being. It should never be forgotten that the neglect of being inevitably leads to losing touch with objective truth and therefore with the very ground of human dignity. This in turn makes it possible to erase from the countenance of man and woman the marks of their likeness to God, and thus to lead them little by little either to a destructive will to power or to a solitude without hope. Once the truth is denied to human beings, it is pure illusion to try and set them free. (John Paul II 1998, §90; cf. Levin 1988, 1-51)

1.2 RORTY, LONERGAN & THE NEW ENLIGHTENMENT

This work hopes to explain the cause of disillusion and contribute to the defense of the human capacity to know. It hopes to accomplish this redemption without dogmatism or naïve realism but by rationally and critically establishing the possibility of knowing the truth without a god's-eye view. In short, it hopes to offer a small voice of assistance to those struggling for what Fred Lawrence and Hugo Meynell have called the "New Enlightenment", i.e., to clarify, justify and apply rational norms in a way which takes seriously postmodern objections to modernity while rejecting the nihilistic tendencies of postmodernism (Meynell 1999, xi).

To this end, I will study the thought of Bernard Lonergan, SJ, and Richard Rorty on the possibility of knowing. I argue that *while Lonergan and Rorty share similar criticisms of the philosophical tradition's dependence on intuitionism, Rorty's subsequent attempt to jettison the correspondence theory of truth is unsatisfactory given the success of Lonergan's critical realism.* In addition to this larger hypothesis, several particular implications are drawn: (1) Both Rorty and Lonergan are correct in rejecting intuitionism; (2) Rorty commits a false dichotomy by assuming that either we have the certainty of intuitionism or there is no truth as correspondence; (3) Rorty is in what Lonergan calls a counterposition, for Rorty's explicit statements about the impossibility of Truth contradict the performance of his own intellect; (4) Lonergan is capable of answering Rorty's objections and better satisfies Rorty's demands to recognize our historicity while allowing conversation than Rorty is himself capable.

While there are differences in their narrative, both Rorty and Lonergan claim that the philosophical tradition has too often relied on intuitionism. As a result, a classical culture developed believing that genuine knowledge had to be certain while science attained universality and necessity. However, the work of thinkers such as Hegel, Dewey, Heidegger, Wittgenstein, Kuhn, Quine, Davidson, and Derrida has called classical culture into question, resulting in the disillusionment of philosophy.

For Rorty, this disillusionment is not a crisis to overcome but a therapy to welcome and then radicalize. Since we cannot escape our language games and historical situations we can hardly discover the world as it actually is and any form of realism disappears: "there is no method for knowing *when* one has reached the truth, or when one is closer to it than before" (COP 165-166). Furthermore, Rorty no longer thinks that there is even anything interesting to say about Truth and advocates the end of epistemology. Without the concern to "get things right" or discover reality, Rorty suggests versions of epistemological behaviorism and pragmatism in which we accept certain answers as true when others within our language game accept the answers and when the answers allow us to control and predict our environment (PSH 27).

Lonergan responds to the fragmentation of knowledge with transcendental method or intentionality analysis (M 13-15). At root is his cognitional theory discovering that before we answer questions of epistemology we must ask and answer the question "what are we doing when we are knowing?" Lonergan's discovery is that whenever we are knowing we are engaged in a structured set of cognitional operations broadly organized under *experience, understanding* and *judgment* (UB 35-36). The tradition largely has ignored or misunderstood the structure and has given definitions of knowledge inconsistent with the cognitive operations, but Lonergan's cognitional theory allows the redemption of philosophy and the correspondence theory of truth against detractors like Rorty.

1.3 BEGIN AT THE BEGINNING: FIVE BASIC QUESTIONS

Despite agreeing on the flaws of tradition, Rorty and Lonergan reach radically different conclusions on the possibility of knowing. After explaining the positions of each in the second and third chapters subsequent chapters engage in a debate between the two thinkers centered around five questions:

1. Does Rorty suffer from Cartesian anxiety, the fear that if there are not absolutely certain foundations then Truth is not possible? Does Lonergan avoid this fear? There is reason to believe that Rorty commits a false dichotomy by agreeing that knowledge, if it is to be objective, must have certainty.

2. Can Lonergan's understanding of cognitional theory demonstrate that Rorty's statements about knowledge and truth performatively contradict *how* he presents his case? If we pay less attention to what Rorty says and more to how he says it, will we see that Rorty acts exactly as Lonergan predicts?

3. Can Lonergan survive Rorty's critique? Lonergan's theory depends on the dynamism of the human intellect and our pure, disinterested desire to know Being. Rorty argues that such a desire does not exist—not truth but power is the goal of inquiry. Has Lonergan remained in the classical consciousness, assuming a reason purer than possible?

4. Can Lonergan survive the linguistic turn on which Rorty depends? Some commentators argue that Lonergan has not come to terms with the linguistic turn and thus remains trapped in the world of the transcendental subject with its improper notions of meaning, language, communication and thought (Kerr 1975).

5. Rorty argues that the end of epistemology leads to a hermeneutic situation where we no longer seek the truth but attempt to keep the conversation going and grow in self-enlargement. But, given the normative standards inherent in the Transcendental Method, can Lonergan (a) provide more adequate notions of epistemic progress, and (b) provide a more adequate motivation for ongoing conversation and thus co-opt Rorty's own position?

Due partly to the different traditions of Rorty and Lonergan and partly because Lonergan has not received the attention he deserves, there is very little literature devoted to comparing the two thinkers. What exists is written by students of Lonergan and supports the claim that both Lonergan and Rorty reject the tradition's reliance on intuitionism but that Lonergan's cognitional theory provides a foundation for knowledge without intuitionism (Barden 1986; Beards 1997; Fitzpatrick 1995; M. McCarthy 1990; Meynell 1985). There is, to my knowledge, no literature written by Rorty or a supporter of Rorty concerning his relation to Lonergan or critical realism (Bradley 1994, 149).

But while the literature establishes the common rejection of intuitionism and provides the basic rationale for a comparison between the figures, there is no extended study devoted solely to comparing Rorty and Lonergan. The literature consists of shorter articles or chapters in books dealing with broader topics. Consequently, the debate is not exhausted, particularly on the questions of the pure desire to know and the linguistic turn. Of course students of Lonergan have examined his position on the pure desire to know and his understanding of language, but this has not been applied specifically to Rorty and his objections. In addition, Lonergan's potential to co-opt Rorty's demands for an ongoing conversation while providing better justification to converse has not been examined.

Further, the commentary comparing Lonergan and Rorty often focuses on the foundations of knowledge as presented in *Insight* rather than the more historically minded Lonergan of the *Method* period. The most exhaustive comparison of the two thinkers, Michael Mc-

Carthy's *The Crisis of Philosophy* (1990), while excellent as an exposition of the history of thought and the roles of Rorty and Lonergan within that history, leaves untapped Lonergan's appropriation of intersubjectivity, history and meaning. Critics of Lonergan, most notably Fergus Kerr (1975), argue that Lonergan remains trapped within a Cartesian framework; ignoring developments in Lonergan's later work makes him appear more classically minded and less sensitive to non-Cartesian historical and linguistic questions than he actually is.

Finally, Rorty has been called "America's most influential professor of philosophy," (Lawler 2002, 75) while Lonergan is generally unnoticed in the general philosophical community. As such the presumption is against Lonergan and in my judgment his students have not yet met the burden of proof. The literature explores Rorty's rejection of intuitionism and how Lonergan as a non-intuitionist escapes Rorty's critique. This is a sensible and intelligent approach as it grapples with an issue of basic similarity between the thinkers but it tends to leave unanswered other facets of Rorty's project such as the contingency of the self, the role of language and the pragmatic denial of the quest for truth. These positions, if true, are potential defeaters of Lonergan's solution. Since Lonergan is relatively unknown, the existing literature explains and introduces Lonergan, again a sensible tactic. But since there is a relative paucity of literature, and since what exists are shorter articles or segments of books, the arguments most damaging to Lonergan are not, in my judgment, adequately addressed. This is ironic, since Lonergan is perhaps strongest and most coherent at addressing these points and most capable of turning the tables on Rorty and demonstrating his performative contradictions.

I.4 HISTORY OF THE PROBLEM

The comparison between Rorty and Lonergan is not simply arbitrary or expressive of an idiosyncratic interest, for both agree that knowledge is not somehow taking a look at reality. But while they agree that intuitionism is a mistake, much of the philosophic tradition rests on this mistake. But intuitionism is not exactly nonsense, as evidenced by the common sense reliance of everyday language on ocular metaphors to explain knowledge—knowledge seems "enlightening" after the darkness of ignorance, a particularly intelligent student is "bright", we "see" what the other means, writing can be "clear", and so on. Recognizing the propensity to relate knowing and sight, Hans Jonas (2001) investigates its attributes in "The Nobility of Sight: A Study in the Phenomenology of the Senses". He discovers that properties of sight inform both common sense and philosophic notions of what constitutes knowledge. The more familiar act of seeing is used to explain the more complicated act of knowing, resulting in the following three assumptions about knowledge:

1. *The Simultaneity of Vision and the Metaphysics of Presence.* Sight, says Jonas, "is unique already in beholding a co-temporaneous manifold as such," and is *"par excellence* the sense of the simultaneous" (136). When we see, all is revealed in a moment, in simultaneity. Objects near and far, moving and still, are juxtaposed in a single instance as "co-existent parts of one field of vision" (136). Even objects which are moving or otherwise exhibiting change are still revealed in one act of sight. Hearing, on the other hand, provides "only dynamic and never static reality," as, for example, when listening to a song the end is not yet present and upon arriving the beginning and middle are no longer present except in memory (137). Touch results in the presentation of a simultaneity—we touch the book—but we arrive at the presentation of simultaneity only through succession, that is we first touch one cover, then the pages and finally the back cover before touch presents us with the presence of a single object. Touch works from one surface, then another until a single shape is presented. While it is true that we can look at first one cover, then the pages and finally the back cover, this is all present in one field of vision and we perceive this as one act. In this way sight is the sense of presence, of simultaneity, and allows the notion of the unchanging to emerge.

2. *The World Confronted Already-Out-There-Now and the Confrontation of Reality.* Hearing and smell are essentially passive, we have no control over the fact *that* we hear or smell. We perceive odors and sounds with complete dependence on the object, for if the object produces an odor or a sound we cannot simply shut up our nose or our ears—there are no eye-lids for the nose or ear—and despite our wishes, if the object produces no odor or sound we will not hear or smell (146). Taste and touch differ, for they allow a high level of control. We can choose to touch or taste an object or refrain from touching or tasting. True, if something touches us we feel it, but there remains a high level of activity on the part of the subject (145). Sight is unique in being both active and passive. Sight is active in that we can shut our

eyes and if we wish refrain from looking. At the same time, if we open our eyes we passively see what is already there. Whereas we can touch whatever we wish, we see what is already there. Whereas we hear when the object makes a sound, we can refuse to look. *Theoria* mirrors this process, for in the Platonic vision of the Forms one is to confront what is already real, as opposed to creating the real or abstracting the real, but one can refuse to look, i.e., to think, one can remain in the darkness of the cave.

3. *The Objectivity of Distance.* Sight is the only sense in which distance has an advantage over proximity (149). We cannot touch or taste without proximity, and while hearing and smell can operate over distance they are never benefited by distance, but sight is often advantaged by distance. We cannot focus on what is too close, and we often step back in order to gain perspective or to see more clearly. Light also travels farther than sound or smell, so the distance that we can step back is often very great. But this ability to step back, to see things in perspective or to see the "whole picture" gives sight the status of disinterestedness or of objectivity. Disinterest is such a prevalent conception of thought that Husserl can identify the philosopher as the disinterested person: "Man becomes the disinterested spectator, overseer of the world, he becomes a philosopher" (Lauer 1965, 172). Rather than being entangled in the situation or context, sight allows us to survey the field from an objective standpoint and see what is really going on, perhaps why we often imagine God to perceive the world from a great distance.

It is these qualities—unchanging presence, the confrontation of reality and the objective disinterest of the spectator who confronts—from which I derived my definition of the god's-eye view: *universal and necessary knowledge of the world as it actually is without any mediating factors that skew or slant the perception of reality.* When the properties of sight are imported into cognitional theory, knowing is defined as somehow taking a god-like look at reality (intuitionism). In the following sections I examine several representative and enormously influential thinkers who illicitly imported sight into their cognitional theories and by so doing trapped the tradition in inconsistencies and contradictions. This examination is merely representative and not exhaustive, but however partial and incomplete it may be it reveals the philosophic tradition's lengthy imprisonment by a metaphor and the resulting incoherence. Since this is a narrative of captivity I do not include Aristotle or Aquinas in the current discussion, for as I explain in subsequent chapters the Aristotelian-Thomistic theory, as appropriated by Lonergan, provides an escape from intuitionism.

1.41 Plato

On their face, the early Socratic dialogues give little hint of the ocular metaphor, most likely because they demonstrate more about Socrates' method and character than any particular doctrine. Further, the dialogues are aporetic: Socrates is committed to rational investigation and the search for universal definitions against the undifferentiated conventionality of common sense, but he proclaims his ignorance and the dialogues end with no certain answers. But even within these dialogues, and especially as the insights of the earlier dialogues become Platonic doctrine in the middle dialogues, Plato fundamentally relies upon visual images and metaphors, so much so that his position is not simply a *metaphorics* of light but also a *metaphysics* and *epistemology* of light (Blumenberg 1993, 33). Despite the Divided Line's distinction between levels and degrees of reality, Plato does not grasp the distinction between perceiving and knowing, merely importing brute empiricism—knowing is perceiving—into the intellectual sphere. Plato is, to use Lonergan's phrase, a *sublime empiricist*, since knowing is a mental looking, a strict analog to physical looking (I 437).

Claiming that Plato is a sublime empiricist seems slightly absurd; of all the philosophers, Plato seems least likely to appeal to the ocular metaphor given his distrust of the senses and his devotion to reason. For instance, the Socratic commitment to questioning and arguing (*Apology* 21a-23c; *Crito* 46b-48b) demonstrates the value of *logos* over sensation. This distinction is perhaps most extreme in the *Phaedo*, with its harsh indictment of the body and suggestion that philosophers are practicing for death by separating their reasoning soul from their body as much as possible. On this account, the senses are distracting and polluting and interfere with the acquisition of knowledge (*Phaedo* 65a-e), although of the senses sight is the most reliable (*Laws* 12.961d) and sensation in general may be the occasion giving rise to recollection or reasoning (*Phaedo* 73c; *Timaeus* 47a-c; *Republic* 7:523a-525a; *Symposium* 210b; *Theatetus* 184b). It seems that if we are to follow Plato's advice, we would turn away from the world of images and sight that blind the soul to reality and instead rely on *logos* (*Phaedo* 99e-100b).

In addition to his distrust of the senses, Plato seems to reject empiricism when he argues that perception is simply insufficient to attain knowledge. In the *Theatetus*, for instance, the equation of perception with knowledge cannot explain how knowledge exists of events in the past, for we are no longer perceiving what is past, or how a distinction could ever be made between what appears to be so and what actually is the case (*Theatetus* 151e-168). An individual with disordered sensation would know even though their perception is faulty and misleading. Further, if bare perception equaled understanding, there would be no distinction from the person who merely perceives and a person of understanding, which is problematic. Again, in *Republic* VI Plato insists that sensation operates only in the world of becoming but knowledge is of what *is*, attainable only by reason. While Plato realizes the problems with defining knowledge as justified true belief (*Theatetus* 201d-210d) he consistently affirms "that holding an opinion which is in fact correct, without being able to give a reason for it, is neither true knowledge—how can it be knowledge without a reason?—nor ignorance—for how can we call it ignorance when it happens to be true?" (*Symposium* 202a; *Meno* 97e-98a). For Plato, unraveling a definition of knowledge requires giving an account or a reason (*logos*) which hardly seems like taking a look.

Despite his objection to the senses and his reliance on *logos*, a close examination reveals the empiricist inconsistency within Plato. Even in the early dialogues, before the mature theory of Forms, Plato insists that understanding requires a universal element relevant to all particulars included in the class. In the *Meno* for instance, Socrates chastises Meno for simply giving a list of virtues instead of providing the essential element common and necessary to any and all particular virtues:

> I seem to be in luck. I wanted one virtue and I find that you have a whole swarm of virtues to offer. But seriously, to carry on this metaphor of the swarm, suppose I asked you what a bee is, what is its essential nature (*ousia*) and you replied that bees were of many different kinds. (*Meno* 72a-b)

Instead of a mere list, Socrates requests the underlying nature, *ousia*, of that to be defined. On first inspection, the discovery of *ousia* through the giving of an account (*logos*) is non-ocular, but almost immediately

Socrates switches to a visual metaphor when relating to Meno that even if there are many virtues "yet at least they all have some common character (*eidos*) which makes them virtues" (*Meno* 72c; *Protagoras* 349b). Now the non-ocular term *ousia* is replaced with the visually laden *eidos* (*eidos*=that which is seen; *idein*=to see). This is not simply a matter of the use of metaphor but discloses an inner tension within Plato's account of knowing: the apparently discursive and non-ocular notion of knowledge as including an account or reason (*logos*) devolves into an account of knowledge dependent on taking a look at the Forms. The *Meno* insists that the difference between opinion and knowledge is that knowledge includes working out a reason, but Plato is unable or unwilling to actually work out a reason discursively without reliance on intuition. In fact, in the early dialogues no definition of virtue is ever given, not simply because of the famous Socratic ignorance but because "when he asks for the nature of areté he does not want a definition for an answer...The answer to 'What is a virtue?' is not a definition, but an Idea" (Jaeger, 1986, 163). At the end of the *Meno*, Socrates explains what providing an account would entail, namely, *recollection* of an Idea (98a). Earlier, Socrates demonstrated through the slave boy that what is often taken for learning is actually recollection, but even though the slave boy is able to finally solve the problem of the diagonal he cannot explain the exact relationship of the diagonal to the shorter sides and does not yet have full knowledge, as Socrates admits (85c). The implication of this failure is that while definition is perhaps necessary for knowledge it is not sufficient; definition is not even the process of working out an account—that process is recollection's task, and recollection, both in the *Meno* and *Phaedrus*, is explained explicitly in terms of intuition rather than discourse.

The distinction between working out an account understood visually as opposed to discursively is subtle, but important. In the *Phaedrus* Plato says that to define is to "bring a dispersed plurality under a single form, seeing it all together [*idean sunorônto*=to put under one form]" (265d). In this language, definition involves a *seeing*, and the condition of possibility of this seeing is recollection. In the *Phaedrus*, as in *Meno*, knowledge is possible only given recollection, or the remembrance of what was once known in a disembodied state. Recollection, the ability to see many particulars under one Form or idea (*idean sunorônto*) is in essence remembering a past vision. Plato explains the source of our recollected ideas as an intellectual intuition of reality, fundamentally similar to the god's vision of reality:

> It is there that true being dwells, without color or shape, that cannot be touched; reason alone, the soul's pilot, can behold (*theatê*) it, and all true knowledge is knowledge thereof. Now even as the mind of a god is nourished by reason and knowledge, so also is it with every soul that has a care to receive her proper food; wherefore when at last she has beheld (*thêorousa*) being she is well content, and contemplating truth she is nourished and prospers.... (*Phaedrus* 247c-d)

Here knowledge is linked to theory (*theôreô*=to see, to look) and knowing is to take a look at reality, admittedly not with sensible sight but with the eye of the mind in an intellectual intuition. As a look, knowledge is immediate, not mediated by the body or language, but is direct and unencumbered. In a sense, Plato is consistent, for sensible perception cannot provide access to the world of immaterial reality and at best is an occasion of remembering, but Plato rather inconsistently understands definition as requiring a type of sight enabled by a prior intellectual vision.

While the term recollection falls from favor in the later dialogues, little changes in Plato's reliance on visual images. The *Republic* replaces recollection with dialectic, which is "viewing all things in their connection [*sunoptikos*]" (537c). The earlier recollection and the later dialectic share a fundamental similarity, namely, that working out an account is to *see* or *view* the *eidé* underlying particulars (Jaeger 1986, 160-166). As such, the disappearance of recollection as an operative term in the later dialogues might have implications for the nature and survival of the soul, the moment when knowledge is gained and the role of myth in Plato, but the *nature* or constitution of knowledge remains fundamentally similar whether symbolized as recollection or dialectic.

In the image of the cave, the prisoner is compelled to turn and ascend from the cave, from the darkness of shadowy images to the light of day and finally to the sun itself, but the mind is seeking "to get sight of those realities which can be seen only by the mind" (*Republic* 510e). The good itself is compared to the sun, for like the sun the good is needed to illumine all things and ensure their intelligibility; the good makes things luminous for the mind to view. But now we are full circle, for what is known are the Forms, the *eidé* or what is looked at, and *nous*, the intellectual faculty for knowing the Forms, becomes simply a superior mental ability for seeing. The slow education out of the cave (the world of images) to physical things, to hypotheticals and finally to reality, is an education or habituation in mental sight. Plato refers to the turn from the shadows to the light as a conversion (*periagoge*), but while there is a conversion on the ontological plane—from becoming to being—there is fundamentally a lack of conversion on the cognitive level. This is surprising, as Plato takes great pains in the dialogues to emphasize the distinction between types of cognitive activity—argument versus passion in *Crito* (46b-d), opinion versus knowledge in *Theatetus, Meno, Sophist, Phaedrus, Phaedo* and *Republic* VI, wonder versus dogmatism in *Apology* and *Theatetus*. His protestations to the contrary, however, the distinction between imagination (*eikasia*) and reason (*noésis*) falls flat; both are fundamentally taking a look at what is already out there to look at, although the reality of what is to be seen is obviously distinct.

The philosopher's education, which is to surpass opinion and attain knowledge, remains trapped in a sort of empiricism. The increasing intelligibility offered in the move from music and gymnastic to arithmetic, geometry, astronomy, harmony and finally dialectic, while perhaps grasping the increasing levels of certainty within those pursuits, does not escape sight. The heavenly ladder of the *Symposium*, like the *Republic's* ascent from the beauty of the particular body to the beauty of reality demonstrates Plato's inability to transcend empiricism. Paraphrasing Diotima, Socrates explains knowledge of beauty itself:

> Whoever has been initiated so far in the mysteries of Love and has viewed all these aspects of the beautiful in due succession, is at last drawing near to the final revelation. And now Socrates, there bursts upon him that wondrous vision which is the very soul of the beauty he has toiled so long for. ...And if, my dear Socrates, man's life is ever worth the living, it is when he has attained this vision of the very soul of beauty. And once you have seen it, you will never be seduced again by the charm of gold...it is only when he discerns beauty itself through what makes it visible that a man will be quickened with the true, and not the seeming, virtue.... (*Symposium* 210e-211e)

It is not altogether ridiculous for Plato to fall prey to the seductions of sight. His own warnings against sensation demonstrate his awareness of the easiness of this temptation. Plato wishes to solve the

question of change and permanence raised by Parmenides and Hera-
clitus as well as overcome the skepticism of the sophists and his metaphysical system of degrees of being is an admirable solution. But the
metaphysical system, if it is to work, must allow for knowledge, and
the language of sight guarantees that the "eye of the soul" and the "light
of reason" preserve the possibility of knowledge. Given the need for his
theory of knowledge to match up with his metaphysics, it is natural,
although given his distrust of the senses a bit unexpected, for Plato to
have recourse to the *metaphorics* of sight (Blumenberg 1993, 33). The
metaphors of sight discussed by Hans Jonas—unchanging presence,
confrontation with reality and the objectivity of the spectator—reveal
how the elements of sight perfectly meet Plato's need for a theory of
knowledge matching his metaphysics. These three elements become
part of the Platonic system, and through Plato essential elements of
the classical system of meaning and knowledge. Knowledge must be
of what is unchanging, of what is already real and it must be free of
baser desires and moods; intellectual intuition, or seeing, is the means
to attain knowledge.

1.42 Augustine

Plato's metaphysics of light and his insistence on the transcendence of
the source of light resulted in what Hans Blumenberg calls the *cosmic
flight of light* (Blumenberg 1993, 34). For Plato the good (*agathon*) is
the source of luminosity and makes visible all below it, but the transcendent nature of the luminous becomes so dominant in later Hel-
lenistic thought that it is seen only as a metaphysical pole, withdrawn,
other-worldly and so distant that its light is not accessible in this world
through reason but depends on some sort of ecstatic revelation:

> The brightness that fills the cosmos like a medium is withdrawn,
> concentrated, objectified as a metaphysical pole. Radiance comes to
> mean a decline, a loss of darkness…The "unnatural" protection of
> the cave is extended to the cavernous nature of the entire cosmos,
> which seizes light, swallows it, and exhausts it…Light, now other-
> worldly and pure, does not allow for theoretical lingering in joyful
> contemplation; it demands extraordinary, ecstatic attention…Few
> are equal to this task. The deadly light must be made available to
> mortals in the more cautious dosages of the *phótismos* of myster-
> ies. Thus, light becomes a metaphor for "salvation".… (Blumenberg
> 1993, 34; cf. Voegelin 1990, 177-181, 212-232)

Being is no longer self-presenting, but is hidden from the grasp of *logos* and *nous*; thus it is no surprise that mysticism and Gnosticism would flourish in the mystery cults and skepticism in the later Academy. Gnosticism, in its Manichean version, and skepticism are both crucial backgrounds to Augustine and his internalization of the source of light.

While the Gnostic cults vary in detail, all, including Manichaeism, hold a dualism of Good and Evil. The cosmos is not created by the God of Goodness and consequently matter and the world are evil. Natural reason is of this world, it is darkened, and salvific knowledge (*gnosis*) is not attained through the soul's (*psyche*) use of reason and theory but through the enlightening of the spirit (*pneuma*) with supernatural *gnosis* (Jonas 1991, 31-37; on Mani see 206-236). Of course, Augustine is a Manichean only for a short time in his youth and much of his work is an anti-Gnostic defense of Christianity. Still, his work must be understood as operating within the cultural framework of the cosmic flight of light—as a response to a particular problem it is influenced by the concerns of that problem—and belongs to the age of Gnosticism in trying to set up a system explaining the role of knowledge in escaping evil (Ricoeur 1967, 4).

Like Plato before him, Augustine is responding to skepticism. Augustine flirted with skepticism (383-384 AD) as it was presented by Cicero in the *Academica* before his interest in Neo-Platonism and subsequent conversion to Christianity (Matthews 2001, 171; O'Daly 2001, 159). In his *Contra Academicos*, Augustine exposes inconsistencies in the skeptic's position and demonstrates, rather broadly, that some truths can certainly be known. For instance, Augustine argues that the skeptic's *epoché* or suspension of judgment is inconsistent so long as they allow action based on probability (*Cont. Acad.* 2). In claiming that something is likely true (*veri simile*) or probable one assumes a tacit and prior understanding of what the truth is; one cannot say *x* is almost like *y* if one does not know *y* (O'Daly 2001, 161). But besides these dialectical devices, Augustine is also eager to defend logical truths such as non-contradiction, mathematical truths and reports of immediate experience (*Cont. Acad.* 3.10.23-11.26). My perception of a blue object might be deceptive, but it is still true that either there is or there is not a blue object, that another of these objects would make two and that I think there is a blue object directly in front of me. While this may be sufficient to expose skepticism's inconsistency,

Augustine realizes a positive account of knowledge is necessary and relies on a thoroughly visual account.

In response to both Gnosticism and skepticism, Augustine is concerned to rehabilitate reason. To do so, he will try to show that reason is capable of attaining knowledge that is both *indubitable* and *self-authenticating*, i.e., knowing for certain that we know and knowing what we know with certainty (Matthews 2001, 173). First, Augustine's visual understanding of the nature of knowledge: Augustine refers to reason as the "eye of my soul" (*Confessions* 7.10), but like Plato he surpasses mere metaphor. The famous argument for the existence of God in *On Free Choice of the Will*, for example, betrays Augustine's assumptions. In this argument, Augustine attempts to sketch the hierarchy of being from bare existence through beings which live and understand until he ascends to God. In his attempt, Augustine provides his understanding of reason in claiming that if there is anything higher than reason then God exists (*De Lib. Arb.* 2.1-20).

Beginning with the exterior senses, sight and hearing are privileged in that several people can see a common object in a manner not available to the other senses. For instance, while we can touch the same object we cannot touch it at the same point at the same time, and we cannot taste or smell the exact same part or effect of an object (2.7). Availability to everyone is taken by Augustine as the mark of reason's objectivity, but while the trait applies to hearing as well as sight only sight is used as a metaphor for reason; in other works, *De Trinitate*, for instance, reason is compared directly to sight alone (*De Trin.* 11.2.6-8).

That which we sense but do not transform by sensing is thus "public property" (2.7) and can be perceived by all. But this element of "public property" is true not only of sensation but also of thinking and reasoning. The order and truth of number (mathematical truth from the *Contra Academicos*), ascertained not by sensation but by an "inner light" or "light of the mind" (2.8) is public; if private answers differ then at least one of the answers must be incorrect (logical truth). Along with mathematical and logical truths, Augustine adds moral truths as held in common. While it may be true that individuals provide differing answers to what is good, just as they might to mathematical and logical problems, the truth is not simply a private matter but is public and objective. Wisdom, in fact, consists of the individual seeing with their own mind what is public and able to be "seen in common by all who know it" (2.9). Since reason is then judged *by its accordance with truth and wisdom* and is not the judge *over* truth and wisdom—simply meaning that our private judgments do not create truth but are true or false in light of objective truth—truth and wisdom are higher than reason proving the existence of God (2.12).

Accordingly, true reason is the contemplation of "true and unchangeable things with the sure eye of reason" (2.13). Wisdom, too, will "shine upon you...and if its brilliance overwhelms your weak sight, turn the eye of your mind back to the road on which wisdom revealed itself" (2.16). It is folly to "turn away from your light," and in such a person "the eye of the soul grows weaker and more inadequate" (2.16). Augustine rather obviously relies on a visual understanding of the nature of knowledge because he assumes reason must mirror sight in perceiving public truth. In one crucial respect sight and reason are similar: Although sight perceives changeable objects it is more truthful than touch or smell since "any form that is seen by the eyes is seen equally by every eye that sees it" (2.13).

Still, this demonstrates only Augustine's understanding of the nature of reason and knowledge, the means of acquiring indubitable and self-authenticating knowledge is not yet known, although Augustine will rely on visual metaphors in this respect as well. Consistently throughout his work, but most explicitly in *De Magistro*, Augustine expounds his theory of illumination. Reminiscent of the *Meno*, Augustine asks how we can acquire knowledge without first knowing what we are trying to know. For instance, Augustine points out the difficulty of using signs to convey knowledge (10.29-11.36). If we are trying to teach someone what a *sarabarae* is, we cannot provide an easy definition if the student does not already understand the significance of the terms of the definition. Even if we can teach the students to parrot a nominal definition—we teach them to say "hat"—if they do not already know what a hat is the nominal definition is meaningless. Ostensive definition does not solve the problem either; saying *sarabarae* while pointing may be misinterpreted to mean the act of pointing itself unless the student first understood how ostensive definition works.

The failure of signs to impart new knowledge combined with Augustine's hesitancy to accept Platonic recollection and its dependence on a pre-existing soul gives rise to his theory of illumination. Signs give knowledge only of other signs and so we must have access to the things themselves. Instead of appealing to some form of abstraction,

Augustine relies on divine illumination or Christ, the Teacher, to act
as inner teacher and revealer of Truth (11.37-13.46):

> But among the things which have been created by God, the rational
> soul, when it is pure, surpasses all and is closest to God. And in
> the measure in which it has clung to him in love, in that measure,
> imbued in some way and illuminated by him with intelligible light,
> the soul sees, not with physical eyes, but with its own highest part
> in which lies its excellence, i.e., with its intelligence, those reasons by
> the vision of which it becomes supremely blessed. (*De ideis*, Ques-
> tion 46, in Matthews 2001, 181).

Beyond simple metaphor, however, Augustine assumes elements of
the visual in his content. First, knowledge is always understood as immediate, as a privileged and intuitive grasp. Since knowledge does not
depend on external signs but on the inner light of God, knowledge is
intuitive rather than discursive. Further, our access to and understanding via the illuminating light must be immediate or else the inner light
would need illumination itself, and so on to infinite regression. Additionally, Augustine's theory of sensation, in which the senses cannot
cause change in the soul because the lower cannot act on the higher
but the soul is simply aware of what is sensed, means that the body
is more of an occasion of sense knowledge than a mediating factor,
especially since the theory of illumination makes sensation somewhat
superfluous. Self-knowledge as well is immediate since we are immediately present to ourselves (*De Trin.* 10.2). Second, as if immediate
knowledge was not enough, divine illumination presents the epitome
of a god's-eye view; it is God's light which enables us to see. Further,
since illumination allows us to see the ideas as they exist in the mind
of God, the content of our knowledge is dramatically similar to the
content of God's knowledge, perhaps so much so that we know the
essence of God when we know His ideas (Gilson 1929, 244-245).
Of course Augustine's ontologism is debatable, but whether we know
God's essence or not, it remains that we know the eternal ideas of God
and we do so in an immediate grasp or flash of illumination unmediated by the body or language. This stretches the finite pole of our existence to the bursting point, our knowledge is like God's. Third, divine
illumination allows the individual thinker to operate without social
mediation—alone with God, so to speak. This is not yet Descartes'
cogito which suspects that other men are automatons, but it does fore-
shadow the solitary individual. Plato's cave is not confining because

of isolation; in fact, one need not leave the cave at all since the light descends into the cave itself and works within the inhabitant. The monastic cell is not a prison but the place of accessing light, as Descartes alone with tent and stove soon realizes (Blumenberg 1993, 38).

1.43 Descartes & Decadent Scholasticism

Like Plato and Augustine, Descartes uses vision for his model of knowledge in his attempt to overcome skepticism, a skepticism caused in no small part by the tradition's reliance on the visual model. In Chapter Three I will examine the Aristotelian-Thomistic solution to knowledge that is not dependent on sight, but the background to Descartes' skepticism is caused in some part by the breakdown of the Thomistic solution in the work of John Duns Scotus and William of Ockham. The medieval breakdown, coupled with Galileo's science and the Renaissance discovery of perspective, prompts Descartes' worries and spurs him to an intuitive solution.

Scotus' epistemology is naïve in that it dogmatically assumes an isomorphism between concepts and reality: if "something has the native ability to produce different concepts of itself in the mind…then the distinction must be in some sense actual" (Wolter 1972, 431). Thus, if we can make a formal distinction in our mind between an object's common nature and its "thisness" or *haecceitas* then according to his isomorphism the object itself must possess these formalities. This assumption of isomorphism, however, weakens the distinction between understanding and judgment. While abstraction rather mechanically results in an understood concept for Scotus, he sees no need to exercise reflective judgment to ensure that the concept matches with the object—isomorphism guarantees the match—and instead judgment merely synthesizes concepts into propositions which are judged true or false. So while abstraction results in some concept, *P*, judgment does not (as it would for Aquinas) investigate the adequacy of the concept to the object but remains on the level of propositions, *P* is *C*. But since this judgment remains merely on the level of ideas, Scotus cannot explain if or how concepts accurately relate to reality. To escape his predicament, Scotus introduces the distinction between abstraction and cognitive intuition.

In abstractive cognition "the intellect can act in such a way that it regards an object with complete indifference to the existence or nonexistence" of the object; abstractive cognition allows one to easily discuss the properties of a unicorn and deduces grand conceptual systems on the nature and habits of unicorns (Day 1947, 49f; Bettoni 1961, 122-123). Intuitive cognition, which is an intellectual and not merely sensible intuition (Bettoni 1961, 122) is the operation by which we apprehend the object as existing and present (Day 1947, 50-70). While this does not *prima facie* result in skepticism—Ockham's innovations are necessary for that—Scotus reverses the Thomistic cognitional theory and reintroduces the chasm between understanding and being. For Scotus, understanding and judging are only dogmatically related to reality—assuming isomorphism between the concept and the real—creating the need for intellectual intuition to guarantee existence. (Sebastian Day, OFM, who famously argues for Scotus against Aquinas, is explicit in claiming that intuition is needed to get back to what is instead of what is merely abstracted.)

Ockham continues the distinction between abstraction and intuition. But since he begins his philosophic system with a theologism, namely, the creedal statement of God the Father Almighty, his concern is to ensure that there are no constraints on God's absolute power. Consequently, universal ideas and God's nature are abandoned as threats to the utter freedom of God (Gilson 1937, 61-91). As a result, the order of the cosmos breaks down: the world does not exhibit God's rational nature or God's ideas but is radically contingent, it is as it is simply because God willed it to be so (Blumenberg 1983, 129-225). Moreover, while God normally operates through secondary causes, He need not as there is nothing contradictory with God acting directly. God may cause intuitions of objects that are not existent or present. Normally, we would intuit a star due to the star's presence, but God can give the intuition of a non-existing star.

In *The Legitimacy of the Modern Age*, Hans Blumenberg argues that Ockham breaks the medieval solution. The cosmos is no longer rational or trustworthy. No divine order is found in it, only the evidence of sheer and absolute will. Additionally, and here Blumenberg finds support from Etienne Gilson (1937), Louis Dupré (1993) and Michael Gillespie (1995), Descartes' hyperbolic doubt and fear of a deceiver God is enabled, or even necessitated, by the arbitrary God of the nominalists. This is a God that can deceive and provide false intuitions, and since human rationality is incapable of attaining the real without the aid of intuitions there is no way of knowing whether our experiences are veridical or not. Since God could be the master illusionist, hyberbolic doubt is not simply a thought-experiment but a real possibility and Descartes is quite justified in his worried attempts to find a method for overcoming the possibility of a deceiver God. If certitude is to be attained, then humans must find a method or technique to guarantee intuition and shine light upon what they wish to know; God is no longer trustworthy as an illuminating source.

In addition to the erasure of judgment in Scotus and the possibility of divine illusion raised by Ockham, Descartes is forced to deal with Galileo's new science of primary and secondary qualities implying that what is sensed is not a quality of the object itself. Even more, Descartes confronts the discovery of perspective in art by Brunelleschi and Alberti resting on illusion to create the appearance of reality (Edgerton 1975, 1-26). These concerns prompt Descartes, from his early works on optics through *Rules for the Direction of the Mind, Discourse on Method* and *Meditations*, to obsess over illusion (Judovitz 1993, 63-86; Levin 1999, 29-59). In his early works on optics Descartes is concerned with physical sensation and the overcoming of optical illusion while later works expand his project to overcoming all illusion, mental and optical. To do so Descartes appeals to the hackneyed project of intuitionism.

In *Rules for the Direction of the Mind*, written three decades before the *Meditations*, Descartes outlines and defines his project, which is to obtain "solid and true judgments" (Rule I) with "certainty and indubitability" (Rule II) (Descartes 1954, 153). This does not sound inherently visual, and in fact is written to escape the visual illusions, but still Descartes is trapped in the metaphor as David Michael Levin (1999) notes:

> Although the rhetoric of vision is not explicit in these words, his subsequent discussion inscribes these "mental powers" of "attention" within the logic of vision. Thus he writes of obeying "the light of reason," a "natural light," in order to overcome "confused reflections" and achieve a "mental vision," a "vision-like knowledge," "a clear vision of each step of the process...." (32)

Descartes plays his hand in Rule III: He wants "what we can clearly and manifestly perceive by intuition or deduce with certainty. For there is no other way of acquiring knowledge" (Descartes 1954, 154). Intuition, as defined by Descartes is not the wavering assurance of the senses, or the deceitful judgment of a misconstructing imagination, but a conception, formed by unclouded mental attention, so easy and distinct as to leave no room for doubt in regard to the thing we are understanding. It comes to the same thing if we say: It is an indubitable conception formed by an unclouded mental mind; one that originates solely from the light of reason. (154-155)

But while Descartes says he allows deduction in addition to intuition, he claims that the chain of inference, if it is to be valid, must itself be grasped in an intuition (Rules III and XI). All knowledge worthy of the name is gained by intuition. Intuition cannot be mistaken, cannot be tricked by illusions and so is the *only* source of knowledge.

Nine years after writing *Rules for the Directions of the Mind*, the project of intuitionism informs the *Discourse on Method*. Beyond simply seeking certain and indubitable ideas, Descartes now engages the world as a solitary Ego, looking from a distance at the world with his "philosopher's eye" (Descartes 1998, 2). Reliance on intuition allows him to put aside the opinions and judgments of others and to shut himself up in his tent convinced that "there is often not so much perfection in works composed of many pieces and made by the hands of various master craftsmen as there is in those works on which but a single individual has worked" (7). Here we have the final result of Augustine's illumination, the cave having first become the monk's cell in which one encounters God and then having become Descartes' *cogito* within the tent. In addition to the separation of the self from others, Scotus' divorce of the judging mind from the physical world is further radicalized—the intuitive mind is separated from the body and the self becomes a thinking/intuiting thing.

Twenty years later, his thinking is expressed most vividly and famously in the *Meditations*. It is ironic that Descartes, like Plato before him, wants to escape reliance on physical senses, especially sight, as well as the faculty most like sight, imagination, only to turn the mind into an internal eye. In the second meditation, after determining that he is a thinking thing, Descartes attempts to explain the status of things other than himself. In the illustration of the wax (Descartes 1998, 67-69) we perceive a piece of wax and are able to sense its shape, color, taste, smell, size, hardness and so on. Upon heating the wax virtually all the sensible qualities change—the wax is softer, warmer, a duller color, a different size and shape, sweeter and so on. Still we recognize this as the same wax. How? Clearly the senses cannot grasp the identity, for from their perspective the wax is evidently different. Instead, Descartes remarks that "I *perceive* it through the mind alone" (68; italics mine). The mind's perception (*mente percipere*) has a different quality than sensible perception, however, as "the perception of the wax is neither a seeing, nor a touching, nor an imagining...rather, it is an inspection (*mentis inspectio*) on the part of the mind alone"[*inspectio*=to look into] (68). Descartes wishes to extract the mind from its dependence on and relationship to the senses, but in order to do so he transfers a quality of the senses—sight—to the mind; the mind looks and gains knowledge.

The nature of the mind's inspection becomes more obvious in the chiliagon example of meditation six. While we cannot imagine a thousand-sided figure but only some indistinct shape, we quite clearly conceive and understand a chiliagon; it must be that imagination is distinct from our intellect, drawn more to the body. Presumably we understand both the wax and the chiliagon through the intellect, through a mental inspection, but now Descartes is more specific on the nature of this inspection: "the mind, when it understands, in a sense turns toward itself and looks at one of the ideas that are in it..." (93). Of course this is only "in a sense", but still Descartes holds that we learn by examining our own ideas, which is to say we have an immediate intuition of our innate ideas. Like Plato, Descartes accepts the confrontation model of truth—we confront ideas—and even though Descartes has us confront internal ideas rather than the other-worldly Forms, both depend on an intuitive moment of confrontation to attain knowledge.

Of course, the problem is that Descartes so successfully divorces the mind and the body that it becomes impossible to join the two again. Clear and distinct ideas are to be had through an internal inspection, an inner intuition, and even though the honesty of God supposedly ensures that an external world exists since Descartes so clearly thinks it does, all knowledge is of internal ideas. There is no bridge by which to join the mental and the external; the subject/object chasm is too wide and Descartes, ironically since he was attempting to answer skepticism, engenders solipsism and skepticism (Gilson 1937, 176-220). The divide between the mind and the physical allows the camps of rationalism and empiricism to form, but rationalism is hard pressed to escape its games of deduction and return to existence while empiricism struggles to overcome phenomenalism or outright idealism. The representative realism of Locke, for instance, is based on a faith that ideas represent reality, but Berkeley savages this faith knowing there is no way to proceed from the ideas of secondary qualities back to the supposed primary qualities and the unknowable substance. Berkeley is right to argue that there is no need to import substance and primary qualities into this structure—ideas are sufficient and to be is to be perceived. Thus, Idealism tends to result from both the rationalist and empiricist accounts. There is a danger of going blind when one stares inwardly for too long.

1.44 Kant

At first glance, the Copernican revolution of the *Critique of Pure Reason* appears to move out of intuitionism, if only incompletely. First, while a vestige of intuitionism remains in the Kantian concern to guarantee the necessity and universality of science, intuition is confined to sensibility alone and non-intuitive understanding is a necessary element in cognition. Kant insists that "our *intuition*, by our very nature, can never be other than *sensible* intuition," thereby making impossible Platonic or Cartesian *intellectual* intuition (B75/A51). Further, all cognition must include the intuitions of sense and the concepts of understanding, for "concepts without intuitions are empty; intuitions without concepts are blind" (B75/A51). While retaining an urge for the apodictic, Kant rejects Cartesian psychology by refusing to extend intuition beyond sensibility and by including sensibility as only one component of cognition (M. McCarthy 1990, 187-189).

Further, sensible intuition does not provide direct or unmediated access to things in themselves, as intuitionists insist. Not only must intuitions be schematized and categorized before they are objects of cognition, and not only does Kant's system allow access only to phenomena and not noumena, but intuitions themselves are mediated by the *a priori* forms of space and time. In the Transcendental Aesthetic sensible intuition "refers to objects directly" and by intuition objects are "given to us" (B33/A19); but while the matter (*Materie*) or content of an intuition is given directly, the matter is "structured—automatically, as it were—in terms of space and time by the forms of intuition" (Kitcher 1987, xxxiv). The matter of sensation is presented only through the *a priori* forms of intuition and consequently the matter of intuition is never known directly but always as an appearance mediated by the *a priori* forms. The mind can never escape the *a priori* forms to glimpse the sensible object as it is in itself; the object is, for us, always mediated.

Finally, like the intuitionists Kant is concerned to respond to skepticism—to Hume, essentially—but Kant is aware that intuitionism has promised more than it can substantiate and by its failure contributes to the cause of skepticism. In the Preface to the Second Edition of the *Critique*, Kant makes clear that the motivation for his Copernican Revolution is the safeguarding of universal and necessary science but that this accomplishment depends on confining intuition to sensibility and making the objects of experience conform to concepts (Bxviii). Only by limiting the power of intuition will philosophy escape the Platonic ideal of an intellectual intuition (B596/A568). It seems that Kant rejects Plato's intuitionism and its god's-eye view as illusory: "What is to us an ideal was for *Plato* an *idea of the divine understanding*, an individual object in this understanding's pure intuition" (B596/A568). Kant accuses Plato of confusing human knowing with God's knowing, and *only* God achieves such intuition (B72; B138-139; B145; B307-309). It would seem that Kant is moving away from intuitionism; he limits intuition to sensibility, he allows no unmediated or direct access to reality and he rejects the god's-eye view. The Copernican Revolution demands the end to a direct grasp of reality and instead forces reality to conform to the mediation of the mind.

However, despite the apparent rejection of intuitionism, Kant is influenced by it to such an extent that Martin Heidegger stated: "To understand the *KRV* one must, as it were, hammer into one's head the principle: Knowledge is primarily intuition" (Sala 1994, 9). But how can we account for the discrepancy between Kant's apparent rejection of intuitionism and Heidegger's claim that Kant is an intuitionist?

Transcendental analysis involves a shift of emphasis from the consideration of objects to the consideration of cognitional acts (Sala 1994, 9) and the method allows Kant to distinguish three cognitional acts—sensibility, understanding and reason—and three corresponding types of representations—intuitions, concepts and ideas (M. McCarthy 1990, 188). Lacking content provided by intuitions, ideas of reason are representations without a corresponding intentional object—ideas, such as God, the world and the soul, do not provide knowledge. Concepts differ from ideas in that intuitions *potentially* provide content for concepts while there are no potential intuitions relating to metaphysical ideas, but concepts are similar to ideas in that they do not represent intentional objects—concepts, after all, are mental categories. Unless there are *actually* intuitions concepts are blind. Of the three types of representations, only intuitions intentionally represent an object. If Kant rejected the confrontational model of knowledge this would be irrelevant, but since Kant assumes that knowledge requires the relation of subject and object, merely reversing the usual order of subject to object, the cognitional act relating object to subject is thus the model of knowledge, as Giovanni Sala (1994) explains:

> [For Kant] there are many activities which contribute to the constitution of our knowledge; but if we ask what constitutes knowledge as knowledge *of an object*, and hence as knowledge at all, we have to answer: It is intuition. No matter how many mediated relations other activities are able to establish with the object, if we wish to avoid the nonsense of a series of mediations, no one of which reaches the reality to be mediated, we must say that there is a type of cognitional activity whose very nature consists in setting up a bridge between knower and known. This is intuition. Knowledge is essentially intuition; therefore intuition is found in all knowledge. (9)

According to Sala, Kant insists that a cognitive act is objective only insofar as it is analogous to sight, but does so only because he has not undergone the Lonerganian turn which distinguishes between the intentions of understanding and judgment. Understanding intends what is intelligible in data while judgment intends what is real (Sala 1994, 11). By assuming that an object of cognition must be something confronted, something potentially seen or intuited, Kant assumes, just as all intuitionists do, that a real object is always already-out-there-now—something very much like a material body. A non-intuitionist, like Aquinas or Lonergan, could say that there is more than the object of intuition, since understanding provides an *intelligible* object and judgment the *real* object. By reducing the real to that which has bodily presence, Kant is unaware, claims Sala, that knowledge is objective insofar as it relates to being, to the real, and the real is not simply what is already-out-there-now—the Pythagorean theorem is objectively real as is the law of non-contradiction but neither is "out there" somewhere. This Lonerganian account is developed more in Chapter Three, but for the moment Kant's insistence on intuition as the only source of objectivity betrays his reliance, although certainly not such a naïve reliance as Descartes, on intuitionism.

Scotus' hidden influence is revealed here, for just as Scotus thought that only intuition related to existing objects, thus relegating understanding and judgment to the interplay of ideas, so Kant relies on intuition to provide the object while reducing understanding and judgment to merely the relation of concepts to each other (M. McCarthy 1990, 190). Kant assumes that judgment is the ability to "apply to appearances the concepts of understanding," i.e., judgment deals not with the object but with concepts only (B171/A132):

> But in such judging, a concept is never referred directly to an object, because the only kind of presentation that deals with its object directly is intuition. Instead the concept is referred directly to some other presentation of the object (whether that presentation be an intuition or itself already a concept). Judgment, therefore, is the indirect cognition of an object, viz., the presentation of a presentation of it. (B93/A68)

Judgment is the *presentation* of a *presentation*, and no object (the real) is intended in a judgment. A judgment relates to the real only indirectly, i.e., only if the intuition presented relates to reality. Intuitions, however, are "but the presentation of appearance. The things that we intuit are not in themselves what we intuit them as being...they cannot exist in themselves, but can exist only in us. What may be the case regarding objects in themselves...remains to us entirely unknown" (B59/A42). Judgment is the conceptual organization of appearances and does not relate to things in themselves. Intuitions access only the appearance, and there is no guarantee that the appearance relates in any manner to the thing in itself.

Kant's attempt to save reason from dogmatism and illusion results not only in the jettison of metaphysics as he openly admits, but of any reliable contact with the real. Kant is trapped by the intellectual tradition by assuming that only intuition provides access to objects, but, like Ockham, Kant discovers that intuitions offer no guarantee that reality is intuited. God alone knows the real through intellectual intuition, as "an *object of a nonsensible intuition*...an intellectual one" (B307). Humans, lacking such intuition are able to speak of the noumena only in the negative, "*insofar as it is not an object of our sensible intuition*" (B307). The noumena are *objects* of knowledge only because they can be intuited, at least by God; to us they are not objects simply because we cannot intuit them. This amounts to the belief that only a god's-eye view is knowledge of the real but humans do not have this view. Plato, Augustine and Descartes all assumed that only a god's-eye view provided knowledge of the real, but they all agreed that humans could attain this view; Kant agrees with their impossibly high standard of knowledge while acknowledging it is impossibly high!

Humans, then, lacking intellectual intuition, have no contact with things in themselves and understanding and judgment merely organize appearances into intelligible (not real) concepts and propositions. Since intuitions themselves are only appearances (not the real), no method exists by which to ensure that any cognitional act confronts, as Kant assumes it must, the real to result in knowledge. In the end, Kant has difficulty even establishing the existence of the real since he has no access to it and must *assert* that the real causes sensation.

Of course, the Absolute Idealists reject the noumena since Kant derives them either from an illicit application of the categories to non-intuited objects or as a remnant of a brute dogmatism simply asserting their existence. But while the Idealists provide speculative pyrotechnics for a time, Darwin and Hegel's historicism guarantees the ascendance of naturalism in counter-movement to Idealism. Rejecting any hint of transcendental subjectivity, the naturalists move philosophy and thought back into the history, society and culture often overlooked in the Platonic-Cartesian-Kantian picture. But naturalism has tended towards a truncated picture of the subject as merely immanent. The immanentist subject favors the project of psychologism and scientism, thus reducing epistemology and cognitive theory into the genetic investigations of factual conditions in which knowledge claims develop. Kant's project refutes itself, if not logically at least historically.

Thus Kant's failure makes him the transition figure from the unquestioned supremacy of the intuitionist tradition to the current disillusion with philosophy noted in the beginning of this chapter. While implicitly retaining intuitionism, for all practical purposes he sounds the death knell of intuitionism as an explicit project. Philosophy's disillusion demonstrates that the god's-eye view picture of philosophy in the Platonic-Cartesian-Kantian is not accepted as a viable project, for intuitionism is irrational and not up to the task of refuting skepticism. The current disillusionment with philosophy noted at the beginning of the chapter results from the abandonment of intuitionism by the major figures of philosophy and the vacuum resulting from the abandonment. Continental philosophy in Heidegger, Foucault, Merleau-Ponty, Levinas, Derrida, Gadamer and Habermas rejects intuitionism as dehumanizing, forgetful of being, logocentric and co-ercive (Levin 1988, 3-49; 1993, 1-29; 1999, 170-234). The linguistic school provides the criticism of the later Wittgenstein, Sellars, Kuhn and Davidson against intuitionism and its reliance on direct, non-linguistic givenness (Levin 1999, 94-114; M. McCarthy 1990, 140-169). Dewey leads the pragmatist charge in rejecting the spectator theory of knowledge for forgetting instrumentality and action (Kulp 1992, 1-19; M. McCarthy 1990, 186-199). Finally, some Thomists, by no means all, reject intuitionism as an incomplete understanding of the subject known through Transcendental Method. Clearly, the project of the tradition is in jeopardy, but what, if anything, fills the vacuum?

1.5 CONCLUSION

While this history is brief, it demonstrates the central place of the ocular metaphor in the tradition. Too often, however, the tradition has been taken captive by the metaphor, even while attempting to overcome it. We are left with the question of what should fill the vacuum now that the tradition itself is in jeopardy, a crisis caused by the collapse of philosophy's ability to meet the standard of intuitionism. Philosophy's claim to arbitrate the other disciplines by providing universal and necessary knowledge is now undercut by the collapse of intuitionism and so we wonder what to do after philosophy.

Richard Rorty and Bernard Lonergan offer answers to these questions. Rorty, much more influentially, has argued that philosophy is now simply another genre of writing, and he makes this claim by defeating the possibility of direct and immediate access to reality that philosophy pretended to allow. But if philosophy cannot provide intuitions of the real, its role is no greater than that of the poets. Bernard Lonergan, on the other hand, also has a thorough-going critique of the tradition and of intuitionism, but Lonergan promises to deliver an alternative model of knowing capable of freeing the tradition from the metaphorics of sight. The rest of this work, then, attempts to explain the two thinkers and offer a critical defense of Lonergan's account. In the end, Rorty was incapable of freeing himself from the Siren call of intuitionism, and so his proposal fails. Lonergan, though, breaks from the trap of ocularity and thus allows a rational account of knowing. The next chapter of the work investigates Rorty before turning in Chapter Three to Lonergan's *aggiornamento* of Thomism. The relative merit of these two choices—Rorty's version of hermeneutics or Lonergan's intellectual conversion—are the subjects of Chapters Four through Six before I offer my conclusions in Chapter Seven.

CHAPTER 2

FROM EPISTEMOLOGY TO HERMENEUTICS

It is as when one who lacks skill in arguments puts his trust in an
argument as being true, then shortly afterwards believes it to be
false—as sometimes it is and sometimes it is not—and so with
another argument and then another... It would be pitiable...when
there is a true and reliable argument and one that can be understood, if a man who has dealt with such arguments as appear at
one time true and another time untrue, should not blame himself
or his own lack of skill but, because of his distress, in the end gladly
shift the blame away from himself to the arguments, and spend the
rest of his life hating and reviling reasonable discussion and so be
deprived of truth and knowledge of reality.

(Plato, *Phaedo*, 90b-d)

2.1 PUTTING INTUITIONISM TO THE TEST

In Chapter One I argued that for much of the Western tradition
knowing was understood as an analogue to seeing. Consequently,
anything less than a god's-eye view was not considered knowledge.
The desire for immediacy, for the intuitive grasp of a completely present reality, results in the inordinate fear of any activity on the part of
the knowing subject, since the subject's active role in creating knowledge raises the danger of the subject himself placing a mediating factor between the mind and reality. As John Dewey noted in his 1929
Gifford Lectures:

> The common essence of all these theories, in short, is that what is
> known is antecedent to the mental act of observation and inquiry,
> and is totally unaffected by these acts; otherwise it would not be
> fixed and unchangeable. This negative condition, that the processes
> of search, investigation, reflection, involved in knowledge relate to
> something having prior being, fixes once for all the main characters
> attributed to mind ... they *must* be outside what is known, so as to
> not interact in any way with the object to be known. The theory of
> knowing is modeled after what was supposed to take place in the
> act of vision. The object refracts light to the eye and is seen; it makes

a difference to the eye and to the person having an optical apparatus, but none to the thing seen. ... A spectator theory of knowledge
is the inevitable outcome. There have been theories which hold that
mental activity intervenes, but they have retained the old premise.
They have therefore concluded that it is impossible to know reality.
(Dewey 1929, 23)

Since any activity of the subject threatens knowledge, a dedication
to realism is often thought to imply a concomitant commitment to the
spectator theory. The knower opens their eyes (either their literal eyes
or a metaphorical Eye of the Mind) and looks upon reality, they are a
spectator [*specere*=to look] discovering a reality completely independent of them. But what if intuitionism is untenable? What if there is
no immediate access to the real? Since realism is historically conjoined
with intuitionism, is a realistic epistemology doomed? Richard Rorty
thinks so. In this second chapter, I investigate and summarize the central tenets of Rorty's rejection of epistemological realism. Rorty puts
forth a devastating critique of intuitionism and any realism dependent upon an immediate access to the real, but I argue in subsequent
chapters that he too quickly conflates realism and intuitionism. If realism is not dependent on intuitionism then Rorty is guilty of a false
dichotomy, for he assumes that either we have clear and unmediated
access to the real or realism fails.

2.2 DETHRONING PHILOSOPHY
IN FAVOR OF DEMOCRACY

Rorty (1931-) was educated in philosophy at the University of Chicago and at Yale and has taught at Wellesley, Princeton and the University of Virginia. He is currently a member of the Department of
Comparative Literature at Stanford. His early work concerned the
philosophy of mind and the linguistic turn in analytic philosophy. Beginning with his influential anthology, *The Linguistic Turn* (1967), he
argued that analytic philosophy is not capable of solving traditional
philosophical problems and will eventually, as will the Continental
tradition, turn pragmatic. He augments and furthers this claim in
Consequences of Pragmatism (1982), a collection of earlier articles, and
in his enormously influential and controversial work, *Philosophy and
the Mirror of Nature* (1979). Since then he has released *Contingency,
Irony, and Solidarity* (1989), three volumes of collected papers—*Ob-*

jectivity, Relativism, and Truth (1991), *Essays on Heidegger and Others* (1991) and *Truth and Progress* (1998)—as well as *Achieving our Country* (1998), *Philosophy and Social Hope* (2000) and numerous articles and chapters in books. He is unique in his facility with both Anglo-American and Continental philosophy, arguing that both have or will abandon epistemology in favor of pragmatism, in his familiarity with literature and in his political concerns. Although his appropriation and understanding of pragmatism is controversial, he is considered by many to be the current face of pragmatism and perhaps the most influential intellectual in the United States.

Rorty argues that philosophical problems are not perennial or logically necessary but are products of historical choices and questions. By means of a historical narrative (*Geistesgeschichte*) which is less concerned with accurate reconstruction of history than with exposing philosophical problems as contingent historical choices and thus as pseudo-problems, Rorty hopes to provide therapy to the disastrous mess that philosophy has become (Rorty 1984, 56-59; cf. Hall 1994, 16, 27). More specifically, Rorty hopes to dethrone the image of Philosophy (upper case) developed in early modernity as the discipline which "sees itself as the attempt to underwrite or debunk claims to knowledge made by science, morality, art, or religion" (PMN 3). Philosophy sees itself as having a "special understanding of the nature of knowledge and of mind," and is thus "foundational in respect to the rest of culture because culture is the assemblage of claims to knowledge, and philosophy adjudicates such claims" (PMN 3). Understood in such a manner, Philosophy is reducible to epistemology and specifically an epistemology of representation:

> To know is to represent accurately what is outside the mind; so to understand the possibility and nature of knowledge is to understand the way in which the mind is able to construct such representations. Philosophy's central concern is to be a general theory of representation, a theory which will divide culture up into the areas which represent reality well, those which represent it less well, and those which do not represent it at all (despite their pretense of doing so). (PMN 3)

Not at all convinced that this is possible or desirable, Rorty attempts to demonstrate that Philosophy's reign over the theory of knowledge and subsequent status as judge of other cultural pursuits depends upon an untenable intuitionism. Once exposed, Philosophy becomes merely another genre of literature, with no more claim to supremacy than any other genre. The first part of Rorty's project, then, is to overcome the epistemological foundationalism of modernity. Once modernity is weaned off of epistemology the concern to "get things right" will vanish and Rorty can push for the second half of his project, i.e., the fulfillment of the political aspirations of modernity. In his reading of modernity, heavily influenced by Hans Blumenberg's *The Legitimacy of the Modern Age*, modernity is characterized not only by the foundationalism of Descartes but also by the self-assertion of Francis Bacon in response to the theological absolutism of late scholasticism. Rorty rejects the foundationalist project but accepts the project of self-assertion, essentially the liberalism of modernity stripped of any pretense of natural foundations. Liberalism places a strict separation between the private and public spheres of existence, the private sphere allowing the pursuit of personal perfection, however defined, while the public sphere's only goal is to minimize cruelty (Hall 1994, 40). But unlike political projects which feel the need to provide some foundational grounding, Rorty does not assume that living well depends upon the Truth—virtue and happiness are not reducible to knowledge as in Platonism (Lawler 2002, 78-80). Rorty wants Democracy to be prior to philosophy, solidarity prior to objectivity.

Before Rorty can push for the democratic end of his project, he must dismantle the Philosophic pretensions of the tradition. Richard Bernstein argues that Rorty uses a two-fold tactic to do so. First, he exposes the contingent nature of philosophical problems, their status as fruits of historical language games rather than any sort of intuitive or necessary problem (Bernstein 1985, 55-59). Second, once exposed as contingent, the problem can be dissolved simply by rejecting its questions and problems and by raising new questions.

2.3 EXPOSING THE CONTINGENCY
OF EPISTEMOLOGY

Rorty argues that from the beginning of philosophy the ocular model was dominant:

> the distinction between the eye of the body and the Eye of the Mind, νοῦς—thought, intellect, insight—was identified as what separates man from beasts. There was, we moderns may say with the ingratitude of hindsight, no particular reason why this ocular metaphor

seized the imagination of the founders of Western thought. But it did, and contemporary philosophers are still working out its consequences.... (PMN 38)

He thinks that the picture of the mind as mirror or spiritual eye has its roots in the Greek and medieval concern with universals. Since universals are immaterial, the soul was also thought of as immaterial, a special sort of faculty capable of knowing more than particulars and thus separating us from the mere brutes. But since the knowledge attained by the soul was modeled on the confrontational model of physical sensation, the soul was explained as the internal eye, the Eye of the Mind, a mirror or a Glassy Essence which was able to see universals. Rorty's account of this is somewhat hasty and less than rigorous, although in fundamental agreement with the exposition of the previous chapter, because he is less concerned with the metaphor in ancient and medieval philosophy than with its impact in modern epistemology. He argues that it is only with the Cartesian turn from universals to an obsession with certainty that the ocular metaphor transforms into epistemology and claims the title of First Philosophy. In Rorty's judgment, the Cartesian problematic creates modern epistemology's reliance on the ocular metaphor: "without the notion of the mind as mirror, the notion of knowledge as accuracy of representation would not have suggested itself" (PMN 12). But if epistemology is created by the ocular model, he can then overcome epistemology simply by deconstructing the metaphor.

2.31 *The Veil of Ideas & the Need to Mirror in Descartes*

Descartes creates the problem of *representational realism* which results in the veil of ideas and the chasm between mind and reality. When Descartes rejects the Aristotelian *soul* appropriated by the scholastics in favor of *mind* he creates a set of insoluble problems (PMN 45-46). For Aristotle, the soul is the animating force of the body exercising 1 vegetative, sensitive and locomotive powers through the body. Since the soul performs at least some functions through the body there is no possibility of its isolation from the physical world. Further, since the soul is sensitive in addition to intellectual, the soul cannot simply be a thinking thing in contact only with ideas. Rather, the soul is able to become identical with reality through means of sensible and intelligible species which are intentionally identical with the real even if differing in their mode of existence. Soul, then, always implies body and its relation to the world while mind does not (Gilson 1937, 160-161; cf. PMN 47-50).

Since Descartes insists on the dualism between mind and body and on the resulting split between mental subject and physical world he is forced to conclude that the mind has immediate access only to its own ideas. While this introspective access is intuitive and thus the content of ideas are immediately given, the immediate access is only of ideas representing reality and thus not of reality itself: "it is *representations* which are in the 'mind.' The Inner Eye surveys these representations hoping to find some mark which will testify to their fidelity" (PMN 45). Reality is always mediated.

A consequence of the mediation of representations is the threat of skepticism, for "how do we know that anything which is mental represents anything which is not mental? How do we know whether what the Eye of the Mind sees is a mirror ... or a veil" (PMN 46)? Descartes still thinks of the mind as a mirror representing the world, but the question of whether the representations accurately reflect the world is raised (PMN 113). Of course, Descartes is convinced that the bridge is guaranteed by his clear and distinct ideas of the world and the reliance of such ideas given the honesty of God. He depends on a particular class of representations, what Rorty calls *privileged represen-tations*, which have the power to compel and justify belief because of their unique foundational stature. Still, such a solution is tenuous, and Spinoza, Leibniz, Malebranche, Locke, Berkeley and Kant are heirs of a thorny problem, namely, how can we know that representations in the inner world mirror the outer world accurately? Rorty believes that the Cartesian problematic creates the possibility for the "new philosophical genre" (PMN 113) of epistemology attempting to bridge the gap between subject and object.

2.32 Locke's Causal Account & Privileged Representations

While the Cartesian mind creates the basic problems of epistemology, it is Locke and Kant who complete the genre (Vaden House 1994, 32). Prior to their systems, the notion that the discipline of philosophy possessed a unique sphere of operations distinct from science or natural philosophy did not exist (PMN 131). The distinction was possible only on the assumption that philosophy governed the theory of knowledge—epistemology or *Erkenntnistheorie*—and was thus foundational or underlying of the practice of the natural sciences (PMN 132-135). Locke is the key cause of this in that he made "Descartes's newly contrived 'mind' into the subject matter of a 'science of man'— moral philosophy as opposed to natural philosophy" (PMN 137). By studying the "inner space" of the mind Locke hoped for an advantage in the discovery and understanding of the outer world. Of course, it is possible that the study of the inner mind could be performed empirically, but then philosophy would lose its function. Subsequently, if philosophy were to be safeguarded from science's encroachment the study of the inner mind must be non-empirical but the matter of armchair philosophical reflection.

Locke accepts the Cartesian picture of ideas representing the external world and mistakenly assumes that if he *explains* how ideas are formed he will have justified the accuracy of those ideas. Subsequently, he performs an investigation into the processes by which beliefs are formed, a description of the mechanisms of the mind and its faculties (PMN 140; cf. Vaden House 1994, 34). By examining the faculty of understanding, Locke explains how the *tabula rasa* of the mind is "something like a wax tablet upon which objects make *impressions*," and thinks that having an impression is itself knowledge (PMN 142). Assuming that the mind is fundamentally passive with respect to the acquisition of sense impressions he assumes that sensation serves as "a power, not ourselves, which compels us" to have certain beliefs (PMN 157-158). If he can explain the cause of this then he has explained how our ideas represent objects in the world—our ideas are impressions caused by objects and are thus justified. That is to say, the mere presence of the impression is equated with knowing and explaining how the impression arrived on the tablet is thus to explain the cause and justification of the knowledge.

This assumes the ocular metaphor in several ways. First, it accepts the Cartesian version of the subject/object split modeled on the distance between the eye and the object beheld out-there. Second, it assumes that the ideas of the mind must mirror or represent reality in order to attain knowledge. Third, it assumes the spectator theory in that the object gives itself to a fundamentally passive mind and causes the ideas of the mind. Fourth, Locke smuggles in the Eye of the Mind, the inner Eye, which mysteriously has a vantage point from which to observe itself in some super-intuition:

It is as if the *tabula rasa* were perpetually under the gaze of the un-blinking Eye of the Mind—nothing, as Descartes said, being nearer to the mind than itself. If the metaphor *is* unpacked in this way, however, it becomes obvious that the imprinting is of less interest than the observation of the imprint—all the knowing gets done, so to speak, by the Eye which observes the imprinted tablet rather than by the tablet itself.... Since for him impressions were *representations*, he needed a faculty which was *aware* of the representations, a faculty which *judged* the representations rather than merely *had* them.... (PMN 143-144)

In addition to these ocular metaphors, Locke assumes, as did Descartes, that a certain class of representations is privileged or foundational. For Descartes these are clear and distinct ideas, but for Locke sense impressions. We have various types of ideas, some directly caused by impressions (like the idea of this sheet of paper) and others created by ourselves out of the data of sense (the idea of a dragon). But, since nothing is closer to the mind than itself, the eye of the mind is able to distinguish between the various classes of ideas and judge that those directly caused by sense impressions are certain while those caused by ourselves are not. According to Rorty, the notion that sense impressions are privileged because of their certainty is to assume that knowledge is only guaranteed when privileged representations compel belief in the same manner that opening our eyes compels belief in what we see. Without the privileged representations there would be no certainty or foundations: "the notion of 'foundations of knowledge'—truths which are certain because of their causes rather than the arguments given for them—is the fruit of the Greek (and specifically Platonic) analogy between perceiving and knowing" (PMN 157). Rorty continues:

We will want to get behind reasons to causes, beyond argument to compulsion from the object known, to a situation in which argument would be not just silly but impossible, for someone gripped by an object in the required way will be *unable* to doubt or see an alternative. To reach that point is to reach the foundations of knowledge. For Plato, that point was reached by escaping from the senses and opening up the faculty of reason—the Eye of the Soul—to the World of Being. For Descartes, it was a matter of turning the Eye of the Mind from the confused inner representations to the clear and distinct ones. With Locke, it was a matter of reversing Descartes's directions and seeing 'singular presentations to sense' as what should 'grip' us—what we cannot and should not wish to escape from. (PMN 159)

2.33 Kant's Failed Attempt & the Neo-Kantian Mistake

Of course, Locke fails in his attempt, as both Hume and Berkeley demonstrate, and Kant must awake from his dogmatic slumbers and attempt another justification. Kant makes progress by not relying on representations grasped with intuitive certainty such as Cartesian clear and distinct ideas or Lockean impressions. Both had the charm of gripping the knower, compelling them to believe and providing certainty, but Kant realizes that any representation alone—whether of sense of mind—was incapable of compelling assent. Instead of seeking for some privileged inner representation (recognized through introspection) which caused and thereby justified belief, Kant realized that knowledge always resulted from synthesis, or judgment, and so moved dramatically towards understanding knowledge as propositional rather than modeled on perception (PMN 159). Also, he does not think of ideas as pictures or images whose truth depends on their resemblance to the world out-there but instead is concerned to attain coherence among ideas.

Unfortunately, Kant moves only "halfway toward a conception of knowing which was *not* modeled on perception ... Kant's way of performing the shift still remained within the Cartesian frame of reference; it was still phrased as an answer to the question of how we could get from inner space to outer space" (PMN 147). So long as knowledge is guaranteed by an explanation of "causes rather than arguments" Kant remains trapped by the "analogy between perceiving and knowing" (PMN 157). The Kantian answer to the relation of inner and outer is a reversal of the past tradition, of course, for rather than arguing that sensation results in concepts Kant holds that the activities of the understanding organize the manifold of sensation and subsequently constitute the phenomenal outer space (PMN 155). But this is still an explanation of how knowledge comes about, how the apparatus of the mind works to relate the inner and outer spheres to one another, still a "framework of causal metaphors—'constitution,' 'making,' 'shaping,' 'synthesizing,' and the like" (PMN 161).

The Kantian attempt to explain knowledge depends upon the distinction between two sorts of representations—intuitions and concepts. Although reality was not discovered but rather constituted by his solution, Kant's system is still objective in the sense that we cannot help but construct reality and we must necessarily do so according to the nature of our subjectivity. Since an element of necessity remains, the two types of representations—intuitions and concepts—divide into the contingent and the necessary. Kant still assumes that the manifold is *given* in intuition, still caused by the world as it is in itself, and thus Kant still is forced to accept the appearance/reality distinction. Since we can never leap over appearance to the real, objectivity is preserved by the unique role of transcendental philosophy in grasping the necessary structure and synthesizing function of the understanding. To Rorty's mind, the genre of epistemology—both Anglo-American and on the Continent—remains entirely Kantian by retaining the distinction between the content given to intuition and the necessary structure of the mind (PMN 160-162). Philosophy is reduced to epistemology, and since epistemology is the discipline dealing with the structures of belief which provide necessity, philosophy retains its status as grounding the other disciplines which study the contents of intuition but which merely assume the structures of belief.

Transcendental Philosophy was almost overcome by Nietzsche and Dewey, but Russell and Husserl turned back to the problems and revived neo-Kantianism in their respective traditions (PMN 166). In their attempts to overcome psychologism, they reclaim the ground for philosophy as a foundational discipline. Husserl returns to the privileged representation made available through the reduction while Russell and his heirs "linguistify" the Kantian distinction between the contingency of immediately given intuitions and the necessity provided through logical form (now linguistic rather than categories of the understanding) (PMN 165-168; PSH 32).

In Rorty's analysis, the analytic tradition accepted the scheme/content distinction from Kant while presupposing an isomorphism between language and the non-linguistic world (M. McCarthy 1990, 112). As such, it still accepts the subject/object split and still assumes that knowledge is a mirroring or accurate representation of language and the world. To take just one example, the early Wittgenstein of the *Tractatus* clearly falls into this mold. The *Tractatus* attempts to provide an *a priori* foundation based not in experience but in logic that explains how language and thought are related to reality (M. McCarthy 1990, 114). As such, it is both foundational and causal in nature;

it attempts to explain how we get back to the world and does so by appealing to a formal and necessary structure of how representations must work. Wittgenstein finds his solution in the picture theory: A proposition pictures the real by sharing a common form, but in order for the proposition to correspond to reality the structures of the world and of thought/language must be isomorphic (Wittgenstein 1961, 2.16, 2.161, 2.17). In true Kantian spirit, the structure is not discovered through investigating the world (that would merely provide contingent structure) but in analyzing the structure of propositions (M. McCarthy 1990, 114). Furthermore, propositions consist of names, which are primitive signs incapable of further dissection or analysis (Wittgenstein 1961, 3.261, 4.22). Consequently, while names occur only as a nexus within a proposition (4.23), names are the elements within the proposition which stand directly for objects and which "correspond to", or are representatives of objects (3.2, 3.21, 3.221).

This fits Rorty's theory as it is representational, explanatory, and assumes a type of scheme/content distinction which appeals to a special type of representation (the name) within the form of language to guarantee the correspondence of language and reality. Rorty's narrative thus demonstrates the creation of the discipline of epistemology. Beginning with the Cartesian problem of how inner representations can be guaranteed to match up with reality, epistemology attempts to explain how beliefs are formed through a causal explanation, but since representational realism risks solipsism, epistemology is forced into finding a foundation, some sort of special representation which is incorrigible or immediately given and supposedly capable of guaranteeing other representations. As Rorty explains:

> To describe this development as a linear sequence is of course simplistic, but perhaps it helps to think of the original dominating metaphor as being that of having our beliefs determined by being brought face-to-face with the object of belief.... The next stage is to think that to understand how to know better is to understand how to improve the activity of a quasi-visual faculty, the Mirror of Nature, and thus to think of knowledge as an assemblage of accurate representations. Then comes the idea that the way to have accurate representations is to find, within the Mirror, a special privileged class of representations so compelling that their accuracy cannot be doubted. These privileged foundations will be the foundations of knowledge.... Philosophy-as-epistemology will be the search for

the immutable structures within which knowledge, life and culture must be contained—structures set by the privileged representations which it studies. (PMN 163)

So long as philosophy assumes that the mind must mirror reality it remains trapped in the "Cartesian-Kantian picture presupposed by the ideas of 'our minds' or 'our language' as an 'inside' which can be contrasted to something (perhaps something very different) 'outside'" (ORT 12). But to assume an 'inner' versus 'outer' distinction is to accept an optical image, to assume that representations are pictures or images of the outside and that "some transcendental standpoint outside our present set of representations" is necessary if we are to "inspect the relations between those representations and their object" and compare them to each other (PMN 293).

2.4 UNDOING INTUITIONISM

Rorty wishes to oppose the status of a philosophy-as-epistemology superior to other cultural pursuits. He first revealed the contingency of epistemology and its problems. His second move is to undo the god's-eye view upon which epistemology depends. Only then can we escape our supposed need to mirror reality. For Rorty, the concern to have our beliefs correspond to reality is an attempt to humble ourselves, bowing and scraping before the non-human authority of the real world. Philosophers may have liberated themselves from the domination of God, but they have merely replaced God with being. Dewey, more than any other, exposed the abasing quality of the spectator theory demanding our passive obedience to the real and the "priest-craft" of the Philosopher who is able to mediate the real to merely ordinary humans (McDowell 2000, 109-114; cf. ORT 27-28, 38-39).

Instead of the Platonic-Cartesian-Kantian tradition, Rorty has as his heroes Hegel, Dewey, Wittgenstein and Heidegger. These figures, like Harold Bloom's strong poets, reveal the contingency of the real world and the freedom of humans to assert themselves and control the world. Hegel dismantles the necessary structures preached by Kant and reveals their mutable and historic status. Dewey allows us to escape our abasement before the "divine world" in favor of coping and control of the world. Wittgenstein and Heidegger both disclose the paucity of accounts dependent on representing a separate reality in favor of being-in-the-world in a manner recognizing the tool-like status of our encounters and descriptions. In short, Rorty sides against the tradition, against the understanding which grants Philosophy a special status in helping us mold our beliefs to the dictates of the nature of things and promising "salvation" to those who have mastered the vocabulary of *what is.* He sides with Bacon and Darwin rather than Plato. But Rorty is no hack. This is not a sophomoric attempt to convince us that we can do anything we want; Rorty has good reasons to reject the tradition.

2.41 Exposing Unmediated Intuitions

The central thesis of Rorty's critique is that epistemology has confused explaining the causes of belief with justifying belief (PMN 139). If knowledge is justified true belief then the realm of the epistemic should be a realm of justification, reasons, arguments, and not reduced to an explanation of a mechanistic causal process. Further, when the causal account reduces justification to the immediate grasp of a foundational, privileged representation—to intuitionism—it assumes that to see is to justify. This is possible only if knowledge is not defined as justified true belief, says Rorty, since a moment of sight, either of sense or of the Mind's Eye, could never serve as the premise of an argument. It has confused looking at reality with knowing reality.

For example, we might want to test our belief that the earth is flat by observing a ship sail into the horizon. If the earth is flat the ship should merely appear smaller and smaller, but instead it appears to "sink" as it recedes. For an intuitionist, all that would be required is to point at the ship and say "see!" and the belief that the earth is round would be justified. But of course this is insufficient, we must argue that the ship's apparent sinking is possible only if the earth curves downward and not just point at the sight. Knowledge must be obtained discursively rather than intuitively. The same principle is true of contents of our own minds as well. We cannot simply look inward, see something and claim to have justified knowledge of the world. All knowledge claims must be defended with warrants, reasons, arguments—a case must be made.

So not only is an intuitively grasped representation insufficient to justify a belief, but even to assume that any representation is immediately given or privileged is to fall into error and accept what Sellars calls the Myth of the Given (PMN 182-192). For Sellars and

Rorty, any awareness that is epistemically relevant—which exists in the realm of warranted, justifiable assertability—is linguistically conditioned rather than immediately given. A baby or a rat obviously are aware of objects or of raw feels given their discriminatory behavior in response—the baby cries when pinched, the rat sniffs for food—but they are not aware in the sense of operating in the logical space of reasons where one utters sentences in the attempt to justify other sentences (PMN 182). The child clearly seems to experience pain but is unable to know what sort of thing pain is, for to be able to state what sort of thing something is presumes the ability to relate it to other sorts of things (the pain when I am pinched is like x, y, or z). But if this is the case, then non- or pre-linguistic awareness may in fact be the *cause* of knowledge but is not capable of *justifying* knowledge (PMN 183).

Accepting the linguistic mediation of awareness does not mean that Rorty is a linguistic idealist. He does not think that "to be is to be perceived," or "to be is to be spoken," and readily admits the existence of a non-linguistic world (ORT 81). Non-linguistic objects certainly exist and exert causal influence, even belief-causing influences upon us: "there is such a thing as brute physical resistance—the pressure of light waves on Galileo's eyeball, or the stone on Dr. Johnson's boot.... When the die hits the blank something causal happens...the blank has no choice, nor do we" (ORT 81). But to say that the merely causal forces of the non-linguistic world *justify* our beliefs about these "facts" is to assume that we intuitively capture the world without the mediation of our prior belief structures.

Intuitionism assumes that we are passive spectators of these causal forces and assumes that certainty is guaranteed by a special class of representation, immediately given, which somehow perfectly possess the causal forces as they are in-themselves and which justifies our knowledge by their mere presence. But, while the causal forces of the non-linguistic world are independent of our language, our awareness of these causal forces is linguistically mediated. As such, there is no special class of representations escaping mediation to express itself in the natural language of causality. There is no non-linguistic access to an ahistoric, purely given, bottom layer of infallible representations which are foundational and which perfectly capture the causal world. *All* representations, including the merely sensory, are already descriptions and so exist in the world of linguistic mediation.

To give an example of Rorty's point, traditional epistemology assumed that my statement, "I see a red patch" is justified by a red patch which is simply given or presented in a sensory impression or intuition. However, in order to do so, my listener and myself must first assume that the verbal statement "I see a red patch" is a reliable indicator of the presence of a red patch. But the condition of possibility allowing us to assume the verbal statement is reliable is a prior familiarity with the semantic rules of language which we share with each other and all others in our social context. If there were not prior social rules governing how statements are to be used it would still be true that the red object may cause me to perceive a red patch but the givenness of the red patch alone would not justify my statement that I see a red patch. The statement is 'justified' because the prior social rules of language govern when and how such statements are to be made and the rules of the language cannot be reduced in any way to the perception of a red patch itself. Since the rules of language use are learned through prior lessons and experiences (e.g., my parents pointing to a red ball and saying "this is a red ball"), I am justified now in saying "I see a red patch" only because of this prior knowledge. Dr. Johnson's kicking of the stone indicates an argument against idealism only because everyone has already understood what is being talked about, what the terms mean and what sort of evidence would count.

Further, Quine's attack on reductionism demonstrates that there is no one-to-one correspondence between a moment of observation and a belief; an intuition alone is insufficient for justification (Orenstein 2002, 85). While logical empiricism might hope that an individual belief is proven or disproven by a single observation, there is no way to escape the background web of beliefs intrinsically tied up with the belief in question. To return to our example of the roundness of the earth based on the appearance of the ship "sinking" into the sea, we assume this is because the earth is curved and the ship has not sailed away in a straight plane but has followed the curve. In fact, this assumes a background such as our belief that light travels in a straight line. And our assumptions about the behavior of light assumes a great deal about light and about space—we cannot test any hypothesis in a vacuum free from other assumptions (Orenstein 2002, 81-82). Also, since every assumption rests upon others, there is no bedrock of infallible assumptions free from criticism and the need to be tested. If this is true, then our awareness of a sensory "given"—shown by Sellars to already be linguistically conditioned—is also not isolated. Any representation which we hoped would be privileged and foundational is already placed holistically in a pattern of previous assumptions, language games and beliefs—we cannot burrow down to a bottom layer of immediately given representations (Orenstein 2002, 84-85).

If we cannot examine any belief in isolation from other beliefs, then observational data cannot with certainty be used to verify or falsify the belief in question, for it is always possible that the observational data relates not to the belief in question but to another belief. For example, the ship's sinking into the sea may not indicate the curvature of the earth but perhaps the curvature of space or the erratic patterns of light; either description would adequately account for the observational data. Further, since the observational data, or at least any epistemically relevant awareness of the data, are already conditioned linguistically, it is impossible to attain a privileged representation or a foundational, intuitively certain idea:

> The ubiquity of language is a matter of language moving into the vacancies left by the failure of all the various candidates for the position of "natural starting-points" of thought, starting points which are prior to and independent of the way some culture speaks or spoke ... the regress of interpretation cannot be cut off by the sort of "intuition" which Cartesian epistemology took for granted. (COP xx)

2.42 A Non-Representational Account of Language

This would be unproblematic if the Kantian assumptions of much of linguistic philosophy were true, if like the Wittgenstein of the *Tractatus* we could simply uncover the necessary schemes underlying the contingent and linguistically conditioned content of our intuitions. It might be that intuitions are conditioned by language (just as they were by the forms of space and time for Kant), but necessity is guaranteed by the permanent and objective structures of the schema (here language substitutes for Kant's categories). Philosophy of language which is neo-Kantian assumes that knowing the underlying structures of language provides "a permanent ahistorical framework for inquiry in the form of a theory of knowledge" and still assumes that these structures are representational or correspond to the world 'out-there' (PMN 257). This is still part of the genre of epistemology, for it still assumes the subject/object distinction and is trying to determine a way to get back to the object:

> If we stick to the picture of language as a medium, something standing between the self and the nonhuman reality with which the self seeks to be in touch, we have made no progress. We are still using a subject-object picture, and we are still stuck with issues about skepticism, idealism and realism. For we are still able to ask questions about language of the same sort we asked about consciousness. (CIS 11)

Rorty rejects the scheme/content distinction by appealing to Donald Davidson's overcoming of this "third dogma of empiricism." If we take the neo-Kantian approach of a given reality and various conceptual schemes distinguished from the world, then the schemes are maps which organize and carve up the given world in different ways. Since the schemes are ubiquitous there is no way to step outside our schemes and see the world as it actually is, but there is supposedly an isomorphism between the schemes and the structure of reality (Nielsen 1991, 86-87). Of course, if there are alternative schemes, say between cultures or times, then the various realities are not only untranslatable to each other but impossible to defend as better than the others. A representationalist account would then necessarily devolve into skepticism or relativism, and indeed intuitionists and representationalists always suffer this risk (ORT 25-26).

Rather than supposing that language is a medium between the subject and object, and rather than supposing with the early Wittgenstein that language pictures or mirrors reality, and rather than supposing that understanding the structure of language exposes the structure of reality, Rorty advocates that language is simply a set of socially constructed practices to be used as a tool in accomplishing some task (ORT 97-101). If language has an underlying scheme which is necessary and ahistorical then understanding that scheme uncovers what is to be considered as rational, but if language is merely social practice then it is historical and contingent.

Language is not a thing. We ought not reify it, but should do for language what Ryle did for the mind—look to behaviors instead of trying to uncover underlying substance (CIS 15). Just as Ryle's "solution" simply erased many of the traditional mind/body problems so too is a therapy reached if we stop thinking of language as a thing, as a "third thing intervening between the self and reality" (CIS 14). In practice, language "is an exchange of marks and noises, carried out in order to achieve specific purposes. It cannot fail to represent accurately, for it never represents at all" (PSH 50). In this view, influenced heavily by the later Wittgenstein and by Davidson, language does not derive its meaning by any reference to the non-linguistic world, for that is merely a repetition of the Cartesian problematic, merely substituting "words" for "ideas," but by its use within a certain vocabulary or language game. We speak to accomplish some task; when we are on the construction site we say "hammer" to indicate we wish for the hammer to be passed to us and "five apples" in the store so that the store-keeper will give us fruit. Of course, these words have meaning only because of their underlying social usage. Unless we accept this Darwinian account where language is simply a tool for communication and coping we risk "treating Language as a quasi-agent ... something that stands over and against human beings" (EHO 3).

But vocabularies are not intractable or necessary by nature, for social practice is not necessary by nature; it changes:

> On the contrary, revolutionary achievements in the arts, in the sciences, and in moral and political thought typically occur when somebody realizes that two or more of our vocabularies are interfering with each other, and proceeds to invent a new vocabulary to replace both. For example, the traditional Aristotelian vocabulary got in the way of the mathematized vocabulary that was being developed in the sixteenth century by students of mechanics. Again, young German theology students of the late eighteenth century—like Hegel and Hölderlin—found that the vocabulary in which they worshipped Jesus was getting in the way of the vocabulary in which they worshipped the Greeks. (CIS 12)

Just as Hegel's *Phenomenology of Spirit* undid the Kantian transcendental categories, so too does any reliance on the scheme or structure of language give way to the later Wittgenstein and Davidson when they revert to the meaning of language occurring in social practice, "languages are made rather than found" (CIS 7).

Rorty's insistence on the contingency of language underlies his belief that (1) non-linguistic entities (such as pain and causality) are epistemically irrelevant and cannot justify belief, (2) language is contingent upon use and (3) meaning is produced within a language game by using words in familiar ways (Hall 1994, 90). All of this is anathema to an intuitionist, but Rorty has been attempting to expose, in what Bernstein calls the softening phase of his argument, the genealogy of epistemology and the implausibility of intuitionism. They result from historical choices, namely Descartes' creation of the veil-of-ideas problematic and the attempts of Locke and Kant to solve this problem while subsequently attempting to retain a purpose for philosophy. The modern face of Philosophy arose as it put itself forward as the ruler of epistemology and the arbiter and judge of what other cultural pursuits could be counted as rational. But not only has the modern foundational project been softened by Rorty's *Geistesgeschichte* which exposes its contingency, but the intuitionist presuppositions behind epistemology begin to be called into question. Immediate access and a priori structures are pipe-dreams, always conditioned by language, by the background web of beliefs and by social practice and vocabularies. Rorty does not stop with the softening approach, however, but proceeds to cheerfully accept the failure of epistemology and Philosophy.

2.5 ABANDONING TRUTH & EPISTEMOLOGY FOR HERMENEUTICS

Rorty considers realism and antirealism as variations on a theme, namely, both are concerned with the *representational* but differ on the possibility of accurately representing reality. In his reading, both assume a theory of truth in which reality is "out there" and a true statement is one in which the "out there" is accurately mirrored or corresponded by the statement (ORT 38; COP xxv). But since arguments like those of Sellars, Quine and Davidson seem to demonstrate that there is not really any way to get to the *Ding-an-sich*, Philosophy in the Cartesian-Lockean-Kantian tradition always worries about skepticism. It is only on the assumption that truth is correspondence or accurate representation of the out-there that the problems of realism and antirealism emerge. Both worry themselves sick about whether what we think and say is accurate to the facts of the matter.

Instead of remaining stuck within the impasse or realism and antirealism, Rorty instead suggests that we abandon the project altogether. Instead of proposing new theories of truth or new solutions to the questions of representationalism, we should admit that the very questions have become tired and useless and should not be asked anymore! There is nothing interesting to say about truth if we suppose it to be representation of reality and every attempt to explain and defend the correspondence thesis has failed. If we abandon the project of representationalism altogether—if we are not antirealists but *antirepresentationalists*—then we escape the problems of skepticism, relativism, realism and antirealism in one nifty trick (ORT 39). If we abandon the fly-bottle trap of thinking we need to picture reality we escape not only the need to find some theory which coherently explains this but we escape the entire genre of Philosophy-as-epistemology. Of course, to a representationalist this is the worst heresy, but Rorty has already demonstrated that the tradition of epistemology, i.e., the tradition attempting a theory of truth by which to explain representations, was the result of a historical choice and is neither necessary nor intrinsic to the enterprise of thought—we are committing heresy only against a mutable and suspect orthodoxy. We can stop worrying about "getting it right" or accurately representing reality.

Instead of a representational epistemology, Rorty advocates an antirepresentational epistemological behaviorism, the attempt to explain "rationality and epistemic authority by reference to what society lets us say, rather than the latter by the former" (PMN 174). Epistemology failed to discover any necessary and universal epistemic norms and its failure reveals that knowing is something humans do, a behavior we engage in, and the matrix of terms that we use to speak of this activity—truth, justification, certainty—are governed by the linguistic rules that the community comes up with (PSH 48; cf. Vaden House 1994, 88). The criteria by which a belief is determined to be justified rest upon the historic decisions made by a linguistic community. For example, the Church's use of Scripture against the Copernican theory is thought by the modern scientific community to be completely illegitimate since it includes religious and cultural considerations into what should be purely scientific deliberations (PMN 330). To us moderns, this perhaps makes a great deal of sense, but only because we are children of Galileo and his defenders who "refuted" Bellarmine and the Church by appealing to the distinction between science and religion. This was an historical choice, one which did not make sense to Bellarmine but which does to us, but only because we operate within a sphere of rationality that accepts Galileo's defense—it might have been otherwise. All that remains is our acceptance of the fact that if we understand the rules of a language game, we understand all that there is to understand about why moves in that language game are made, i.e., we will understand why certain beliefs are considered justifiable while others are rejected. In the end, beliefs which are considered objective, even incorrigible, are thought so simply because most people within the linguistic community have not thought to question the belief or propose another answer; beliefs thought to be "subjective" have simply not attained consensus (PSH 51).

Epistemological behaviorism claims that epistemology, i.e., Philosophy, loses its special status as judge of the rationality of the various disciplines and cultural practices. Rather, it is simply "the study of the ways in which human beings interact" (PMN 175) and has "no more to offer than common sense...about knowledge and truth" (PMN 176). But without some sort of necessary or ahistorical vocabulary, changes in social rules of justification cannot be considered as progressing or regressing from an ideal norm. Rorty follows Thomas Kuhn's *The Structure of Scientific Revolutions* in this respect, understanding that vocabularies accepted for long periods of time begin to appear natural or "normal" to the members within the vocabulary. Normal discourse with its canons of justified discourse—the Aristotelian understanding of physics until the scientific revolution, for example—is challenged by an incommensurable "abnormal discourse" which cannot be proven or disproven by the norms of normal discourse or disprove normal discourse with its own norms. Tension builds, neither discourse is capable of conclusively proving or disproving the other, but each is capable of making sense of the empirical data, until the tension breaks in a revolution where the abnormal discourse is accepted for no conclusive reason; usually the proponents of the older normal discourse simply become old and die before the younger adherents of the abnormal discourse. Eventually, the once abnormal discourse becomes normal, accepted as the new standard and presumed to be natural and permanent, until challenged and overthrown by another rival which now takes is considered abnormal (PMN 323-333).

It would be one thing if Rorty were merely describing the ways in which he thought standards of justification historically occurred. If that were the case, epistemological behaviorism would amount to nothing more than a rejection of the solitary Cartesian Ego in favor of a community of investigators and an awareness of history. However, Rorty is adamant that epistemological behaviorism is not simply a description of the fact that we indeed accept community standards but is a complete rejection of any standard, especially the standard of correspondence, that claims to amount to anything more than what is accepted by a community:

> There is no activity called 'knowing' which has a nature to be discovered, and at which natural scientists are particularly skilled. There is simply the process of justifying beliefs to audiences. None of these audiences is closer to nature, or a better representative of some ahistorical ideal of rationality, than any other....
>
> It may seem strange to say that there is no connection between justification and truth. This is because we are inclined to say that truth is the aim of inquiry. But I think we pragmatists must grasp the nettle and say that this claim is either empty or false. Inquiry and justification have lots of mutual aims, but they do not have an overarching aim called truth ... we do not need a goal called 'truth' to help us ... any more than our digestive organs need a goal called health ... There would be a 'higher' aim of inquiry called 'truth' if there were such a thing as *ultimate* justification—justification before God, or before the tribunal of reason, as opposed to any merely finite human audience.
>
> ... Such a tribunal would have to have what Putnam calls a "God's eye view." (PSH 37-38)

Justification "is a social phenomenon rather than a transaction between 'the knowing subject' and 'reality'" (PMN 9); "justification is not a matter of a special relation between ideas (or words) and objects, but of conversation, of social practice" (PMN 170). In this case knowledge is "not a relation between mind and object, but, roughly, ... the ability to get agreement ..." (ORT 88) while opinion is just a belief more difficult to get most people to agree to (ORT 23). In this case, we have simply and completely abandoned the hope to represent reality, and even the change of vocabularies is not progress in the sense of better getting at reality, although it might be progress in the sense of controlling or coping with reality. 'Truth' is simply what your audience accepts from your attempts to persuade them.

To a representationalist such a picture of science or philosophy is scandalous. Since the various discourses are incommensurable and incapable of being proven or disproven by a neutral framework it is impossible to consider the history of revolutions in science or philosophy as making progress towards some final discourse which gets it right at last: "When the notion of 'description of the world' is moved from the level of criterion-governed sentences within language games to language games as wholes, games which we do not choose between by reference to criteria, the idea that the world decides which descriptions are true can no longer be given a clear sense" (CIS 5). The transition of discourses is not moving towards getting it right; there is just a different discourse and odds are good that there will be yet another, and then another after that. The change of discourses may be motivated by any number of reasons or causes, but none are able to claim to be final. As for Philosophy, since it abandons the claim to adjudicate between various discourses and areas of culture, it is no more useful than poetry, science or literature (COP xliii). The acceptance that Philosophy-as-epistemology is a dead end and is not a special master science spells the end of Philosophy in favor of philosophy and Epistemology in favor of hermeneutics.

Philosophy (upper case) accepts the Platonic questions of trying to get to *what is* while philosophy (lower case) is simply "an attempt to see how things, in the broadest possible sense of the term, hang together, in the broadest possible sense of the term," and accepts that "Blake is as much a philosopher as Fichte, Henry James more of a philosopher than Frege" (COP xiv-xv), which is to say that professional philosophers have no more to say than any other bright and insightful thinker. Hermeneutics abandons the epistemological quest for commensurability or for attaining the master vocabulary which would provide a perfect vantage point, a god's-eye view, from which to understand and control the meanings internal to every other vocabulary. Instead, hermeneutics is the practice of abnormal discourse or the attempt to mediate between apparently incommensurable discourses and vocabularies. Hermeneutics is not foundational, does not claim to solve the disputes between various vocabularies (that would be epistemology), and does not allow escape into a presuppositionless ether (Vaden House 1994, 97). In fact, hermeneutics does not even have inquiry into truth as its goal. It merely attempts to allow an ongoing conversation, a cooperation, between various discourses, which allows us to cope with life:

> We cannot regard truth as a goal of inquiry. The purpose if inquiry is to achieve agreement among human beings about what to do, to bring about consensus on the ends to be achieved and the means to be used to achieve those ends. (PSH xxv)

The attempt to engage in conversation trying to seek consensus about what should be done is called *edification* by Rorty. In his (mis)reading of Gadamer's hermeneutics,

> Rorty uses Gadamer's notion of *Bildung* to characterize a break with epistemologically centered philosophy. *Bildung* for Rorty, describes an interest in edification and self-formation that contrasts with an interest in certain knowledge. The point of an edifying philosophy is not to discover either foundations for our beliefs or a basis upon which to criticize them. Neither is its concern a final, irrevocable understanding of "truth" or the way the world is. Its point is rather to foster an awareness of different possibilities of coping with the world, of different life-options and, indeed, of new modes of self-description. From the point of view of edification what is important is not "the possession of truths" but our own development. (Warnke 1987, 156-157).

Rorty feels strongly that choosing edification over truth is an epochal-making decision, for the choice to do so is to move from either a religious or philosophical world which tries to get either the will of God or the nature of the world right to embracing a literary world which is concerned to embrace as many alternative vocabularies and modes of discourses as would help to attain consensus and cope with the world (Rorty 2000).

Unless we understand that Rorty is not advocating another foundation by which to judge between competing viewpoints we will not understand the radicality of his position. In his mind, modernity had two guiding impulses, one of which he accepts and one which he rejects. The Cartesian, epistemological project is rejected by Rorty and in this respect he is a postmodern who is incredulous towards meta-narratives and who rejects any and all foundational or transcendental projects. On the other hand, if we understand modernity as fundamentally a project of Baconian self-assertion then Rorty is a modern (Hall 1994, 31-34). He rejects the epistemological foundationalism of modernity but accepts the attempt to master our own fate and create the world in our image rather than passively wait for the whims of providence and the will of God. When we attempt to attain consensus, edification and self-improvement, we do not do so based on any Truth or Goodness which is out-there, we do so based on our own desires to avoid pain and cruelty, nothing more.

2.6 HOPING FOR ANOTHER TYPE OF REALISM

To my mind, Rorty provides a compelling critique of the intuitionist project, exposing it not only as a historical choice but as a fundamentally untenable choice. But, since Rorty assumes that the ocular tradition of epistemology is merely a choice and not intrinsic to the philosophic enterprise which attempts to see how things hang together, he risks committing a false dichotomy when he assumes he has exposed realism as a pipe dream merely by exposing direct and representational realisms as untenable. My own *Geistesgeschichte* of Chapter One and that of Rorty are in fundamental agreement with each other, for both argue that the Western epistemological tradition has held itself captive to the ocular metaphor. So such theories do not work, but to claim that realism is overthrown simply because versions of realism which are dependent on the ocular, intuitionist metaphor are overthrown is to assume that *all* realisms are ocular. If there is a realism which is not at all based on the ocular metaphor it might escape Rorty's critique.

To argue that we can defend a realism without a god's-eye view is to escape from what Richard Bernstein has called *Cartesian Anxiety*, "the grand Either/Or—either there is some basic foundational constraint or we are confronted with intellectual and moral chaos" (Bernstein 1985, 72-73). If Lonergan can provide a realism without a god's-eye view then he escapes the false dichotomy of Cartesian Anxiety as well as Rorty's critique. But if that is the case, it would begin to appear that Rorty has too quickly conflated realism and the god's-eye view. In fact, it would then appear that Rorty is himself guilty of Cartesian Anxiety although he is quite willing to accept the "or" side of the dilemma, the side of self-assertion and chaos. Bernstein himself suspects that Rorty has committed this error:

> Rorty ... [tries] to help us to set aside the Cartesian Anxiety—the Cartesian Either/Or—that underlies so much of modern philosophy. But there is a variation of this Either/Or that haunts [Philosophy and the Mirror of Nature]—Either we are *ineluctably* tempted by foundational metaphors and the desperate attempt to escape from history *or* we must frankly recognize that philosophy itself is at best a form of "kibitzing." (Bernstein 1985, 77)

I attempt to demonstrate Rorty's Anxiety in the chapters to follow.

CHAPTER 3

COGNITIONAL THEORY & SELF-KNOWLEDGE

> Brother, I don't pretend to be a sage,
> Nor have I all the wisdom of the age.
> There's just one insight I would dare to claim:
> I know that true and false are not the same.
>
> (Molière, *Tartuffe*, Act I. Scene 5)

3.1 PREAMBLE

The last chapter concluded with Richard Bernstein's suggestion that Rorty is guilty of Cartesian Anxiety, the fear that either we have indubitable and certain foundations or realism is impossible. Since a dichotomy is only false if a legitimate alternative exists, Rorty's argument stands until an ocular-based epistemology is justified or until a non-ocular realism is established. The first two chapters investigated the failures of the ocular model, and as I do not wish to repeat those failures, I will not attempt to overcome the dichotomy with a renewed defense of intuitionism and its type of foundationalism. Rather, this chapter argues that a non-ocular realism is possible if one undergoes an intellectual conversion in which all versions of the ocular metaphor are rejected and the structure and processes of cognition are affirmed. Of course, it would be premature to argue that Rorty is thereby disproven, but in this chapter I begin to establish that claim, arguing that Rorty is right to reject the ocular metaphor since it is irrational but that the link between realism and intuitionism can be severed and realism saved. Rorty may be correct: past attempts at realism have been irrational, but the answer is not to abandon realism but to finally give a rational account of it (Meynell 1999, 184-186).

To my mind, the work of intellectual conversion and defense of realism is best accomplished by Bernard Lonergan, S. J. (1904-1984). Born in Buckingham, Quebec, Canada, he was educated at the high school of Loyola College, Montreal, entered the Jesuit Novitiate in 1922 and completed his juniorate in 1926. He studied philosophy at

Heythrop College, mathematics and languages at the University of London and theology at the Gregorian University and taught at the Collège de L'Immaculée-Conception in Montreal, Regis College in Toronto, the Gregorian University, Harvard Divinity School and Boston College (Crowe 1992). His collected writings will fill twenty-two volumes upon complete publication and include such notable works as the *Verbum* articles written between 1946 and 1949, *Insight: A Study of Human Understanding* released in 1957 and *Method in Theology* of 1972. He was invested as Companion of the Order of Canada and Corresponding Fellow of the British Academy. Research centers dedicated to his thought are established in Toronto, Boston, Washington, D.C., Los Angeles and overseas.

It would appear that Lonergan and Rorty never commented on the work of the other (Bradley 1994, 149) but there is a small body of literature by students of Lonergan comparing the two figures (Meynell 1985 and 1999; Barden 1986; M. McCarthy 1990; Fitzpatrick 1995; Beards 1997). Despite the diverse backgrounds of the two thinkers—Rorty's concern with Anglo-American and recently Continental figures versus Lonergan's Scholastic training—the commentators note the fundamental similarity they share in rejecting ocularism. However, Rorty rejects ocularism in hopes of freeing us from the concerns of Philosophy-as-epistemology which tries to get things right while Lonergan overcomes the ocular metaphor in order to finally get it right; Rorty views the ocular tradition as providing false hope of an unattainable goal, Lonergan thinks of ocularism as a form of obscurantism keeping us from attaining the goal.

Lonergan is an epistemological realist, he believes that judgments are true if and only if they correspond to what is in fact the case. Still, the correspondence theory is too easily hijacked by ocular terms to be entirely helpful—mental contents in-here correspond to objective reality out-there. This is picture thinking, for it assumes that thinking takes place in images and correspondence occurs when the mental image reflects or accurately represents nature, exactly what Rorty rejects. But realism can be conceived in terms other than ocular (Meynell 1985, 31) and Lonergan's critical realism is largely motivated by the attempt to escape what he calls the fundamental *cognitional myth* of equating knowing and looking (M 238). To distinguish his version of realism from the false starts of these past thinkers, Lonergan's version of realism will not be called the *correspondence theory* with its almost irresistible Siren call to ocular thinking but rather *cognitive self-transcendence,* or *self-transcendence* for short since we are dealing only with cognition and not with self-transcendence in ethics or religion. Lonergan's realist intention for self-transcendence is indisputable, and he writes:

> Not only does it [self-transcendence] go beyond the subject but also it seeks what is independent of the subject. For a judgment that this or that is so reports, *not what appears to me, not what I imagine, not what I think, not what I wish, not what I would be inclined to say, not what seems to me, but what is so.* (M 104; italics mine)

Lonergan is not tender-minded, however, and realizes that the ocular metaphor is so engrained in the tradition and in our common sense understanding that the move away from the cognitive myth towards self-transcendence requires a radical change in understanding, what he terms *intellectual conversion.* Just as the prisoner in Plato's cave requires a conversion or turning (*periagoges*) to escape so the human knower needs to convert from the mental trap of equating knowing with taking a look. But conversion is not accomplished simply by reading a text or encountering the right arguments; it is not a change of opinion about some proposition but rather changes an entire way of thinking, the horizon of what counts as real and valuable. The struggle of Augustine in *Confessions* 7 comes to mind: Augustine could not simply abandon his conception of God as a body or corporeal substance and struggles through an assortment of false and incomplete answers until he has a mental conversion, is able to think of an incorporeal God and finally defeats the Manicheans. Lonergan is asking us to undergo the same laborious and intense process, one in which any lingering presence of the cognitional myth dooms our ability to comprehend his position.

3.2 THE COGNITIONAL MYTH

The cognitional myth results in three fundamental errors, all intertwined: (1) that knowing is like looking, (2) that objectivity is seeing what is there to be seen, and (3) that the real is what is out there to be looked at (M 238). These three errors will be explained in detail throughout the chapter, but it serves to have a brief explanation in mind before proceeding.

First, Lonergan rejects the account that knowing is like seeing:

An act of ocular vision may be perfect as ocular vision; yet if it occurs without any accompanying glimmer of understanding, it is
mere gaping; and mere gaping, so far from being the beau ideal of
human knowing, is just stupidity. As merely seeing is not human
knowing, so for the same reason merely hearing, merely smelling,
merely touching, merely tasting may be parts, potential compo-
nents, of human knowing, but they are not human knowing itself.
(C 222)

Notice that this passage fundamentally agrees with Dewey's rejection
of the spectator theory; we do not passively gape at reality the way a
cow does. Of course, merely rejecting the notion that knowing is like
seeing is not a positive account of what knowing actually is, but such is
Lonergan's project in *Verbum*, *Insight* and *Method*.

Second, Lonergan argues that the ocular metaphor assumes a notion of the real, of being, which reduces being to what is *already out
there now*, to what can be looked at (SC 76; C 232-236). The empiricist "identifies the real with what is exhibited in ostensive gestures.
What is a dog? Well, here you are, take a look" (M 76). The idealist
objects that merely looking does not take into account the structur-
ing elements which constitute knowing, such as Kantian forms and
categories, but the idealist still assumes that the real is the out-there
that we would look at if we could, we just cannot see it as it is. All such
veil of ideas problematics, including Kant's distinction between the
noumenal and phenomenal realms, assume that reality is out-there,
waiting to be seen by a mind free of categories and capable of a perfect
intuition, just as I argued regarding Kant in the first chapter. In this
account, idealism is a half-way point between empiricism and realism, for it understands that mere looking is insufficient but it does not
develop an account of the real which surpasses the empiricist's naïve
extroversion based solely on sight.

Third, the notion of the real based on what is out there and able
to be seen implies a concomitant epistemology, or at the minimum
a notion of objectivity. If the real is what is capable of being seen or
imagined, then "any cognitional activity that sufficiently resembles
ocular vision *must* be objective" and "any cognitional activity that does
not sufficiently resemble ocular vision *cannot* be objective" (C 232).
Objectivity must be like seeing, but then "knowing, if objective, is like
seeing" (C 233). Moreover, we know that we know when "we see our
knowing ... we see the correspondence of our knowing to the known"

(C 233). Of course, to be able to compare the knowing and the known is to have a super-intuition which sees our mind and the world in a god's-eye view, an impossibility (SC 15).

These three attributes of the cognitional myth are prevalent both in the philosophic tradition at large and in individual knowers (V 20, 192; SC 219; M 238-239). There is no need to reiterate the positions of philosophers such as Plato, Augustine, Descartes, Locke or Kant, and Lonergan would largely agree with the conclusions of the first two chapters. But Lonergan does diverge widely from Rorty by holding that the Aristotelian-Thomistic tradition avoids the error of the tradition of the myth, what Lonergan categorizes as "Platonism" (V 152-155), while still justifying and allowing for cognitive self-transcendence or realism. For the Platonist, which would include all of the epistemological villains of previous chapters, "knowing is primarily a confrontation, it supposes the duality of knower and known" (V 192). In other words, the Platonist commits the cognitional myth and accepts the three postulates that (1) knowing is like looking, (2) objectivity is seeing what is there to be seen, and (3) the real is what is out there (or up-there or in-here, as the case may be) to be confronted in an intuition. The Aristotelian, on the other hand, thinks that knowing is primarily "perfection, act, identity" (V 192). The Lonerganian enterprise is the working out of the Aristotelian account of knowledge as perfection, act, identity, although to be sure Lonergan is no paleo-Aristotelian or paleo-Thomist advocating a simple return to an extinct classicist world (LR 436-440, 545-549).

3.3 VERBUM: CLUE TO A SOLUTION

Lonergan was not a cradle Thomist. He remarks that he came late to Thomas and only after working through Newman, Augustine and Plato (UB 350). In fact, his early textbook exposure to Scholasticism had not impressed him and only upon reading Aquinas directly did he begin to think that the Angelic Doctor was not as bad as was made out. This culminated in an eleven-year apprenticeship to Aquinas in which Lonergan wrote his study of operative grace in Aquinas and the *Verbum* articles (Crowe 1992, 39-57). The *Verbum* articles, in examining Thomas' attempt to work out in Aristotelian form Augustine's Trinitarian analogy of the production of the inner word, reveal Lonergan's take on Thomas's cognitional theory properly understood. It is this study which allows Lonergan to claim the dichotomy between the confrontationalism of the Platonist and the identity theory of Aristotle and Aquinas.

The identity theory of knowing, as expressed by Aristotle in *De anima* 3 and appropriated by Aquinas, holds that that the human mind is capable of becoming all things, by becoming the form of the things it knows. So, when I understand a horse my intellect abstracts from the sensible species and the resulting intelligible species of horseness is identical to the form of the horse. My mind receives the form it has abstracted, it is informed and thus identical with the object. Of course, it is impossible to actually take the form of horse into my mind or I would literally become a horse, so the distinction is made between the modes of existence the form has in my mind and in the natural object. The species as it exists in my mind has intentional existence (*esse intentionale*) while the form of the object has existence in nature (*esse naturale*). That being said, the content of my mind, informed by the intentional species, is identical to the known object. This is not a representational theory, my mind does not have just an image picturing the object, my mind *is* the object in an intentional manner of existence. For an analogy, this is not a photograph of an object but more like the impression made in wax by a signet ring—the impression is the ring in a different mode.

Thomists such as Etienne Gilson have looked to the identity theory to escape the Cartesian problematic: since the contents of the mind do not represent extra-mental reality but *are* extra-mental reality in another mode of existence, the veil of ideas and the problem of the bridge created by the subject/object distinction are pseudo-problems. Thomism is thus able to bypass the major epistemological quandaries that Rorty finds insoluble and guarantees realism. But while the Thomistic revival following Pope Leo XIII's *Aeterni patris* in 1879 produced so much good, it has faltered, so much so that a contemporary epistemologist who largely ignored Thomas' contributions might be considered a poor historian but still a fine epistemologist. So while Thomists everywhere may fulminate, Rorty barely breaks stride from his larger targets to address Thomas; he simply is not much of a concern to Rorty.

Rorty studied at the University of Chicago at a time when Mortimer Adler and Richard McKeon had "enveloped" it in "neo-Aristotelian mystique" (PSH 8) and makes enough references to neo-Thomism and Gilson to indicate his familiarity with the identity theory. He even acknowledges that Aristotle need not worry about the veil of ideas because the identity theory is not representational (PMN 45, 144). The Cartesian problematic is then a radical departure from previous tradition and creates both the problem and language of representational mirroring. Still, Aristotle is not entirely free from ocular images, and while "intellect is not a mirror inspected by an inner eye" it is "both mirror and eye in one" (PMN 45). Aristotle uses the "retinal image" as the "model for the 'intellect which becomes all things,'" (PMN 45), and *De anima* 3 notes a similarity between perceiving, where the eye is capable of receiving the sensible form without the matter, and the passive intellect's ability to become in-formed and receive the intelligible species. Further, Aristotle's fascination with universals retains the classical concern to distinguish human from beast by creating a special type of perceiver, the Glassy Essence, which sees universals and gives us our unique status (PMN 42-44). Still, the mere presence of ocular language does not seem to justify equating Aristotle, and, by default, Aquinas, whom Rorty essentially identifies with Aristotle, with those depending on intuitionism or privileged representations and ignores Aristotle's claim that "thinking is different than perceiving" in that thinking includes "judgment" (*De anima* 3.3 427b29). Again, Rorty presents no real arguments against Aristotle other than a bemused "Aristotle's model may seem merely quaint" and "optional" (PMN 46). He seems to think that the Aristotelian-Thomistic tradition rests upon an outdated metaphysics, dependent on the existence of universals and thus that the hylomorphic account of reality necessitates an account of abstraction (PMN 40-41 n. 8). But since such a metaphysics is historically surpassed if not outright irrelevant he thinks himself within his rights to not take it all that seriously.

Lonergan certainly agrees that the problem of universals is rooted in ocular images (I 438), but in his *Verbum* articles he combats the notion that Aristotelian forms are just immanentized Platonic Ideas. Such accounts are rejected by Lonergan as "conceptualist" rather than genuinely "intellectualist" as Thomas intends (V 195). Conceptualists have not adverted to their own *acts* which they perform in the attempt to know and consequently do not understand the attempts of Aristotle and Aquinas to advert to their own acts of understanding (V 195). Ignorant of their own intellects, conceptualists see only metaphysical or faculty constructs in the terms agent intellect, phantasm, possible intellect, intelligible species, sensible species, intentional existence, first act, second act and so on. Since these terms are not really understood by the conceptualist, they seem to explain an overly static account of knowledge, one concerned with concepts, logic, certitude and not concerned enough with intelligence and understanding (V 194). Knowing becomes like a cognitive sausage machine: data go in the top, a crank turns and out pops concepts, but the process is mechanical rather than intelligent.

The conceptualist sees in Aquinas only a metaphysics of knowledge, but Lonergan says Aquinas performs not a metaphysics but an empirical introspection of understanding: "The Thomist concept of inner word ... is no mere metaphysical condition of a type of cognition; it aims at being a statement of psychological fact" (V 59). Now, Lonergan realizes that Aquinas doesn't leap out of his time into our own; Aquinas is not doing phenomenology. On the other hand, Aquinas' cognitional theory has the appeal it has even today, says Lonergan, because "Aquinas explicitly appealed to inner experience and ... Aristotle's account of intelligence ... has too uncanny an accuracy to be possible without the greatest introspective skill" (V 5). Still, and here is the warning, while Aristotle and Aquinas used introspection, and "did so brilliantly, it remains that they did not thematize their use, did not elevate it into a reflectively elaborated technique" (V 6). They were, in fact, performing an activity that they themselves did not yet have the categories or the motivation to explain. As Lonergan says, "performance must precede reflection on performance, and method is the fruit of that reflection. Aquinas had to be content to perform" (V 10). But the lack of thematization allows the conceptualist to easily overlook the performance and focus instead on the metaphysical categories in which Aquinas, a product of his times and limited by the language of Aristotle, was forced to express himself.

The tradition has too often ignored Thomas' introspection and his subsequent intellectualism because it has understood him through the lens of Scotus. As a conceptualist, Scotus is unable to explain the intelligent process whereby universal concepts are attained but simply posits a "spiritual look at a universal" that is inexplicable and unverifiable on any but metaphysical grounds (V 195). Consequently, Scotus takes concepts for granted, they just result through a faculty of the soul, and is concerned to explain the deductive relation of concepts to each other (V 39 n. 126). But this ignores the importance of understanding—*intelligere*—in Aquinas and reduces the second act of the intellect, judgment, to a purely discursive function of relating concept to concept. The clue, then, is to understand what Aquinas, not a Scotist version of Aquinas, said about the first and second acts of the intellect and how the acts are recognizable through introspective access into the actions of our own intellects.

The two acts are two kinds of understanding, the first results in insights into phantasms and the conceptualization of insights, while the second results in judgments concerning the truth or falsity of the first act. The first act deals with the quiddity of the thing, the essence, and responds to the question "What is It?" in its various forms. In the *Posterior Analytics*, Aristotle notes that one can ask: (1) whether there is an *x*, (2) what is an *x*, (3) whether *x* is *y*, and (4) why *x* is *y* (V 26). The first and third versions are empirical, they can be answered by adverting to the facts of the matter, to the data, while the second and fourth ask for a cause, for the source of intelligibility. Intelligibility is not attained by mere observation—one cannot simply gape at the data and expect to grasp the formal cause or the essence of the composite object. Rather one needs insight into the data, the phantasm in Thomistic terminology, which is not a matter of a secret peek into the form of an object but the perhaps difficult and lengthy reasoning process of grasping intelligible relations in the sense data.

Our insights are not constant, for unlike angels or God we have only occasional acts of understanding and must reason to understanding (V 44-47). Further, while insights grasp a possible relation of intelligibility in the data, i.e., a cause, they are not yet expressed in a definition. The production of the *verbum*, contra Scotus, does not proceed mechanistically and is not imposed automatically upon us from without by the intelligible object (V 46-47). Instead the process is one of intelligence. We reason, perhaps having multiple insights (acts of *intelligere*) which are compounded together by yet higher insights, until the process of reasoning is completed and a definition (the expression of *intelligere*) emerges from our intelligent processes (Byrne 1986, 45). But the conception or definition is not automatic, "conceptualization comes as the term and product of a process of reasoning" and "as long as the reasoning, the fluctuation of discourse, continues, the inner world is as yet unuttered" (V 51). This is to say that while our inner discourse—questioning, puzzling, thinking, wondering—continues we do not yet understand but "are thinking in order to understand" (V 51).

This "thinking in order to understand" is accessible to our introspective investigation and within the free control of our intelligence, as opposed to a mechanical account of abstraction (V 53). In abstraction we ignore the here and now of our investigation (an insight into quantum physics is true both here and in Copenhagen), ignore the accidental sensible qualities of the data (the size or imperfect rendering of the triangle is irrelevant to the geometer), and finally ignore all matter in order to arrive at concepts of being, potency and act (V 53-55). But this sort of abstraction is a far cry from the common explanation of Aquinas whereby the active intellect ab-stracts or ex-tracts a form from the matter. Such ab-straction is conceptualist, for we really have no idea how the intellect performs this miracle absent a faculty metaphysics, and moreover confuses *form* understood as intelligible cause with *Form* understood as Platonic Idea removed from heaven and inserted into matter over-there. To think of abstraction as uncovering or removing form which is "in" matter is to remain trapped in picture thinking, it is to assume that a form is a semi-invisible thing, a hazy figure that is in the object and then *removed* by abstraction and placed as a hazy image in the intellect. But, while the intellect uses images to gain the data of investigation, insights into the data and definitions of the insights are precisely not imaginings or picturings of a form but an understanding of the intelligible cause of a thing.

When the process of reasoning is complete, when the quiddity of the object has been fully understood, then understanding has received the species. The understanding, with respect to this object, is fully in act and the understanding *is* the act of the object, the understanding and the species of the thing are identical (V 83-85). But while strictly speaking the first act of understanding results in identity and thus knowledge of reality, the first act is incapable of knowing that it knows and the second act of judgment is necessary (V 61, 71-72). For a Scotist, the language of judgment, i.e., composition and division, means only the synthesis of concepts—S is P, S is not P—and prescinds from the question of how to determine if the understanding is true or not (V 63). Judgment, however, is not only synthesis but "positing of synthesis" or assenting to the second question of understanding, "Is it So?".

The question is not "Do I understand the species?" as that already answered by the first act but "Is it So?" or "Is the intelligible *species* I have understood indeed the intelligible form of the sensible image I originally puzzled about?" (Byrne 1986, 51). For anyone under the Cartesian spell this last question would necessitate asking if the idea/ image in my mind matches up with the thing out there, but if one can compare the two it implies a super-intuition from an external vantage point which can see and compare mental and extra-mental reality directly. Not only is the status of this vantage point questionable, but if we possess such a super-look one wonders why we need the redundant—we could just look at reality and know. That being said: "to judge that my knowing is similar to the known involves a comparison between the knowing and its standard; but either the standard is known or it is not known" (V 72). But to what standard? If we do not compare the results of the first act directly to extra-mental reality, then to what?

In *De veritate* I.9 Aquinas argues that truth is known insofar as the intellect *reflects upon itself*. Lonergan will thus distinguish the two acts of *intelligere* into direct understanding and reflective understanding: direct understanding attains identity while reflective understanding attains knowledge of the identity or truth. Reflective understanding reflects upon itself, not by an extroverted leap out into extra-mental reality or by some inward-upward look that confronts divine reality as demanded by the various shades of intuitionism: "our knowledge of truth is not to be accounted for by any vision or contact or confrontation with the other, however lofty and sublime" (V 85). The standard is not seen but understood and the standard is reflection on our own essence. In an older Scholastic terminology, the standard is in the principles of the intellect itself and truth is determined through a *resolutio in principia*, to principles of the mind (V 72-73, 86, 95).

The principles, of course, are the first principles of the intellect, but while these can be taken as explicitly propositional, whereby one deduces backwards until a=a is reached and the principles of identity and non-contradiction used, they are more relevant as performative or operational principles of the mind's intelligent and dynamic exigencies:

> Thus, what is meant by "intellect measuring things by its own principles" turns out to be ... the way in which the consciousness of intellect itself, present in every act of understanding and every

movement of reflecting, determines what is required to satisfy intellect's demand for unconditioned understanding.... the principles of intellect occur and are only known performatively, that is, in the concrete, intelligently acting subject.... (Byrne 1986, 59)

The human intellect stops wondering and inquiring at some point and accepts or rejects an answer when satisfied that sufficient evidence is attained to make a judgment. We distinguish poor from strong arguments, clarity from obtuseness, and so on.

Now, *Verbum* is not a complete solution. As primarily a historical investigation into Aquinas it provides preliminary hints but not the more complete solution of *Insight*. Still, it provides the principles with which to reject intuitionism while retaining realism:

1. There is a distinction between the conscious levels of sensation, direct understanding and reflective understanding.

2. These conscious levels are knowable to us, we can experience and understand them as performative in our own intelligence.

3. The process of knowing is not a mysterious Rube Goldberg contraption which mechanically churns out propositions and beliefs but intelligent and intelligible.

4. A metaphysical account of knowledge may be, at the very least, supplemented by an introspective psychology.

In short, what is required is an intellectual conversion, but we do not yet fully know what that entails.

3.4 WHAT AM I DOING WHEN I AM KNOWING?

If we are to overcome intuitionism we must convert the pervasive reliance, sometimes imperceptible or inchoate, on the ocular myth in theoretical accounts of knowledge. As such, a definition of knowledge must not be assumed leaving us to ask only whether we have such knowledge or not (I 11). To do so risks committing Descartes' error: thinking he knew what knowledge was, he developed all further questions upon this principle, but since his definition was not consistent with the operations of human intellect, all further answers too were inconsistent. Instead, Lonergan begins by asking of the nature of knowing since only after defining knowing is it sensible to ask what beliefs can be counted as knowledge and what as mere opinion. There are, then, three questions: What am I doing when I am knowing? Why is doing that knowing? What do I know when I do it? The answer to the first question is *cognitional theory*, the second *epistemology* and the third *metaphysics* (M 25). Cognitional theory must be tackled first or else risk an irrational and unrealistic epistemology, one with the tendency to intuitionism if history is any clue.

The place to begin with is the common act of insight: "It is not a recondite intuition but the familiar event that occurs easily and frequently in the moderately intelligent, rarely and with difficulty only in the very stupid. In itself it is so simple and obvious that it seems to merit the little attention that commonly it receives" (I 3). In other words, we perform the act of insight so frequently, or hope we do to avoid the charge of stupidity, that it seems too common to count for much. But since performance is prior to reflection we must now pivot our attention to this mundane action and understand what occurs in the act of insight. We must have "insight into insight" for it "is not only a mental activity but also a constituent factor in human knowledge. It follows that insight into insight is in some sense a knowledge of knowledge" (I 4). The means to attain an understanding of insight is to follow Aquinas' method of empirical introspection and "discover, to identify, to become familiar with, the activities of one's own intelligence" (I 14) or to attain *self-appropriation* whereby one becomes present to oneself and quite easily is able to answer "What am I doing when I am knowing?"

Insights are commonplace, a dime a dozen, so we should be able to find them in our own intellectual performances. Moreover, if cognitional theory is not to apply solely to ourselves we should expect to find insights in others. Lonergan is fond of the story of Archimedes struggling with the problem of determining whether base metals had been added to the crown of King Hiero. He worries until with a "Eureka!" he rushes naked from the baths having grasped that the principles of displacement and specific gravity allow a solution by weighing the crown in water (I 27-28). The "Eureka!" moment is the moment of insight, the moment when a previously obscure set of data or a seeming unanswerable question suddenly makes sense, is intelligible, when we see what must be the case. Examples of insight abound. The slave boy in the *Meno* grasps the relationship of the diagonal to the area of the square, not because he has recollected squareness but because he finally gets it, "Aha!" Newton is hit by the apple and suddenly has an idea, Einstein boards a bus after struggling with a problem and in a moment relativity is born. We can confirm this in ourselves, we have insights, it is a verifiable experience. We have suspicions about the characters in the mystery novel, the Sunday crossword puzzle begins to make sense, the truth table is organized, the joke understood, the blueprints made intelligible, and no mysterious mental eye was needed to suddenly discover intelligibility in what was previously confusing.

There are five basic elements of insight, none of which are argued for deductively but all available to self-appropriation:

1.   Insight is a "release to the tension of inquiry" (I 28). We are confused but want to know, struggling to make sense of it all, at times incapable of sleep as even our subconscious obsesses over the problem until the "click," until the "flash," and the inner tension dissolves into satisfaction.

2.   Insight comes "suddenly and unexpectedly" (I 29). There is no master method guaranteeing insights; if there were, all teachers and students would be equal. But some students grasp the matter before the teacher has finished the example, other students never will. Some authors write several important articles a year, others take years to arrive at a good idea. Often insights occur when we stop wishing for them to happen and take a walk.

3.   Insights are not functions of outer circumstances but of inner conditions (I 29). While one has very little control over what is seen or heard it is erroneous to think that the mind is fundamentally passive and that insights are mechanically caused by the world imposing its intelligibility onto the mind. If that were the case all functioning minds would have insights in response to data, but it remains a fact that not everyone in the baths of Syracuse shouted "Eureka!" but only those who asked "Why?" and had a particularly alert and inquisitive habit of mind. Answers will not arise unless intelligent questions are asked.

4.   Insight "pivots between the concrete and the abstract" (I 30). Insights occur in response to concrete problems and result in concrete applications—Archimedes asks about this particular crown and decides to weigh this particular crown in water. Thus geometers draw diagrams, teachers give examples, we worry about strategy in this particular hand of cards, but while the problems and applications are concrete the insight is into something quite general. Insights are about the principle of displacement, the relationship of

interior angles of all triangles, the odds of probability for any and
every deck of cards and so on.
5. Insight "passes into the habitual texture of one's mind" (I 30).
Prior to the insight the problem seems insolvable, once the insight
occurs we wonder how we missed something so obvious. Moreover,
we can reproduce the insight almost at will, can teach it to others,
can apply the insight to other related questions. In short, once we
understand the relationship of interior angles of a triangle we will
never again suffer the same confusion as the student struggling to
understand for the very first time.

Still, if we reflect on our performance we realize that "it is one thing for
you to have an insight and quite another to state clearly just what it is
that you have understood" (Flanagan 1997, 18). An insight grasps an
organizing principle within the data, but this click or flash is not yet
expressed and formulating what is understood is often difficult. The
citizens of Athens could recognize injustice as well as Socrates but
struggled mightily to define justice. To put it more simply, "conception,
then, expresses generally what is essential to having the insight, and
that is a matter of abstraction" (UB 42). Abstraction, defined earlier in
Verbum, progressively ignores the here and now of our investigation,
ignores the accidental sensible qualities of the data and finally ignores
all matter in order to arrive at concepts of being, potency and act (V
53-55). This puts into a formula that which the insight discovered and
which is capable of reproducing the insight in oneself or in another
(UB 42).

An example helps to clarify (I 31-35; Flanagan 1997, 20-23): Imagine we begin with a cartwheel with its hub, spokes and rim and ask
of the cartwheel "why is it round or what makes it round?" We could
simply answer that it is circular, that its rim is a line that goes around
and meets itself again. This is inadequate, for although it accurately
describes how a cartwheel appears to observation and exhibits an ability to use language in the customary fashion, it involves no insight into
the intelligibility of the wheel, it does not answer *why* the cartwheel
is round. In other words, it does not grasp the formal cause of the
cartwheel but only describes its appearance. A better clue is to begin with the spokes which in the cartwheel are roughly, if the cart is
not to be terribly bumpy, of equal length from hub to rim. Of course
the spokes of the cartwheel are unlikely to actually be equal even if

crafted with care, but we have the clue in that we can abstract from this particular cartwheel with its imperfect construction and imagine a cartwheel with a point in the middle and equal radii emerging. The greater the number of equal radii the more likely the circle is actually circular rather than uneven or bumpy. Still, points and radii are imaginative constructions and deficient in representing what is meant. The concept "point" is a location in space without magnitude and the radii represent "lines" which have extension but no width. Clearly our imaginings are of a "dot" rather than a "point" and of "marks" rather than of lines since our dot has magnitude and our marks have width. So if we move from the image to what is meant by the image, namely a set of coplanar points equidistant from a center point, we abstract from the concrete cartwheel and the concrete image to an explanatory definition of why the cartwheel is round, provided that we have the relevant insight into why a greater number of equal radii results in a better approximation of a circle. We can then provide the Euclidian definition "a set of coplanar points equidistant a center point," or the symbolic expression of Cartesian coordinates, $x^2+y^2=r^2$.

This is a simple example, and Lonergan, to the chagrin of many readers, follows it up with examples from calculus, statistics and the sciences. But the point is not to model philosophy on mathematics or the sciences, rather the exactness of mathematics merely allows us more easily to understand how the mind works. It is not at the moment necessary to understand all of Lonergan's discussions regarding insight in math and science, but it is important to grasp how invariant and pervasive the acts of insight and formulation are in the performance of knowledge regardless of the field.

One of the points to emerge from his discussion is the development of insight. Insights begin to cluster together and allow further insights to emerge. In the simple cartwheel example several insights coalesced together allowing us to continue. For instance, we had the insight that a description was incomplete and not what we were after, we had the insight that imagining a circle with radii from a center point would be helpful, we had the insight that our imagined circle was not really a circle since it contained a dot rather than a point and marks rather than lines and so on.

Taking another example: A child learning their tables begins with 1+1=2, 2+1=3, 3+1=4 and etc. (I 38-42). Beyond the mere memorization, the child must realize that what is of key importance in this sequence is actually the *etc.*, for they must grasp that the series of positive integers is infinite and that the relationship of plus and equal signs is not true simply of the tables memorized to this point but for all positive integers. Further, once the child grasps the table they are equipped to understand that if 1+1=2 then 1+1+1+1 is the same as 2+2, and have made a connection that was absent previously. Further, once they realize that 1+1+1+1=4 they are ready to understand that 1x4=1+1+1+1 and so until they eventually, and after a great many accumulated insights, arrive at the differential calculus. The same is true in studying the history of philosophy; after a bout with Platonism we read Aristotle and begin to ask what good it does to reproduce reality, but after reading Augustine we wonder how Aristotle explains the efficient cause of the universals and so finally end up with Aquinas as a potential solution. In all of this insights became habitual, part of the fabric of the mind, and so accumulated to allow even further insights to occur.

We must realize that Lonergan is proceeding piecemeal. Rather than simply providing his finished theory he requires self-appropriation or the discovery of what we are doing when we are knowing. There is no immediate grasp of what we are doing but rather the slow, even tedious, task of finding the various elements of what we do until the structure is complete. What we have discovered so far is the fact of insight, five elements of insight, the distinction between insight and conception and the accumulation of insights. We must return and pay more attention to the fact that insights are not products of external circumstances but of inner conditions. Insights occur when we ask questions about the data, when we seek a structured order or intelligibility within the data which until this point is not intelligible.

3.5 INTELLIGIBILITY & INTELLIGENCE IN VARIOUS ENDEAVORS

Now we remember from the *Verbum* articles that Aquinas distinguished the first act of the intellect from the second, the first act asking "What is it?" or what Lonergan now calls asking questions of intelligence. To ask "What is it?" is to seek an intelligible structure in the data now under inquiry, thus *questions of intelligence.* In the older tradition we would begin to distinguish terms such as essence, form, formal cause, quiddity, accidents, properties and so on, and while this nexus of terms was intelligible within an Aristotelian framework of science which searched for necessary and universal causes modern science ignores these very terms. So while Aristotle is correct in the *Posterior Analytics* to point out that we ask "What is it?" his conception of the intelligibility we search for is perhaps too limited. What we search for is heuristic, an anticipation of intelligibility [*heurisko*=I find] not limited in scope to the universal or necessary (LR 390-401). While we do not yet possess the knowledge we are asking about, since we would not ask if we knew, we do have an apprehension of what we are looking for, namely intelligibility. So we know what we are looking for, we know already what the answer will be like, what form it will take, but we do not yet have the content of that answer.

A few examples will clarify. The Socratic heuristic structure is one of universal definition; Socrates asks for a universal definition and rejects any definition that fails to satisfy this criterion. If Meno paid more attention to Socrates' past encounters he would have known that a mere list of the multiple virtues would not answer what Socrates wished to discover. Aristotle, too, was looking for a universal, just a universal with a different metaphysical status, and he expected to slough off all accidents in order to abstract to the formal cause. Galileo, turning to a modern heuristic, did not look for a formal cause, instead he sought intelligibility in the mathematical relationships of data. Consequently, he can not simply think through the relationship of mass to velocity in falling bodies but must do the experiment, his heuristic demands it, and he must climb the steps in Pisa. Still, he assumes that there is intelligibility in the data, he expects to find [*heurisko*] a correlation between the mass and the velocity. When he does not, since the objects land at the same time, he does not then assume that all is chaotic and unintelligible but puts forth a hypothesis resulting in the intelligible relationship between distance, time, velocity, acceleration, gravity, mass, weight and resistance.

Lonergan's point is that the expectations of what counts for knowledge change. The ideal, what we are expecting to find, can vary. Geometers look for necessity, Galileo for mathematical relationships, classical science for the nature of x or the law of x, while statisticians look for probability or correlations. In short, the ideal changes over time, quantum physicists are not looking for what Aristotle expected, but still they "are expressing an anticipation of intelligibility in the data" (UB 62). Thus in the contemporary scene we study much more than the ancients since the merely probable, the non-necessary or accidental, becomes open to expectations of intelligibility, and while we distinguish between classical, statistical, and genetic heuristics, there exists a complementarity between them all—they all begin with a question about data, assume there is a possible answer to the question and wonder and ponder until insights begin to occur and the insights are conceptualized into definitions, formulae, charts, graphs and whatever expressions of the insight are relevant.

In addition to mathematic and scientific questions and their corresponding heuristics there are questions of common sense. Common sense is concerned with knowing, not for its own sake, but for specific ends, for "purposes of developing more intelligent and successful ways of living" (Flanagan 1997, 70). Living occurs in the concrete, distinguishing common sense from the scientific, for while scientists begin with the concrete data and verify their answers concretely they are primarily concerned with the general. Further, common sense is concerned with know-how, how to drive, how to fix the leak, set the broken arm, extract the tooth; common sense is concerned with experience rather than with first causes, as Aristotle puts it, and in the realm of the concrete the person of experience is as successful as the person of science. Moreover, common sense is not concerned to move beyond description, it is satisfied to express how data appear to the subject rather than expressing with Galileo how data relate to other data. If we want to purchase a red car we are happy enough if it seems red to us, we do not worry about the light spectrum and the laws of reflection (I 197-204).

Still, the person of common sense is not unintelligent. Even Socrates recognized the skill of the mason or carpenter. The person of common sense still asks questions of intelligence, they still want to know "What is it?", only now they might ask "What is it that makes the roof leak?" or "What is it that will make me a great deal of money in the market?" Obviously the expression of the question will hardly be this static, but still there is a common sense heuristic, an expectation that there is an answer to the pressing practical questions and that the answer is intelligible and available. Further, the answer arrives with an insight, following all the five elements of insight, for not everyone has an insight of why the brakes squeak or when to sell rather than buy—the insights do not happen until we wonder.

3.6 PATTERNS OF EXPERIENCE, BIAS &
THE COGNITIVE MYTH

Moreover, the most theoretical scientist, including Socrates, is engaged in practical concerns of common sense a great deal of the time—no one remains in pure theory. But if no one remains merely theoretical, and since even the most commonsensical of persons is capable of theory, we must admit that the intelligence of the concrete human subject is polymorphic, we exercise our intelligence in a variety of ways. Lonergan refers to this possibility as a *pattern of experience* (I 205). A pattern of experience might best be defined as a pattern of "conation, interest, attention, purpose" (I 205). This is to say that the human can pay attention or direct their consciousness and concern in various ways: "Thales was so intent upon the stars that he did not see the well into which he tumbled. The milkmaid was so indifferent to the stars that she could not overlook the well. Still, Thales could have seen the well, for he was not blind and, perhaps, the milkmaid could have been interested in the stars…" (I 205). A pattern of experience, then, is the pattern of those things a person is interested in and concerned with.

The biological pattern of experience is common to all animals. An animal must hunt or forage, reproduce, protect themselves against danger and so on. Consequently, sensation, memory, imagination and emotion are directed towards the ends of finding food, a mate and safety. The biological pattern, then, is "a set of intelligible relations that link together sequences of sensations, memories, images, conations, emotions, and bodily movements" for the "terminal activities of intussusception or reproduction or, when negative in scope, self-preservation" (I 206). Further, the biological pattern is one of extroversion, for consciousness is interested only in external stimuli and their importance to the terminal goals of reproduction and self-preservation and does not engage in critical self-reflection or self-knowledge. Only external stimuli are of interest, and "when the object fails to stimulate, the subject is indifferent; and when non-conscious vital process has no need of outer objects, the subject dozes and falls asleep" (I 207).

The intellectual pattern of experience "forgets its primitive biological function to take on a selective alertness that keeps pace with the refinements of elaborate and subtle classifications" (I 209). The intellectual pattern inquires, a feat escaping the concern of the biological pattern, and directs its concern and interest towards inquiry and solving the question. In the intellectual pattern the faculties of the human are directed away from the merely terminal biological interests and "memory ferrets out instances that would run counter to the prospective judgment. Imagination anticipates the shape of possibilities that would prove the judgment wrong. So deep is the penetration...that memories and anticipations rise above the threshold of consciousness only if they possess at least a plausible relevance to the decision to be made" (I 206). This is not merely passive receptivity, for the senses and memory and imagination are directed in a particular direction. Moreover, consciousness does not doze off when external stimuli hold no interest, for the intellectual pattern demands perseverance and can take "years in which one's living is more or less constantly absorbed in the effort to understand" (I 210).

Since we are not simply animals or automatons but fully existential subjects, we also dwell in aesthetic and dramatic patterns of existence. In the aesthetic pattern of experience there is an "exuberance above and beyond the biological account books of purposeful pleasure and pain" (I 207). Experience can be had merely for the sake of experience, not for utility but for pure enjoyment. Thus children play and artists create.

Further, in the dramatic pattern practical concerns, like eating, mating, dressing and making an existence, are conducted not simply with skill but with aplomb. We do not simply cook the meal but attempt to make it peaceful and enjoyable, we do not merely sit to dinner but set the table and establish rituals and hierarchies of serving the meal. These customs are relative to time, place, even the desire of the participants, but still we find our practical concerns caught up in meaning.

Focusing on the patterns of existence may seem on face to be irrelevant to the attempt of self-appropriation, or at least incidental, but the patterns of experience account for two vital elements of self-appropriation, namely, they begin to explain (1) oversight or the flight from understanding and (2) the cause of the ocular myth.

Besides the common experience of insight, we also have the experience of oversight. A wiser person than I reads a play by Shakespeare and comes away with a brilliant idea, a scientist observes, perhaps, the same data as I and is not bewildered, the mechanic knows how to stop the brakes from squeaking and so on. It is a fact, verifiable to experience, that we overlook relevant data, forget to ask the proper questions, stubbornly refuse to admit the possibility of some answers and act stupidly. Of course, this could be explained simply by appealing to a native intelligence, Einstein was just smarter than most, but this would ignore the differences between persons of roughly equal intelligence and essentially claim that the entire matter was a result of chance, luck good or bad, and rather beyond any other explanation. Lonergan believes that the flight from understanding, or oversight, is explicable, both on the individual and cultural levels.

Oversight can be caused by *bias*, a refusal to admit certain possibilities or the ignoring of certain insights when they occur. First is *dramatic bias*:

> Just as insight can be desired, so too can it be unwanted. Besides the love of light, there can be a love of darkness. If prepossessions and prejudices notoriously vitiate theoretical investigations, much more easily can elementary passions bias understanding in practical and personal matters. Nor has such a bias merely some single and isolated effect. To exclude an insight is also to exclude the further questions that would arise from it, and the complementary insights that would carry it towards a rounded and balanced viewpoint. (I 214)

Such dramatic bias results in the stifling of the natural desire to ask questions and the insights that result. *Scotosis* occurs, an unconscious process censoring insights. Either insights occur but the person refuses to follow them with the further questions that naturally emerge or the insights occur but the person refuses to accept them and attempts to rationalize some reason to reject them. In *repression* the censorship serves to "prevent the emergence into consciousness of perspectives that would give rise to unwanted insights" and actively excludes the development of insights deemed, for some reason, undesirable. The sick soul, suffering from what Eric Voegelin terms pneumopathology, will be *inhibited*, incapable of adverting to images or affections which would lead to insight and will suffer in the normal *performance* of their intellect (I 214-231).

In addition to dramatic bias there is *individual bias*. One lives in community and the normal function of a subject involves concern for the common good. Still, one can pursue individual satisfaction at the expense of the good. Not only will such an egoist direct all their attention towards satisfaction but they will reject the affections and questions that would prompt them to abandon their own concern and embrace a world of value beyond their own wants. While individual bias wishes to overcome the normal intersubjective feelings, *group bias* finds support by these very feelings (I 247). The group tends to overlook those bits of data, those questions, those insights, which challenge the suppositions and satisfaction of their group. Here the group sticks together at all costs and rejects the questions and demands of those external to the group.

Perhaps more relevant to our immediate concerns is *general bias*, for I will suggest in the upcoming chapter that Rorty is guilty of this error. General bias is not so concerned with a group or with the psychosis or selfishness of an individual but is trapped within the concerns of common sense. Concerned with the practical, those questions which do not immediately seem to meet some need but justify themselves simply with the desire to know are deemed irrelevant, useless, pie-in-the-sky. General bias occurs when the common sense begins to exclude the intellectual pattern of experience with its desire to know simply for the sake of knowing. While group bias can result in a shorter cycle of decline—class conflict, for instance—general bias can also result in a longer cycle of decline whereby the possibility of progress effected by the clustering and accumulation of insights is damaged by the insistence to remain only within the practical domain to the neglect of the intellectual.

We are still continuing piecemeal, Lonergan's full account of knowledge is still emerging, but what he has already revealed allows an explanation of why the cognitive myth emerges. In the first chapter I referenced Hans Jonas' argument that the introduction of sight as a metaphor of knowledge results in (1) a metaphysics of presence, or knowledge of the static and unchanging, (2) knowledge as confrontation, or we know what is out there, and (3) knowledge as objective, implying a distance whereby subjectivity is lessened. Lonergan arrives at fundamentally similar conclusions but rather than merely point to the inclusion of a metaphor in the accounts of knowledge he adds the distortive effects into the performance of knowing, in what we do. Lonergan refers to the previously explained patterns of experience, and discovers that the biological pattern of experience allows us to know *bodies* whereas the intellectual pattern of experience allows us to know *things*. A body is an 'already out there now real', as Lonergan argues:

> 'Already' refers to the orientation and dynamic anticipation of biological consciousness; such consciousness does not create but finds its environment; it finds it as already constituted, already offering

opportunities, already issuing challenges. 'Out' refers to the extroversion of a consciousness that is aware, not of its own ground, but
of objects distinct from itself. 'There' and 'now' indicate the spatial
and temporal determinations of extroverted consciousness. 'Real',
finally, is a subdivision within the field of the 'already out there now':
part of that is mere appearance; but part is real; and its reality consists in its relevance to biological success or failure, pleasure or pain
(I 276-277).

Bodies, then, are known by the biological pattern of experience; a kitten in a kitchen confronts 'bodies' that are sources of external stimuli
whether those be the terrifying scrape of a chair on the floor, the light
dancing on the wall serving as a plaything or the saucer with milk that
satisfies thirst. Reality for the kitten is comprised of those external
'bodies' that are of interest insofar as they relate to the terminal concerns of survival.

A 'thing', on the other hand, is defined by Lonergan as "a unity, identity, whole in data" (I 271). A 'thing' is not necessarily an observable or
even imaginable 'body' out there upon which the observer can cast their
gaze, but instead is a grasp of *intelligible* unity, identity and wholeness
in the data. For example, the Pythagorean theorem is not an observable body 'out-there'. Still, the theorem exhibits a real understanding of
the relationship of the diagonal to the sides—in the data an intelligible
unity-identity-whole can be grasped. Again, velocity could be said to
be a 'thing' in that from measuring distances and times an intelligible
unity-identity-whole can be grasped in the data, but obviously velocity
is not a 'body' already out there now that the kitten could possibly find
of concern.

There are, then, two types of knowing, one proper to animals and
the other to beings capable of inquiry (I 277). The knowing proper to
animals is of the biological pattern of experience and is "constituted
completely on the level of experience; neither questions for intelligence
nor questions for reflection have any part in its genesis" (I 277). On
the other hand, in *fully human knowing* experience provides no more
than data for questions and data in which acts of intelligence grasp
intelligibility. The difference between the two types of knowing poses
no difficulty *per se*, for a human is both animal and rational and knows
both 'bodies' and 'things', but a great confusion arises when "one shifts
unconsciously from one type to the other" (I 278). To the biological
pattern of experience inquiry and intelligibility seem like a tangled bit

of nonsense, "what they want is an elementary knowing of the 'really real', if not through sense, at least by imagination" (I 278). The biological pattern wants immediate knowledge of what is 'already out there now real'.

The reader will already have noted the similarities between the 'already out there now real' and the vision model of knowing: the vision model is extroverted and thinks of knowledge as confronting an object out there and wants access to the object in some way analogous to seeing. Thus, the vision model of knowing rests on a confusion, for it seems as though the proponents of a vision model have unconsciously shifted from human knowledge to "settle down like good animals in our palpable environment" (I 582). And so, "when Descartes maintained that material substance must be identical with spatial extension, his material substance was the 'already out there now real'. When Kant argued that primary and secondary qualities are merely phenomenal, he meant that for him the reality of the 'already out there now real' was mere appearance" (I 277). Of course, this unconscious shift from proper human knowing to the knowing of the biological pattern brings with it the tendency to think of knowing as seeing. This causes no end of grief for epistemology as it demands some faculty analogous to sight—it demands the Eye of the Mind and all sorts of intellectual contortions to justify the Mind's Eye. Lonergan argues that a mistake was made in the tradition for it confused elements proper to knowing 'bodies' with elements proper to the fully human knowing of 'things', and while Rorty and Lonergan take different routes they arrive at a similar conclusion—looking, either sensibly or mentally, is not fully human knowing. So, we must ask further questions: What is fully human knowing for Lonergan? How can Lonergan justify a correspondence theory without assuming items of knowledge as privileged representations?

3.7 FROM INSIGHT TO JUDGMENT

So far we have been dealing with the first act of the intellect, responding to the question "What is It?" and discovering that questions lead to insights while biases can lead to oversight. But if we remained only in the first act of the intellect Lonergan would provide very little response to Rorty. Rorty is no intellectual dullard or sluggard, and while he does not preach self-appropriation he is very clever, has multiple insights, and would likely admit that the preceding pages are all very fine and well, they just do not establish realism. Questions do lead to insights, insights do accumulate and coalesce into higher viewpoints, stupidity or bias does result in oversight, but these are just ideas contingently conditioned by our language and history. Some of these ideas are more useful or beneficial than others and so profitable to believe, but insights and the concepts that result from them do not provide knowledge of Truth out there or of the real. Kuhn, for instance, or at least as Rorty uses Kuhn, would point out various conceptualizations in the history of science that asked good questions and provided good answers, but none had it more right than any other answer—astrology is just less useful than astrophysics (PMN 322-324, 328-331).

Lonergan would agree. The first act of the intellect with its direct insights and concepts is not knowing:

> When one reaches the expression or conception of an insight, one can utter in words a definition which may be nominal, explanatory, or implicit; one can present a whole hypothesis; one can present a whole theory. But is it true? Is it so? That is a question that need not be answered yet.... definitions, propositions, hypotheses, theories, even if they are spread over hundreds of pages, may be simply objects of thought. (UB 110)

Questions of intelligence asked "What is It?" and there is little sense in answering "yes" or "no," instead, one answers in the affirmative or negative to the question "Is it So?" Insights may be clever or silly, sublime or obvious, but strictly speaking we have not committed to them, and thus cannot be right or wrong until we assert that the insights are true or false, until we judge. Consequently, for knowledge to occur we must move from Aquinas' first act of the intellect—direct understanding—to the second act of the intellect—judging or reflective understanding.

In common experience, especially of events we are familiar with, insight and judgment occur virtually simultaneously as the object is so "well-known" that the question "Is it So?" is simply assumed rather than asked. To return to the circle example given previously, we now are familiar with circles and rarely ask about them, but for a toddler playing with blocks or a sixth-grader learning geometry the circle is a source of wonder, delight and confusion. If asked, "What is a circle?" the child will point to the appropriate block while the adolescent will most likely provide a basic definition. Upon further *reflection*, i.e., upon asking if the definition is satisfactory, the reasonable student will decide that "round" is not a good definition and will try again. Perhaps they will go through several steps, "a circle is a line that curves and meets itself," or "a circle is a set of points equidistant from a center point," but in each case the definition will be unable to answer certain critical questions and will be judged inadequate. Finally, a sufficient definition is reached and the tension of inquiry ends.

A similar process is involved in other pursuits. In attempting to plan a chess move the player has multiple insights into various possibilities but discards all but one as inadequate, and the good chess player will hardly pick the first move that comes to mind (unless, perhaps, chess is so familiar to them that they have attained a habitual understanding and can play essentially without deliberation having mastered the opening or defense). The same is applicable to purchasing stocks, fixing a car, solving an ethical dilemma or positing superstring theory; insights occur and provide a possible explanation to the *intelligent* person who asked questions about the data rather than staring like a dullard, while the *reasonable* person does not buy the first stock that seems a winner or automatically replace the alternator when the car does not start but reasons through the various possibilities before judging which hypothesis best makes sense of the data.

There is, then, a distinction between questions of intelligence— "What is It?"—and questions of reason—"Is it So?"—and questions of reason end in judgment. We can experience judgment ourselves, like insight we perform the act frequently. Examination of the act reveals that "we perform acts of reflective understanding" when "we have grasped the sufficiency of the evidence for a judgment on which we have been deliberating" (I 304). The chess player looks for sufficient evidence to support one move versus another, the honest mechanic considers the evidence before replacing a part, the scientist marshals the evidence before publishing an article, the financial advisor considers various prognostications before buying. In these examples, and Lonergan would say in every example we could think of, the judger begins with the question "Is it So?" about a possible account of intelligibility, that is about the result of some previous insight, and then deliberates until sufficient evidence is found. Obviously what counts as sufficient evidence differs from inquiry to inquiry: the geometer will be unsatisfied with a statistical correlation, a juror considers reasonable doubt and probable cause, the gambler determines odds and so on. In a sense, then, Lonergan would agree with Rorty that it is relevant to consider what your peers will let you get away with saying, for every sphere of inquiry develops its own standards of what counts as sufficient evidence, and the person thought of as respectable or reasonable in a particular sphere may be considered too exacting or lax in another. In good Aristotelian terms, it demands a certain level of prudence or good-schooling to understand what counts as sufficient evidence, and the well-schooled person does not confuse mathematics and rhetoric.

But while the standards of sufficient evidence may vary, the *form* of judgment remains constant in the various spheres. To "grasp evidence as sufficient for a prospective judgment is to grasp the prospective judgment as virtually unconditioned" (I 305). There are two cases of the unconditioned, formal and virtual. The formally unconditioned has no conditions whatsoever, there are no antecedents upon which it depends. To be conditioned is to be contingent, dependent upon an antecedent condition or conditions that must obtain in order for the conditioned to be met. For instance, in the statement "If A then B" the event B is contingent upon its condition A. To be formally unconditioned, or to be free of any conditions whatsoever, would be to escape contingency, and consequently only God, a necessary and uncaused being, is formally unconditioned (UB 118). The virtually unconditioned, on the other hand, has conditions and is thus contingent upon those conditions obtaining, but the conditions *have been met* (UB 118). In the following syllogism "B" represents a virtually unconditioned as its conditions have in fact been met: "If A then B; but A; therefore B." All judgments follow this form. In reflective understanding one grasps that the conditions for B have been met and one thus judges that B is true.

It is important to realize that judgment is a type of understanding, namely reflective understanding, for one must understand when the conditions have been met and must understand what standards apply in the given context. This is not some sort of mechanistic process whereby the judger runs through a checklist or master method and so guarantees their results, although it is certainly true that the more exact domains of inquiry have developed determinate standards for their community of inquirers. Still, the standards are not self-evident and are themselves the results of previous judgments of what counts as a good method in this field of inquiry. Consequently, the ultimate cause of standards of sufficient evidence rest in the human intellect itself; it is not science but scientists who determined their method. But if one must understand when conditions have been met, and if it is the human intellect that ultimately determines the standards of when a judgment is virtually unconditioned, then we must discover within the human intellect the standards of judgment.

In our discussion of the *Verbum* articles Lonergan referred to the *resolutio in principia*, or resolution to first principles (V 72-73). This does not mean that all judgments are virtually unconditioned only after a *logical* or *conceptual* deduction to the principle of non-contradiction or identity, although it certainly is possible that some judgments do reduce to these principles. Instead, even the logical first principles themselves reduce to a previous principle, namely the *operational* distinction between a vulnerable and invulnerable insight (I 309):

> Now this reveals a law immanent and operative in cognitional process. Prior to our conceptual distinction between correct and mistaken insights, there is an operational distinction between invulnerable and vulnerable insights. When an insight meets the issue squarely, when it hits the bull's eye, when it settles the matter, there are no further questions to be asked, and so there are no further insights to challenge the initial position. But when the issue is not met squarely, there are further questions that would reveal the unsatisfactoriness of the insight and would evoke the further insights that put a new light on the matter. (I 309)

A vulnerable insight is one in which further relevant questions remain to be asked, an invulnerable insight is one in which all relevant questions have been asked. Once an invulnerable insight is attained, that is, once all relevant questions have been asked, then the virtually unconditioned is satisfied and the judgment is based on sufficient evidence. Returning to the circle example, the definition "round" did not satisfy all relevant questions and so was vulnerable while $x^2+y^2=r^2$ does answer all relevant questions, assuming one begins from the intersection of the x and y axes, and one can develop a formula which abstracts even from the position at the intersection.

Now, just as with the earlier discussion of the act of insight, attaining an invulnerable insight, which is to have asked all relevant critical questions before judging, is made more or less likely by the honesty and intellectual virtue of the thinker. Intellectual sluggards are likely to be too rash or too hesitant, likely to judge before an invulnerable insight is attained or too loath to commit themselves even when there is sufficient evidence. There is the additional danger of the individual supposing that since no further questions occur to them that there are no further questions, but relevant questions are those relevant to the intelligent, the wise, the experienced and to the broader community of investigators rather than simply the isolated Cartesian subject (I 198; Rehg 1994, 84-87). Further, relevant questions may not occur until much later—Aristotle in the *Physics* did not think to ask about superstring theory—indicating not only that judgments are fallible but also that insights are cumulative since present questions on physics can trace a long genealogy. Also, while the difficulty of some topics warrants hesitant caveats and claims only of probability, it is not the case that every topic is so difficult; there are some invulnerable insights even if few.

So while it is true that there is no "simple formula or recipe" that would allow people of good judgment to "be produced at will and indefinitely" (I 310) or a set of master rules "to be followed meticulously by a dolt (M xi), there is still a difference between a person who is wise, prudent, of good judgment, mature or experienced from a dolt (I 310-311). Further, adverting to our experience reveals that the process of asking questions, i.e., of learning, is self-correcting. Take the circle example, for instance, where inadequate definitions were discarded and surpassed until an adequate answer was attained. The process of verification whereby the possible answers of "round," "a curved line that meets itself" and "a set of points equidistant from a center" were rejected occurred naturally, almost without effort, as if the intellect followed a set of operational principles that disallowed rest until the intellect itself was fully satisfied. We compared answers not to some ideal Form or master answer sheet but simply allowed our intellect free reign to test the answers and compare them to the data. Insofar as we allow insights to accumulate, pay attention to past insights and follow the additional questions that naturally arise from insights we will have a self-correcting, internally dynamic, process of learning (I 311). This dynamism, which I only mention here as Chapter Four discusses and argues for it in depth, is immanent to the human spirit, for human beings desire to know and spontaneously ask questions about their experience and equally spontaneously exercise their critical functions to examine possible explanations about the data:

It is a built-in ideal; it is based upon innate tendencies. Aristotle's *Metaphysics* begins with the statement, 'All men naturally desire to know.' He goes on to add, 'particularly with their eyes,' but the point is that there is a natural tendency, a natural desire to know. (UB 5)

3.8 KNOWING WHAT WE ARE DOING

The preceding has been a description of performance, thus the references to examples, even a phenomenology of what we are doing when we are knowing. Our piecemeal construction of Lonergan's position has reached the point where we can pivot our attention from performance to theory and can symbolize the long work of self-appropriation and be capable of recognizing the experiences which engendered the symbols. In short, after the laborious project of paying attention to what we do when we know we are prepared to define, or conceptualize, what we do and will be able to recognize the definitions rather than be alienated from a definition that means nothing to us (UB 11-13). If we advert to our experience, we discover that what we are doing when we know involves a nexus of operations. These include, "seeing, hearing, touching, smelling, tasting, inquiring, imagining, understanding, conceiving, formulating, reflecting, marshalling and weighing the evidence, judging..." (M 6). To ease matters, the nexus can be further reduced to *experience, understanding* and *judgment*:

> Human knowing, then, is not experience alone, not understanding alone, not judgment alone; it is not a combination of only experience and understanding, or of only experience and judgment, or of only understanding and judgment; finally, it is not something totally apart from experience, understanding and judgment. Inevitably, one has to regard an instance of human knowing, not as this or that operation, but as a whole whose parts are operations. (C 223)

Experience begins with data, either of sense or of consciousness; understanding begins with the question "What is It?" regarding the data and results in insights and then concepts or definitions; judgment asks of the understanding "Is it So?" and returns to the data in further questioning before an affirmation or negation is made. There are a few further observations to be made regarding this structure.

First, the set of operations listed—experience, understanding and judgment—and the fleshing out of them that we have done in this chapter, are available for any knower to discover as immanent and operative in their own instances of knowing provided they undergo self-appropriation of themselves as a cognitive subject. In so doing they will discover and become familiar with themselves as conscious, intelligent knowing subjects and will become aware of the empirical, intelligent, and rational elements of their consciousness. In other words, they will begin to know themselves or appropriate their own consciousness.

Second, the structure reveals itself as impossible to revise (I 359-360; M 19). This is not to say that particular operations could not be fleshed out further, explained more adequately, or that one could even add to it somehow, but the basic structure, properly understood and appropriated, cannot be disproven, it is invariant. To disprove the theory would be to point out some data that it does not account for or does not explain; or to point to a counter-example; perhaps to argue that Lonergan has adverted to the correct data but has misunderstood or misdefined the data; consequently, one would judge his theory to be wrong. However, to appeal to some data or counter-example that Lonergan ignored or cannot explain would be to do exactly as he predicted and appeal to data. To argue that he misunderstood or misdefined the data would be to judge his understanding false, to answer 'No, it is not so,' and provide a different understanding. If one is to disprove his theory in a manner that is at all intellectually respectable, that is to say, in a manner that makes sense of the data in any rational fashion, one will perform the exact operations that he predicted. It is then a performative contradiction to deny his theory by providing good reasons, appealing to the data, asking questions about his theory and so on; but since there is no rational means to deny his theory except by appealing to data, asking questions, providing reasons and so on his theory is impossible to defeat (Meynell 1976, 52-53).

Third, just as the structure is impossible to revise without performative contradiction, so the operational structure is transcendental as opposed to categorical (M 14). Just as Hegel and Rorty argue against Kant, the categorical may differ from time, place, culture, sphere of study and so on. The terms and categories in which one thinks and argues may vary and even the ideal of knowledge and what counts as knowledge changed from the classical to the contemporary, but despite the explicit conceptual changes that may or may not occur the structure and operations of consciousness are transcendental, that is to say, invariant (M 282-283; UB 14). In older terminology, the structure is by nature and thus intrinsic to the human subject (UB 162). Consequently, every intelligent and rational human subject should be able to perform self-appropriation and recognize the structure in themselves, and we should be able to note the operations in others.

Fourth, one of the problems plaguing cognitional theorists is self-referentiality; a theory of knowledge should itself be known in the same manner as the theory predicts other items of knowledge are known. So for instance, is the Platonic theory of recollection itself recollected, or is the materialistic theory of Hobbes known in the same manner as physical objects in the world, or is the verification principle known through experience or through analysis? In fact, these theories, and many more besides, are incapable of proving themselves in a self-referentially consistent manner—the verification principle can itself not be verified (Meynell 1999, 24-26). Lonergan's cognitional theory, on the other hand, is known through experience, understanding and judgment in the process of self-appropriation. If one adverts to what they are doing when they are knowing, then they can experience themselves undergoing experience, can experience moments of insight and conception and can experience moments when they ask critical questions and subsequently reach judgment. If one asks intelligently about what one is doing in these experiences then one can begin to understand what it is to have an experience, or to understand, or to judge. Further, once one has experienced and understood these operations, perhaps after struggling through *Insight* or by performing self-appropriation, one can judge that in fact they do experience, understand and judge; in other words, one can judge that Lonergan's cognitional theory is in fact the case, it is as he describes (M 14-16). To do so, to experience, understand and affirm the operational structure is *self-affirmation*, a judgment of fact that one is exercising these very functions (UB 134-137).

Finally, the discussion allows us to develop norms of cognition that are internal to the operations rather than imposing an artificial external standard. Specifically, just as we observed that a lack of curiosity, biases of various sorts, or carelessness derailed the quest of intelligence to have insights, so too did rashness, hesitation, gullibility, poor judgment, carelessness and lack of critical concern derail the critical rational functions and subsequently the self-correcting process of learning. Further, the structure of cognition is dynamic, we naturally want to know and thus are attentive to data, ask questions of intelligence and questions of reason simply because we have a natural drive to know, an *erotic* dynamism as highlighted so frequently and eloquently by Plato, Aristotle, Eric Voegelin, the Transcendental Thomists and the Straussians. Consequently, the structure exhibits an internal *telos* and the exigencies of the mind itself demand one "to be *attentive* to sensation or feeling; *intelligent* in envisaging possible explanations; and to be *reasonable* in revising, rejecting, or re-affirming our opinions so far as they are or fail to be the explanation which best fits the evidence" (Meynell 1999, 19). Lonergan calls these the transcendental precepts: Be attentive, be intelligent, be reasonable, and insofar as the transcendental precepts are followed, the good or end of the intellect's cognitional structure will be attained and the human subject as cognitive will attain both authenticity, as their innermost possibilities are attained, as well as cognitive self-transcendence is knowing the real. To appropriate our cognitional structure is to affirm ourselves as knowers, as knowing the real.

3.9 INTENTIONALITY & KNOWING THE REAL

The last statement says more than is justified. It is one thing to point out the internal structure and natural tendencies of the intellect, even to argue that it fulfills a natural desire to do so, but surely it is quite another to claim that doing so results in knowledge of the real, in cognitive self-transcendence. Kant recognized the ineluctable desire to know the noumena but thought the project doomed to failure and illusion. Within the world of Thomism those beginning with the desire to know, like Maréchal, Rahner, Rousselot and Lonergan, are sometimes thought to fail in their efforts to overcome Kantian idealism and return to the world of existence (Knasas 1995; Matteo 1992, 116-142; Muck 1968, 205-243). Rorty himself went through a period of accepting the Peircian hope that a theory which can solve all objections at the end of inquiry is true (COP 165) but later rejected it as nonsense: even if you could know when the end of inquiry is reached rather than simply running out of ideas, you still would not know that this end of inquiry resulted in correspondence rather than just simple convenience or coherence (ORT 129-132). So, the question becomes: how was this lengthy explication at all helpful?

Rorty we will return to in the next chapter, but for the moment we discover that Lonergan is not without his defenses. Let us assume for the moment that Lonergan is correct in his cognitional theory, that we experience, understand and judge. Assume also that he is correct in his arguments that this structure is able to be appropriated by all in a self-referentially consistent fashion and that the structure cannot be denied or revised without a performative contradiction. As an aside, I think that he is correct in these arguments and that the structure cannot be consistently denied, but since his arguments rest on *performative* rather than logical or conceptual contradiction the plausibility of his account rests in large measure on the degree to which his interlocutor has accomplished self-appropriation. Readers who have performed appropriation will not need to assume that he is correct; if they have not, I ask for the sake of argument that they grant his account for the moment to see where it leads. So we begin with the structure of consciousness—the various operations symbolized as experience, understanding, and judgment—and ask what the operations intend: to what are they directed?

Intentionality is often associated with Brentano and Husserl, but Lonergan also plays a unique part with *intentionality analysis* (Ryan 1973). In the older faculty psychology of the ancients and medievals, and in their more contemporary proponents like Gilson, the concrete existential subject is reduced to a soul, the essence or form of the human. The soul is a metaphysical postulate and one speaks of it almost as a "thing" (not in the Lonerganian sense of unity-identity-whole, but as an object) or a substance. The soul has certain "parts" or faculties which allow it to perform different activities (LR 424). For example, Plato's tripartite soul of the *Republic* or *Phaedrus* is broken into three parts each of which is a faculty capable of performing a different function. Aristotle and Aquinas, on this account, break the soul into various parts or powers such as the rational soul, irrational soul, appetitive soul, vegetative soul, agent intellect, passive intellect, and so on. On such an account, knowledge is guaranteed in that the faculty is constructed in such as fashion as to grasp reality through the function of its faculty. The Thomistic account, then, is able to become identical or one with all things in that it abstracts and becomes the form of the known object, indeed not the form as it exists in nature but the form as it exists in the mind, as an intentional species. This metaphysical account of the soul, however, is an abstraction rather than a concrete experience of events. Lonergan replaces the metaphysical account of the soul with the empirical and phenomenological account of the subject in self-appropriation and is concerned with actions or operations rather than parts and faculties. Still, if analyzed, the intentions of the operations reveal much.

What do we intend when we are performing the operations? What is it that we are after? "So far we have been talking about knowing, but the natural question is, Knowing what?" (UB 145) We are trying to know, of course, for the very question that started our cognitional theory was "What am I doing when I am knowing?" But knowing, as Husserl rightly acknowledged, is always directed, always intentional; when we know we always know something, and the statement "I know" always implies "I know x," and omitting the variable or the thing known would always lead to the question "*What* is it that you know?" Now, as mentioned earlier in the chapter, the ideal of knowledge varies among pursuits, contexts and historical situations: classical science sought the nature of things, statistics seeks probability, and so on. But despite heuristical variation, or variation of what we expect knowledge to be like once we have it, we always expect, anticipate, or intend knowledge to be of being, the real, or at least one instance of being. We are not after nothing but something; we are after *what is*:

> ... being is the object towards which our intellectual knowledge tends ... to know is to know being; being is the object of the transitive verb 'to know.' We have a fundamental identity: intellectual knowing of the type we have described and explained is identical with knowing being. (UB 149)

There is a sense in which this could come off as merely a semantic trick, that since we pose the questions "What *is* it?" and "*Is* it so?" an affirmative judgment "It *is*" is identified with being simply grammatically, the word *is* implies being. Further, there is the problem of metaphysics: just what is being? Is it the emptiest of concepts and thus entirely unhelpful? Lonergan is not, however, pulling any sleight of hand or empty tautology, but rather pointing out how the intellect functions. Being is simply what is known when one knows, for one knows something when knowing. Since absolutely everything that exists is being, for apart from being there is nothing, being includes all that is known and all that remains to be known, in short, the world of everything to be known, that which is. This definition is both concrete and universal, concrete in that it refers to particular things which are known or knowable, universal in that it applies to the totality of all known and knowable things (I 374-375). Notice that in this account being is not some quasi-mystical entity; we are not here speaking of the Being of beings or any such thing, but simply pointing out that when we attempt to know, we are trying to know what is in fact the case, what is so, and we are trying to know what is real, things which are.

This second-order definition is called by Lonergan a *notion*. It is not a theoretical account and as such is not Aristotelian or Heideggerian or Platonic or neo-Platonic (I 377). A notion is operational; it asserts that since all persons spontaneously and naturally desire to know, and further have an unrestricted desire to know (in that the exigencies of their intellect allow the capacity to ask more and more questions about absolutely everything or anything) operating within this desire to know everything and question everything is an inchoate notion or desire to know being, to know what is, to know absolutely everything about everything. It is why children incessantly question, why philosophers and scientist lie awake at night—they want to know what is—and if they did not desire to know what is they would not ask questions and would never learn anything at all. Again, since this is merely a notion, an operational drive or spontaneous desire rather than an explicit definition or theoretical conception, the notion should be known in self-appropriation; everyone should be able to discover operative in themselves a desire to know, and to know what is, in fact, the case about absolutely everything, assuming of course that they allow their intellect free reign instead of artificially restricting their natural dynamism.

Now one of the many errors in the tradition is to confuse being—all that is known and all that remains to be known—with that which is merely experienced. If one confuses the knowing that occurs in the merely biological pattern of experience with human knowing, then one will mistakenly think that being is that which is *already out there now real* or that only *bodies* are real (Meynell 1998, 62-65). That is, having reduced human knowing to sensation and the ideas caused by sensation, such as Hobbes, Locke, Hume, Berkeley and the positivists do, they reduce the world of reality to the world an animal can experience, albeit an animal with greater facility than most. Still, the positivists and materialists have done exactly what Lonergan has done: they identify what is known with what is real, but since they reduce fully human knowing of experience, understanding, and judgment to the biological pattern of experience, the only real they admit is that which is the already-out-there-now "real" (M 238).

Idealists realize that they wish to know more than what they simply observe; they realize that their knowing is more than just stupidly staring at the world. Consequently, they acknowledge that one thinks, that one is intelligent. But since one's account of the real invariably follows from one's account of knowing, the idealist thinks that the real is what is thought (M 239).

Of course both the materialist and the idealist have incomplete accounts of both the real and of knowing. But since a theoretical account and a performative operation are not the same thing, it follows that a person could perform operations for which they have not theoretically accounted. As a result, all knowers, if they have followed the natural exigencies of their intellect, have performed experience, understanding, and judgment; as such, they intend not merely what they observe, nor what they think; they intend being, what is real, everything that is known and remains to be known.

It follows, then, that we must not confuse what is intended by the various levels of consciousness. In experience we intend or advert to what can be sensed, to what is *sensible*. But since we naturally transcend mere experience to ask questions of intelligence or "What is It?" we heuristically intend an intelligent explanation or what is *intelligible*. But unless we are satisfied with idealism, which performatively we naturally transcend, we will ask critical questions, will be rational and ask "Is it So?" in which we finally intend *being* or the *real*. Each level of consciousness, then, has its own proper intention and the levels and the intentions must not be conflated, but ultimately we intend being and since we have not completed the full operations of knowing until we have judged we do not know being until we have judged truly.

Since each operation has its own intention, various types of objectivity are distinguished. The optical tradition invariably reduces reality to a type of out there now capable of being looked at, even if the out there now is purely intelligible and able to be seen only with the eye of the mind. But when fully human knowing is confused with a type of knowing patterned only after the biological pattern, objectivity is reduced to taking a good look or seeing what is to be seen without any distorting mediation. In other words, Lonergan is able to explain the advent of the god's-eye view; it emerges when the objectivity proper to the level of experience is illicitly elevated to the only type of objectivity

and becomes normative for all levels of consciousness (M 262-264)
But since knowing is not just taking a good look but involves experience, understanding and judgment, "the criteria of objectivity are not
just the criteria of ocular vision; they are the criteria of experiencing,
of understanding, [and] judging..." (M 238). Consequently, the criteria of objectivity are the transcendental precepts: Be attentive, be
intelligent, be rational (Marsh 1975, 256-271; Meynell 1999, 18-21).
Insofar as one performs these functions and allows the natural exigencies of the intellect to follow their dynamic course one is objective.
Somewhat paradoxically, then, genuine objectivity results from genuine subjectivity, or allowing one's own cognitional desires to flourish.
The more that one allows the intellect to follow its own performative
first principles, i.e., the desire to know, the more that objectivity is attained (Marsh 1975, 259):

> Fidelity to the desire to know is the explicit theme of normative
> objectivity. Because the desire to know is unrestricted, it opposes
> the obscurantism that refuses to ask certain questions. Because it
> is detached, it is opposed to inhibitions arising from other desires
> or fears. Because it is disinterested, it is critical of the way other
> desires can tempt one to rationalize and to remain confined within
> a limited horizon. It is the desire to know which grounds the ...
> transcendental precepts.... (Marsh 1975, 256).

As a result, the great discovery of Lonergan's account is that insofar
as one is attentive, intelligent and rational, one tends to discover the
truth, i.e., one tends to know being since the real world is just "what we
tend intelligently to conceive and reasonably to affirm on the basis of
experience" (Meynell 1998, 65; Meynell 1999, 21). Genuine objectivity is attained when a genuine subjectivity is attained, and a genuine
subjectivity results in the knowledge of being, in truth. Of course, intellectual modesty is called for: until we have asked all relevant questions and attained invulnerable insights, until we have attained cognitive authenticity or genuine subjectivity, claims to certainty may have
to be shelved; but the more probable it is that the transcendental precepts were followed the more probable it is that truth was reached.

3.10 OVERCOMING MYTH

But such an account requires intellectual conversion. So long as the
biological pattern of experience is confused with genuine objectivity,

a god's-eye view rather than rational judgments will be sought, and so long as the ocular myth reigns the real will be thought of as what is out there now real rather than what is intelligently conceived and reasonably affirmed. Intellectual conversion demands that the ocular metaphor be replaced with self-appropriation, that an incomplete answer to the question "What am I doing when I am knowing?" is replaced with a complete answer and the self-affirmation of the knower. Intellectual conversion overcomes the three mistakes of the cognitional myth: (1) knowing is not looking but experiencing, understanding and judging; (2) objectivity is not seeing what is to be seen but following the transcendental precepts in genuine subjectivity; (3) the real is not what is out there waiting to be seen but what is intelligently conceived and rationally affirmed.

Once intellectual conversion is accomplished, and once the transcendental precepts are acknowledged, it is impossible to remain a skeptic (Meynell 1998, 3-19). Of course, one can remain skeptical in the sense of being tough-minded, of demanding good reasons and sound judgments, but this sort of tough-mindedness is in fundamental agreement with the precept to be reasonable. But a sort of skepticism which denies knowledge is no longer possible, or at least no skepticism that attempts to give an account of itself. To claim "I am not a knower" is obviously a logical contradiction, for one has provided a proposition that is purported to be true and known; but if one attempts to defend the statement "I am not a knower" in any sort of intelligent and rational fashion—by appealing to evidence, or giving possible explanations or asking hard questions—then one has committed a performative contradiction (I 352-371). One can be a skeptic only if one is silent and attempts no defense of one's position; but such a position, or the holder of a position who attempts no defense, need not be taken seriously as there is no intelligent or rational weight to their position, and as soon as they try to provide some weight they have affirmed themselves as knowers. Further, the natural dynamism of our intellects make it highly unlikely that anyone will want to deny Lonergan's account: Does anyone want it to be known that they have no experiences? Not if they do not want to be thought rather odd. Does anyone want to be known to never ask questions, never to have insights or bright ideas, and never to define insights? Not if they do not want to be thought utter dullards without intelligence. Does anyone want to be known never to challenge first impressions, to believe everything heard or thought, to be entirely uncritical? Not if one does not want to be thought irrational and entirely gullible. Rather, everyone values experience, intelligence and reasonability because they themselves inchoately recognize the value of the performance of their own intellects.

Consequently, and finally, Lonergan provides us with an unshakeable foundation for knowledge. Granted, this is not classical foundationalism with its conceptualist and perceptualist assumptions. There are no appeals to immediately given ideas, incorrigible impressions, clear and distinct ideas, recollected forms, divine illumination, or Rorty's privileged representations. Instead there is a self-referentially consistent, invariant, critically grounded account of a series of operations that if performed consistently tend to lead to the truth, or to knowledge of being if you prefer. There are foundations to knowledge, just not the classical sort that Rorty rightly rejects:

> The first principles of knowing are the dynamic structure of the mind, not a set of statements purporting to express such first principles. Thus, the foundations which Lonergan affirms are not at all like those sought by Descartes, Russell or Husserl. They were correct to look for ultimates, but they looked in the wrong place and for the wrong kind of thing. Rorty is right to reject foundations of this kind. (Barden 1986, 99)

There is, as a result, a fundamental similarity between Rorty and Lonergan: both reject, albeit for different reasons, any sort of foundationalism which rests on the ocular myth. Consequently, both are concerned with *justified* belief, with giving reasons, arguments, an account.

Still, the apparent agreement is overshadowed by the severity of disagreement. While Lonergan is happy to reject the cognitive myth and replace it with his cognitional structure he is not at all worried that justified *true* belief, the correspondence theory of truth, or knowledge *of* the world is replaced with coherence, pragmatism, or a socially constructed set of useful propositions in place of realism. Rorty, on the other hand, not only rejects realism but does so gladly, welcoming the end of the spectator theory and its demand that we bow and scrape before reality. Why the difference? The following chapters will attempt to answer this question, ultimately deciding that Rorty has both an improper notion of knowing and of the real, what Lonergan calls a counterposition, that Rorty has given in to general bias, that Rorty is involved in a performative contradiction, and that Lonergan is capable of answering Rorty's objections and can save cognitive transcendence. None of the arguments has yet been established; I have been explaining Lonergan's position and arguing that self-appropriation will bear him out, I have not disproven Rorty or answered Rorty's objections. However, the responses to Rorty are plausible only to the extent that self-appropriation and the resulting intellectual conversion are effected; absent such conversion, Lonergan's answers will seem insufficient. But since Rorty's arguments against the tradition are too good to ignore, self-appropriation must occur if we are to avoid the spiritual and cultural death that I believe follows from Rorty's position.

CHAPTER 4
THE DESIRE TO KNOW

...man is more than an organism in an environment, more than an integrated personality, more even than a mature and creative individual, as the phrase goes. He is a wayfarer and a pilgrim.

(Walker Percy, *Signposts in a Strange Land*, 246)

4.1 PREAMBLE

The end of intuitionism leads to a crisis in an epistemological tradition which relied so often on the metaphor of knowing as seeing; so long as knowing is modeled on intuition it will be thought impossible. Lonergan solves the crisis through intellectual conversion and a new understanding of knowing while Rorty suggests abandoning the epistemological project altogether. In this chapter I examine the possibility of rejecting the quest for truth as Rorty suggests, asking two questions: (1) Is there necessarily a desire for truth and (2) does Rorty's denial of such desire result in performative contradiction? Both questions are answered in the affirmative. Along the way Rorty's false dichotomy—either there is intuitionism or realism is impossible—becomes more obvious, although the final conclusion on that matter rests in further chapters. I must note that this chapter does not yet ask the question, subject of chapters 5 and 6, of whether we can actually *know* the truth, just whether we *desire* to do so.

4.2 THE DESIRE TO KNOW AS THE MARK OF HUMANITY

The human discovers himself thrown into a world not of his own making, suffers emotionally and physically, is bewildered, confused and faces the inevitable threat of nothingness. Forced into contingency and finitude but gifted with consciousness and the ability to question and wonder, it is natural for humans to define themselves as the being which searches or quests. We are *homo viator*, travelers, questers, wanderers and wonderers, and our knowledge, selfhood and happiness are merely potential, not yet attained. In the history of philosophy and religion we discover numerous nods to the human situation: neither God nor animals but a bit of both we desire to know, for we love but do not yet possess wisdom. Aristotle speaks of a natural desire to know; Plato beautifully expresses the philosopher's erotic desire to know the Good; Scripture discloses our longing for Eden, heaven and the kingdom of God; Augustine speaks of the heart as restless until it rests in God; Heidegger reveals Dasein's special status as the being which has care (*Sorge*) for its world and for Being; C.S. Lewis points to an inconsolable longing (Grieco 1996, 155-163).

In one possible, and overly brief, narrative of Western thought, the desire to know succumbed to the desire to control, thus distorting our best inclinations. In this story, the ages of myth, logos and rev-elation shared an essential unity in pointing to the human quest for the *arche*—the beginning or the beyond—as the natural and necessary *telos* of the human. But such a conception of philosophy—pre-criti-cal, quasi-mystical and naïve—did not survive modernity. Hobbes re-placed the *summum bonum* with the desire to escape a life nasty, brut-ish and short; in other words, fear of the *summum malum* replaced the quest for the Good. Machiavelli dethroned virtue and Bacon preached the pliability of nature and the power of science to force nature to our will. Marx and Comte completed the task of this ideology and subverted the search for transcendent order with the creation of the kingdom of God on earth. Philosophers are replaced with bureaucrats intent not so much on discovering order and bending one's soul into conformity to it but on creating and managing the temporal kingdoms of human will through instrumental reason.

The attitude of transformation has its epistemological consequences as well, for in "contrast with the ancient Greek and Christian medieval understanding of contemplation, the modern turn toward subjectiv-ity stresses the concupiscent side of intellectual desire, and essentially neutralizes the ancient and medieval sense of the transcendent sta-tus and value of being" (Grieco 1996, 160). Rather than the identi-ty or perfection theory of Aristotle or Aquinas in which the object of knowledge has its own underlying reality with which we become united—knowing is a type of loving—modern epistemology ignores the independent value and goodness of being and considers it only as an object of representation. Consequently, the turn to the subject de-volved into a skeptical idealism and gave rise to the realism/anti-realism debates and the need for foundationalism to guarantee objectivity (McPartland 2001, 10-12).

This is only one possible interpretation, of course, but Rorty, for one, certainly recognizes the transformative possibilities of modernity as well as the concomitant epistemological worries. However, he chooses to embrace the transformative aspect of modernity while rejecting the epistemological problems which arise. Free of the metaphysical slavishness attempting to conform the soul to the order of nature or the will of God, the intelligence of the human exists to assert control and dominance over nature and to allow us to cope with the inconveniences of life (Hall 1994, 26-29). In a remarkably consistent move, he refuses to engage in the epistemological quest for objectivity created by modernity since the self-assertive aspect of modernity allows, perhaps demands, an attitude of insouciance towards the nature of things, towards getting it right, and Rorty is not afraid of this consequence. Consequently, hope replaces knowledge, solidarity replaces objectivity, and the liberal concern to lessen cruelty and suffering replaces the Philosophic urge to model society on Truth (ORT 33; cf. PSH 27-28):

> The tradition in Western culture which centers around the notion of the search for Truth, a tradition which runs from the Greek philosophers through the Enlightenment, is the clearest example of the attempt to find a sense in one's existence by turning away from solidarity to objectivity. The idea of Truth as something to be pursued for its own sake, not because it will be good for oneself, or for one's real or imaginary community, is the central theme of this tradition.... By contrast, those who wish to reduce objectivity to solidarity ... view truth as, in William James' phrase, what is good for *us* to believe. (ORT 21-22)

For a variety of reasons, some good, Rorty rejects the tradition of the search for Truth and the natural desire to know as fictional and unnecessary. Lonergan, on the other hand, not only accepts the pure and natural desire to know but bases the validity of his cognitional theory upon it. Consequently, should Rorty disprove the naturalness and existence of the search for truth he would eviscerate the Lonerganian enterprise.

4.3 LONERGAN'S DEPENDENCE
ON THE PURE DESIRE TO KNOW

Lonergan believes that cognitional theory reveals both the existence and the properties of the pure, unrestricted desire to know. This is not an abstraction but is revealed concretely by paying attention to the performance of our own intellects. Questioning is an empirical fact, we do it constantly and only someone with severely impaired intelligence and reason would be incapable of questioning. Further, questioning is spontaneous, natural, for children exhibit curiosity even before they can speak and once they acquire language ask questions so incessantly as to be annoying to their parents:

> But to put these questions is natural: it supposes no acquired habit, as does playing the violin; it supposes no gift of divine grace, as do faith and charity. Hence, since the questions are natural, the desire they manifest must also be natural. There exists, then, a desire that is natural to intellect, that arises from the mere fact that we possess intellects, that is defined by the basic questions, *an sit* and *quid sit*. (C 84)

Since performance of our own intellects reveals the desire to know, the nature of the desire is understood through reflection on our performance. By critically examining our questioning we can define the pure desire to know as "the dynamic orientation manifested in questions for intelligence and for reflection" (I 372). As a definition this is a touch thin, but we can expand upon it a bit more. First, the desire itself is not the verbal utterance of questions or the conceptual formulation of such questions, nor is it an insight, a conception or a judgment, but is the condition of possibility for those events (I 372). If we imagine a person devoid of any curiosity, of any wonder at all, they would not formulate questions. Of course, since intelligent and reflective persons ask questions with some frequency we may assume that they possess the condition of possibility for those questions, namely, the desire to know. This can be verified in ourselves, for we ask questions only when curious, and since we ask a great many questions we must be highly curious.

Second, the desire to know serves as the condition of possibility for understanding. Insights and concepts occur only given a question, for insights are the products not of external circumstances forcing their way into our consciousness but of inner conditions—not everyone shouted Eureka! in Syracuse but only Archimedes. Of course, the presence of the desire to know is a necessary but not sufficient condition of attaining understanding; there are questions which we do not know how to answer and which we do not yet understand (I 660).

Third, just as the desire to know allows understanding it allows judgment. Since we are not content with any possible answer but wish to answer all relevant questions, the desire to know is operative in the critically self-correcting and progressive structure of knowing (I 372). We do not simply answer our questions but spontaneously ask if our answers are right and continue the line of questioning until we have reached further and cumulative insights beyond the first. Of course this may take a great deal of time, generations even, and not everyone is curious about the same problems or as diligent in following the exigencies of intellect to their terminus, but still the corrections and progress internal to the structure of knowing is possible only given a dynamism arising from within the questioner and not from any external source.

Fourth, the desire to know is pure (I 373). It is pure in that the desire to know manifests itself most strongly in the intellectual pattern of experience free from the everyday interests more properly of the biological or dramatic patterns of existence. We can lose ourselves in inquiry and become absorbed in the problem at hand, not for the sake of some practical gain but purely for the sake of knowing, simply because a question remains unanswered, some event not yet understood. There is a "joy of discovery" because it delights us to know (I 373).

Fifth, the pure desire has the objective of knowing being (I 373). Questions of intelligence seek to attain intelligibility or form while questions of reflection intend the real, what is. The content of intelligent conception and rational affirmation is being, what is. Initially totally unknown as our knowledge is merely potential, we begin to know being and the more we know the more of being that we know. Being is the "objective of the pure desire to know," and since we desire to know everything about everything, both what we actually now know and what remains to be known, being is the totality of all that is known and unknown (I 372). This indicates that we do not question for the sake of questioning but for the sake of knowing; it is the content of knowing which allows the mind to end its internal dynamism and rest.

Sixth, since being is the real, it follows that the desire to know the real is a desire for the truth (I 573). Judging "yes" or "no" to the question "Is it?" makes a claim about the real, about the way things are and explicitly and implicitly implies a commitment to a truth claim. Of course, judgments made on hazy grounds are hasty, but supposing that a virtually unconditioned is attained one in fact makes a statement about what is and either affirms a truth or a falsehood. Consequently, the desire to know results in a commitment to the correspondence theory of truth for one makes a judgment about what one believes to be actually the case in the real world (I 575).

Seventh, in affirming a virtually unconditioned, one is making a truth claim universal in its implications. Of course, there are various degrees of certainty or probability, but in either event one claims that *x* probably or certainly is the case. But this claim, assuming one has followed the desire to know to its completion, is about the virtually unconditioned. The event or state in question is conditioned, it has antecedent conditions, but that those conditions are in fact satisfied. To do so, to say "if *y* then *x*; but *y*; therefore, *x*" is to make a statement about what is real, what is in fact the case, and thus is a statement universal in intent. To say "if an acid is present the litmus paper should turn a certain color, but it does turn this color" states not only a truth for you, the statement concerns reality. Even statements that vary in time such as "It is in fact the case that the Supreme Court is considering the University of Michigan's affirmative action guidelines" which you claim to be true now but which would be false in 1992 or 2022 is a universal statement about the real as it exists at the moment, the contingency and variability of the real notwithstanding.

Eighth, the desire to know and the expression of the desire in understanding and truth claims implies an expectation of intelligibility. The very process of asking questions exhibits a commitment to expecting the real to disclose answers to those questions. Of course, answers may not be forthcoming and it may in fact be the case that the full intelligibility of the real is not made known; even if that is so, one cannot ask questions without implicitly committing oneself to accepting the ontological truth, or inner intelligibility, of the real (I 576). To deny this would commit a performative contradiction, for the performance and intention of the question demands an expectation of an answer. To ask a question is to assume that there exists a virtually unconditioned judgment at the finality of the questioning process, even if one does not expect to be able to attain that finality alone or even in one's lifetime.

Obviously, much here is debatable and in no way defeats Rorty *a priori*, but it does, I think, express the centrality of desire to Lonergan's project. It also reveals what is at stake in Rorty's commitment to irony or mere acceptance that we ought to stop trying to get it right and simply be satisfied with what is good for us to believe. If Rorty is right and the pure desire to know is a chimera then the Lonerganian project fails entirely. For the moment Lonergan's arguments for the existence of the pure unrestricted desire to know will be passed over and Rorty's objections examined.

4.4 RORTY'S FIRST OBJECTION: CORRESPONDENCE THEORIES ARE EMPTY

The first objection argues that the conception of Truth as correspondence is unintelligible. We do not know what Truth means, and so intending Truth as the terminus of inquiry is nonsensical. In *Philosophy and the Mirror of Nature*, Rorty attempted to dissolve the thorny perennial problems of mind and knowledge by exposing their contingency (PMN 6-7). Not only did all attempts to solve these problems fail but the problems themselves are optional, arising from historical choices, especially the acceptance of the Cartesian veil of ideas and its corresponding problems of skepticism and solipsism. But things could have gone differently, another set of problems or vocabulary could have been accepted and consequently we can drop those questions without any twinge of conscience (PMN 8-9). Beginning with *Consequences of Pragmatism*, Rorty performs the same maneuver with respect to the problem of truth. All theories of truth are pointless and conceptually incoherent, but if the concept of truth as correspondence is incoherent then it makes little sense to intend it as the object of desire and we can drop the problem as unnecessary (COP xiii).

Broadly construed, there are two types of realists. An intuitive realist, Nagel or Gilson, for example, feels that philosophical problems such as mind-body relations or the theory of truth are justified, even if we do not know how to solve them, simply because we have the intuition that there are more to pains or feelings than simple brain states and that there is a difference between something appearing to be so and actually being the case (CP xxix). Thus philosophy serves a function simply because the question "Are these appearances real?" seems inescapable—we easily and naturally ask this question. Consequently, the intuitive realist considers the pragmatist's claim that it does not matter whether something really is the case so long as it serves our interests as intellectually dishonest. But Rorty does not deny the existence of such apparently natural and intuitive questions. We are, after all, products of a social environment and an intellectual heritage, Platonic through and through; but these "intuitions" are not natural or necessary, they result from a contingent choice to value Socrates over Protagoras or Gorgias:

> *Of course* we have such intuitions. How could we escape having them? We have been educated within an intellectual tradition built around such claims—just as we used to be educated within an intellectual tradition built around such claims as "If God does not exist, everything is permitted" [and] "Man's dignity consists in his link with a supernatural order" ... But it begs the question between the pragmatist and the realist to say that we must find a philosophical view which "captures" such intuitions. The pragmatist is urging that we do our best to *stop having* such intuitions, that we develop a *new* intellectual tradition. (CP xxx)

So, having done away with the intuitive realist who says we *must* answer these questions and have a theory of truth, Rorty turns his attentions to what he terms "technical realists" (CP xxi). Technical realism is nothing more than a reaction against pragmatism, arguing that (1) pragmatic objections to the correspondence theory of truth are answerable and (2) that the pragmatist underestimates the importance of traditional philosophical problems (CP xxi-xxii). The second objection falls back into intuitive realism, but again that begs the question concerning the necessity of our choices. So the real debate concerns whether the correspondence theory is defensible.

Rorty responds that there is unlikely ever to be a profitable and philosophically interesting theory of truth and we should abandon the attempt. For instance, if we examine several statements that are acknowledged to be true—"2+2=4," "George H. W. Bush and George W. Bush both served as Presidents of the United States," "Love is better than hate" and "Bacon did not write Shakespeare"—it is unlikely that we will discover any feature common to all statements by virtue of which they are true (CP xiii). Pragmatists doubt the existence of a common feature just as they doubt that a common core of Goodness is discernable in "the morally praiseworthy actions as Susan leaving her husband, America joining the war against the Nazis, America pulling out of Vietnam, Socrates not escaping from jail" and so on (CP xiii). These were desirable actions, but no common feature makes them good, just as no common feature is found in all true statements, no property (Truth) by virtue of which they are true. Further, the lack of a common property explains why attempts to discover a theory of truth have proven so unfruitful (CP xiv). In fact, "several hundred years of effort have failed to make interesting sense of the notion of 'correspondence' (either of thoughts to things or of words to things)" (CP xvii; Malachowski 2002, 77). These theories are uninteresting because they cannot *explain* how true statements correspond to reality without tautology. For instance, Tarski's notion that "p" is true if and only if *p*, or "Snow is white" is true if and only if Snow is white, is uninteresting and non-explanatory. One might as well say that an action is right because it corresponds to the Moral Law or opium makes one sleepy because of its dormative power (CP xvii, xxiv). In essence one is saying that an action is right because it is right, opium makes you sleepy because it has the power to make you sleepy and a statement is true because it is true. Absent some explanation of what makes a statement correspond to reality a theory of truth is empty verbiage. One should simply say that the world exercises causal forces upon us which naturalistically and physiologically leads to belief. We have some beliefs because we are caused to believe them and others because we persuade ourselves—truth is an unnecessary addition to this explanation.

Should the attempt be made to explain just how language corresponds to the world an illicit appeal to the god's-eye view is made, for it is impossible to take a "meta-verificationist" step outside of language and see where and how language hooks up to the world:

> One cannot see language-as-a-whole in relation to something else to which it applies, or for which it is a means to an end ... The attempt to say "how language relates to the world" by saying what makes certain sentences true, or certain actions or attitudes good or rational, is, on this view, impossible. (CP xix; 160-166)

One can, of course, offer a verificationist approach to truth within a language game, but that amounts to nothing more than what your peers will let you get away with saying, or what is accepted within a certain vocabulary; but to step outside that vocabulary to check if it matches up, or corresponds, to the world is impossible without the discredited notion of the super-intuition of meta-verification. In the end, the technical realist is not much more than an intuitive realist, they figure that there just must be some reason to assume realism because it seems that it must be so, but that is really not much of a reason at all (CP xxix). It is no better than the early Wittgenstein's brute assertion of isomorphism between words and the world they picture.

This objection is not so much an attack on the existence of the desire for truth as the meaning of such a phrase. If no one can say exactly what they mean by 'truth' it makes little sense to talk about the desire for truth—it is jabberwocky. This is, then, a tactical argument, a stratagem, by which Rorty hopes to preclude intentionality analysis. The burden of proof is on the defender of the natural desire for truth to defend both the naturalness and the meaning of such desire.

4.5 A LONERGANIAN RESPONSE

This objection, that a theory of truth is useless if not impossible, does not worry the Lonerganian all that much. First, the objection would worry an epistemologist—whether intuitive or technical—but not someone performing cognitional theory. As opposed to epistemology, cognitional theory is not so concerned with the properties of truth as with the functions of knowing. Since we are concerned with performance rather than with logical properties it would not matter if various true statements x, y, and z lack a common property 'Truth.' Rather, what matters is that they share a common *knower*, the person having attained a virtually unconditioned judgment; we are not looking for a common property but for a performance had in common by all knowers. Beginning with abstract definitions rather than reflection on concrete performance results in a definition of truth which will indeed seem like empty verbiage, even alien to the concrete operations we perform (UB 13). Until self-appropriation is completed the problems of formulation are insurmountable, for one is attempting to define what is still unknown. So I am able to reject the assumption that we must begin with the analysis of the concepts of truth and instead turn to concrete practice.

Second, turning to the concrete practice of cognitional theory allows the development of a minimal correspondence theory of truth which is useful, normative and explanatory. I borrow the minimal correspondence theory from Hugo Meynell (1998, 20-21). He defines such a theory as involving the following three elements:

> (a) "p" is true if and only if *p*;
> (b) in typical cases one does not make *p* to be the case by affirming "p"—the world is generally what it is regardless of whether anyone makes statements about it or not;
> (c) one tends to know what is the case and make true judgments about it to the degree that one follows through with the exigencies of one's own intellect as symbolized in the functions of experiencing, understanding and judging.

Statement (a) is the standard expression of the correspondence theory, in itself non-explanatory and thus in need of (b) and (c). Statement (b) expresses the commonsense notion that the world and its properties do not depend on anyone speaking or knowing about it. There are a few exceptions to this rule, for instance the statement "It is true that I am making a statement *x* at this moment *t*" is true only if I say *x* at *t*. But the vast majority of statements—"George Bush is President," "God exists," "Water is composed of hydrogen and oxygen"—have conditions antecedent to my statement. Now, the difficulty for the theory, and note we are discussing the usefulness of the theory and not yet the possibility of attaining true judgments, is that the theory must also explain how the statement corresponds to reality. We need to explain how language matches up if we are not to just say a statement is true because it is true (Meynell 1998, 21).

We solve the problem by providing a second-order, or notional, definition of reality as *that which we would come to speak about if and when we follow the threefold process of knowing* (Meynell 1998, 21; I 374). Lonergan's definition of being is notional, it does not define the content of being but "how that meaning is to be determined," i.e., the meaning of being is determined by examining the objective of the pure desire to know (I 374). We desire to know, the object of that desire we call being. Since we desire to know everything about everything being is all that is known and all that remains to be known (the totality of intelligent formulations and reasonable affirmations). We can thus expand or articulate Meynell's statement (c) by the following:

(1) being is all that is known and all that remains to be known,

(2) knowing is accomplished as the terminus of the threefold process of attending to relevant experience, intelligently conceiving and rationally judging in a virtually unconditioned judgment,

(3) it follows that being is known in a virtually unconditioned judgment.

(4) from (a) and (b) on the preceding page, it follows that in any virtually unconditioned judgment "p" is true if and only if *p*,

(5) from (3) it follows that *p* as an instance of being is known in a virtually unconditioned judgment,

(6) but "p" is affirmed in a virtually unconditioned *judgment*,

(7) thus, from (5) and (6), "p" is affirmed about a known *p*. So we have explained how "p" matches up with *p*.

As I see it, this solves Rorty's problem as it does explain how a statement corresponds to reality in a true statement—a true statement is one which we *would* say after following the threefold process and attaining a virtually unconditioned judgment. For *if* and *when* we attain a virtually unconditioned judgment we know the real and have made a judgment about the real, concluded in (7). Granted, we may never actually attain a virtually unconditioned judgment, we may never attain all relevant data, ask all relevant questions of intelligence and all relevant questions of reflection, but that is irrelevant since the only burden was to explain what it would mean to make a true judgment that corresponds to reality. So while we may not know if a given statement is true, we are able to define the nature of a true statement (I 573-575). A true statement is a statement about what is known once reality is known in a virtually unconditioned judgment. Reality is what we *would* know at the terminus of inquiry and truth is the affirmation of that known reality.

Third, the definition is also useful, disproving Rorty's assertion that there is no use to a theory of truth. I grant that Tarski's definition hardly gets the blood racing, nor does it help to so solve the problem of whether any particular statement is true or false. Lonergan's theory, as fleshed out by my additions to Meynell, does contain an element of normativity and criticism. If we know that statement "p" is true if and only if *p*, and that *p* generally obtains whether or not "p" is articulated, and that "p" tends to be a true statement about *p* if "p" is or converges upon a virtually unconditioned judgment, then we know that insofar as "p" tends to converge on a virtually unconditioned judgment that it will tend to be correct and presumption is in its favor. On the other hand, a statement "x" that tends not to converge on a virtually unconditioned judgment—the judgment is made before the threefold process is anything near completion—may be correct but prudence withholds judgment. Thus, we have a standard, derived from the theory of truth itself, of what sort of judgments we should trust and make and what sort of judgments should arouse our suspicion—the theory is both normative and critical. Particular problems, then, such as whether one person wrote all of Shakespeare, whether superstring theory is correct, and what we should do about a leaky faucet can be approached with some criterion, namely, to what extent have the natural exigencies of the intellect been followed in arriving at a particular conclusion. Or more briefly, have the transcendental precepts been followed? Obviously the theory of truth does not solve particular problems, only experience, understanding and judgment can accomplish that task, but the theory does provide a test by which we hasten or hesitate to judge.

4.6 RORTY'S SECOND OBJECTION: THERE IS NO DESIRE FOR TRUTH

The preceding discussion exhibits the importance of the desire to know. I responded to Rorty's claim that we need not consider the desire for truth since 'truth' is unintelligible by arguing that 'truth' becomes intelligible if and only if from the desire to know we arrive at the notion of being as that which we would know at the terminus of inquiry, or at the satisfaction of the desire to know. If Rorty is able to disprove the fact of the desire to know, then not only will my defense of the intelligibility of 'truth' fail but so will the normative status of Lonergan's cognitional theory and his defense of realism.

Rorty's second objection rests not on the conceptual meaning of terms but on the possibility of desire. Again he backs his way into the argument, for he does not simply assert that he cannot discover desire in his intellect but rather that since there is no possibility of attaining knowledge of the way things really are we *ought* to abandon as chimerical the desire for truth. His argument runs broadly as follows: If there is no way things really are it is impossible for there to be truth about the way things are, and if there is no truth about the way things are there can be no desire to know the truth. He then redescribes the desire operative behind inquiry in a more pedestrian fashion.

Rorty makes the counter-intuitive claim that there is no way the world really is which we could know. Since there is no 'way things really are,' desiring to conform our intellects to reality, i.e., desiring the truth about things, is a waste of time. His reason: all awareness and all knowing is linguistic, we can never "step outside our skins" and see the world as it is in and of itself without linguistic description, but a non-knowable noumenal realm of being is pointless (COP xix). Now the notion that all awareness and experience is linguistically conditioned does not in itself necessitate the rejection of the 'way things are.' One could very well reject the tradition of intuitionism, admit that all awareness and knowledge of reality "out-there" is mediated by ideas or historicity or embodiment or language and still retain the notion of reality existing in itself. Kant, for instance, attempts to make this move, insisting that our *a priori* forms and categories necessitate a distinction between the phenomenal and noumenal realms, but there still is a noumenal realm causing our intuitions. The standard objection to Kant is that he justifies the existence of the noumenal realm through the category of causation—we know there must be a noumenal realm because our intuitions are caused and must be caused by something—but since causation applies only to the phenomenal world we cannot use the category to deduce the noumenal. Rorty makes a similar objection, insisting that to speak of a non-linguistic world of essences and forms is unintelligible since they are absolutely nothing to us. If we are to consistently and whole-heartedly reject intuitionism and accept our contingency and the mediated status of knowledge, the world *an-sich*, in-itself, must be rejected. It is nothing to us, unknowable, and thus mere metaphysical baggage. It makes no sense to conjecture about such things and we should simply stop doing so:

> Platonism ... attempts to get free of society, of *nomos*, convention, and to turn to *physis*, to nature. But ... there is no such thing as *physis* to be known. The *nomos-physis*, convention-nature distinction goes for the same reason that the appearance-reality distinction goes. For once you have said that all our awareness is under a description, and that descriptions are functions of social needs, then 'nature' and 'reality' can only be names of something unknowable—something like Kant's 'Thing-in-Itself'. (PSH 48-49; cf. 1997, 17)

4 ᴓ *The Desire to Know*   123

To take an example: What is the essence of the number 17? What is 17 "*in itself*, apart from its relationships to other numbers" (PSH 52)? To account for the essence or nature of 17 a definition would be needed that is radically different from the following: "less than 22, more than 8, the sum of 6 and 11, the square root of 289, the square of 4.123105" and so on (PSH 53). We would need to come up with a definition in isolation of 17's relation to other numbers, for all of these descriptions or relations to other numbers do not in any way get close to 17 in and of itself. Now, it might be possible to axiomatize arithmetic and reduce numbers to sets, but "if the mathematician then points to his neat little batch of axioms and says 'Behold the essence of 17!' we feel gypped. There is nothing very seventeenish about those axioms, for they are equally the essence of 1, or 2..." (PSH 53). In short, there is no essence of 17 other than the descriptions we give to it as it relates to other numbers, but those numbers themselves are defined in the same fashion and thus not helpful. Rorty suggests that we think of everything in the same fashion as we do the number 17, that everything we speak about is nothing more than the sum of our descriptions. (This account of reality is counterpositional, not to mention nihilistic—more in Chapter 7.)

Rorty is a tough-minded anti-intuitionist. Having overcome the hope of unmediated access to reality he demands that the notion of reality in-itself is utter nonsense, a pipe dream (COP 160-166). If the subject, or the subject within a language game, constructs all knowledge there is nothing to be known outside of the language game; even to assert the *existence* of something outside the language game illicitly assumes a god's-eye view of what is unknowable. Thus Rorty demands that we become anti-representational (ORT 1-17) and consign the whole claptrap philosophical baggage of realism and skepticism to the flames. Those issues and debates make sense only if we are trying to accurately picture the world correctly, but if there is no world to represent then the realist's claim that we do this well and the skeptic's claim that we do not know if we do it well are irrelevant:

> Pragmatists reply to seventeenth-century arguments about the veil of appearances by saying that we need not model knowledge on vision. So there is no need to think of the sense organs or our ideas as intervening between a mental eye and its object ... They reply to nineteenth-century arguments about the distorting effect of language by saying that language is not a medium of representation ...

It cannot fail to represent accurately, for it never represents at all. (PSH 49-50)

However, if there is no intelligible world in itself, then what sense does it make to speak of a desire for truth? According to Rorty, "giving up the representationalist account of language obviously throws doubt on the use of the word 'Truth' to name an object, *even an object of desire*"(1997, 22; italics mine). Instead, we look only for "reliable tools" since there is no "specifically human activity called the quest for truth" (Rorty 1997, 22-23). We are questing for control, not for truth or getting things right: "the use of the noun 'Truth' as the name of an object of desire is a relic of an earlier time: the time in which we believed that there was a natural order to be grasped" (Rorty 1997, 23). Replacing *love of truth* or *desire for truth* is either (a) an attitude of intellectual curiosity, not in the sense of wonder about the natural order, but "simply open-mindedness: curiosity about opinions different from [one's] own, tolerance for the existence of such opinions and willingness to let [one's] own views be corrected ..." or (b) being true to oneself, having "the courage to stick to [one's] guns" even when everyone else thinks you are crazy (Rorty 1997, 25-26). The ancient notion of the pure unrestricted desire to know was a mistake, relic of a spectator theory hoping for blessedness by bowing and scraping before a non-existent natural order. The desire to know mutates into a tension between "conversability and stubbornness," and in Rorty's liberal dream both poles of the tension are given free reign in a culture allowing for the pursuit of private perfection but demanding tolerance and the minimizing of cruelty in the public sphere (PSH 3-20; CIS 73-121).

Reducing the desire for truth to public conversability and private stubbornness does not entail irrationalism (COP 166-169). Humans are not satisfied with nonsense and try to make sense of their world, but they do so not "because they love truth but because they cannot help doing so" (Rorty 2000, 15). The mere fact of language requires this, "there is no language without justification, no ability to believe without an ability to argue about what beliefs to have" (Rorty 2000, 15). Consequently, we pursue conversability and stubbornness for three reasons: (1) a need to make beliefs coherent, (2) the need for the respect of one's peers and (3) curiosity. (Rorty 2000, 14-17). Undergirding these three reasons is Rorty's naturalism: our brains are not constructed to withstand the neuro-chemical imbalances which are the physiological correlate of incoherence, as members of a social community we derive standards of justification internal to that community, and as Darwinian animals we need the influx of new ideas to develop new and better ways of coping.

To construct coherent webs of belief for ourselves, gaining the respect of our peers and searching for better coping mechanisms demonstrates not a desire for truth but a concern to *justify our beliefs*. The traditional definition of knowledge—justified true belief—says too much; we are not concerned with justified *true* beliefs but simply with justified beliefs or warranted assertability (Rorty 2000, 4-5; PSH 27-32; ORT 23-32, 98). Of course, there are as many standards of justification as there are communities rather than one best or natural vocabulary—presumably fortune tellers value the judgments of someone who is wise in the use of Tarot cards more than the judgments of Martha Nussbaum—but without a natural vocabulary there is no concern for truth:

> All the idea of truth does is to say, "Bethink yourself that you might be mistaken; remember that your beliefs may be justified by your other beliefs in the area, but that the whole kit and caboodle might be misguided, and in particular that you might be using the wrong *word* for your purpose.... The *only* cash value of this regulative idea is to commend fallibilism, to remind us that lots of people have been as certain of, and as justified in believing, things that turned out to be false as we are certain of, and justified in holding, our present views. (Rorty 1990, 635)

On the face of it, these arguments sound the death knell for Lonergan. His position assumes: (1) that the intellect's natural exigencies towards understanding and judging have as a condition of their possibility the pure unrestricted desire to know, that (2) the natural *telos* or intention of this desire is being, the real, and that (3) cognitive self-transcendence, or knowledge of the real, occurs or tends to occur insofar as the pure desire to know is allowed free reign. Now, Rorty's argument cuts off (1) at the knees—there is no desire to know but only the desire to control and use, makes (2) meaningless since we cannot desire to know being as there is no real being absent our social and linguistic constructions and thus defeats (3). Lonergan's natural desire to question mutates into either the desire to control the world or remain socially and personally virtuous.

4.7 LONERGAN'S RESPONSES

Lonergan is not all that concerned to defend the fact of the desire; he assumes that everyone finds this desire too self-evident to need much defense, "it is beyond doubt" (I 28, 660; cf. Morelli 1990, 57). Those who would deny it have made a decision for "the deeper hopelessness that allows man's spirit to surrender the legitimate aspirations of unrestricted desire and to seek comfort in the all too human ambitions of the Kantian and the positivist" (I 723). Further, the skeptic doubting the hope of inquiry does not do so "without first arguing that the effort is useless or enervating or misleading or illusory" and by so arguing demonstrate the existence of the very desire to know (I 661; Morelli 1990, 57). But such confidence needs support, and while Lonergan's arguments are pithy, they do, at least cumulatively, offer a strong defense. Here I examine two of Lonergan's arguments and find that they reveal a performative contradiction in Rorty's reasoning.

4.71 *Desiring Coherence is Performatively Identical to Desiring Truth*

Lonergan first defends the desire for truth by appealing to the empirical fact of inquiry—people simply do ask questions of intelligence and reflection:

> Deep within us all, emergent when the noise of other appetites is stilled, there is a drive to understand, to see why, to discover the reason, to find the cause, to explain. Just what is wanted has many names. In what precisely it consists is a matter of dispute. But the matter of inquiry is beyond doubt. It can absorb a man. It can keep him for hours, day after day, year after year, in the narrow prison of his study or his laboratory. It can send him on dangerous voyages of exploration. It can withdraw him from other interests, other pursuits, other pleasures.... (I 28)

Further, "neither centuries of inquiry nor enormous libraries of answers have revealed any tendency for the stream of further questions to diminish" and so both the child, the scientist, the philosopher and the common person continue to ask "What is it?" and "Is it so?" (I 661).

The problem with this argument, as Elizabeth Morelli notes, is that "from the standpoint of a Nietzsche or a Foucault [or a Rorty] one can easily admit this continuing history of intellectual pursuit and yet deny the existence of a pure desire to know," for the desire could be explained as "will to power or a civilized libido" or simply the desire to make our web of beliefs consistent and comprehensive (1990, 58). That is to say, it begs the question to argue that the fact of intellectual pursuit necessitates classifying this activity as a desire for *truth* rather than some other desire. Rorty's explanation—that we desire coherence, public esteem and better beliefs—could then subsume and redescribe the intentions of intelligence and reflection.

Such a redescription goes against the intuitions of most inquirers. When we inquire we think of our questions as intending to get things right, to get to the heart of the matter and figure out what is really going on. Still, Rorty would respond that these intuitions are neither natural or necessary—he advocates abandoning these intuitions and redescribing them as a desire to make sense of things given our situation rather than knowing the world as it really is. We may assume that questions have answers, but there is no reason to believe that any answers intend the way things are let alone actually discover pre-existent order within the world. Further, as products of the Western-Platonic tradition, it is easy to explain why our "natural intuitions" would "intend" the really real—this is simply the vocabulary of our inheritance, but things would have turned out remarkably different if someone as capable as Plato wrote treatises defending Thrasymachus or Protagoras. In that event, our "natural intuitions" would be that justice is the advantage of the stronger and that the human is the measure of all things.

There are, to be sure, a few minor problems with Rorty's account. First, Rorty is overly hasty in assuming that our supposedly natural intuitions are merely products of Platonism. One could show that "'non-Platonic' cultures also have context-transcending senses of truth and reality" (T. McCarthy 1990b, 360; for an example of this method see Crowe 1993, 89-107). For instance, the Hebrew scriptures, the Koran, various pre-philosophic cosmological myths and other non-Western philosophical accounts of reality would all claim to disclose important truths about the way the world is. However, while such ethnomethodological studies could very well disprove Rorty's claim that only Platonism leads to intuitions of realism, just as such studies eventually damaged the claims of moral relativists, they would do nothing to counter Rorty's comeback that the problem may be wider than philosophy but still each system is just a way of making beliefs gel together in an advantageous fashion.

Second, one could argue that Rorty's epistemological behaviorism should serve merely a descriptive role, discovering how various communities in practice go about determining standards of justification rather than reforming our commonsense assumptions. It seems amiss for a behaviorist to argue that one, or as it may turn out, many communities, should change their standards since the behaviorist lacks any transcendent reason by which to justify the change. Consequently, since our community has, and despite Rorty's best efforts, probably will continue to use "universal, context-transcending notions of truth and reality, right and good," a consistent epistemological behaviorist would need to remain content in describing how such systems operate and is compelled to play by those very rules if speaking within that system (T. McCarthy 1990b, 361). Given his epistemological behaviorism and ethnocentrism, he should be content to allow us to do what we have always done, i.e., appeal to universal, context transcending notions of truth and falsehood, appearance and reality, right and wrong.

These arguments do cast some doubt on Rorty's ability to consistently advocate a change in cultural standards and the way philosophy operates. Still, he has shown a remarkable ability in works such as *Philosophy and the Mirror of Nature, Objectivism, Relativism and Truth, Essays on Heidegger and Others* and *Truth and Progress* to work from within the context of philosophy itself to show how the project becomes incoherent according to its own principles. At the point he succeeds at internal criticism it is less egregious to suggest that the particular context and vocabulary of philosophy do not sustain its web of beliefs. It should be kept in mind, however, that Lonergan too rejects the claims of wrongheaded philosophy and for many of the same reasons as Rorty. Consequently, if Rorty is not to commit the fallacy of division—philosophy is incapable of supporting its claims, Lonergan practices philosophy, thus Lonergan is incapable of supporting his claims—the burden would be on Rorty to demonstrate that Lonergan commits the same errors as the broader tradition.

However persuasive these arguments might be, a far stronger response is simply that his distinction between truth and justification is unresponsive since the desire to coherently justify one's beliefs is *performatively* identical to the desire for truth. There is obviously a conceptual or logical distinction between truth understood as self-transcendence and coherence understood as lack of tension between beliefs, but in practice one does the same thing whatever one intends, or at least if one is attempting a coherence which is intelligent and reasonable. Let me give a simple example of the search for coherence, and while it is rather basic I see no reason why the mechanisms and process of more complicated webs of belief would be different. (For similar examples see Quine's *The Web of Belief*—the simplicity of such examples allows us to more readily observe the process.)

A very young boy, Tommy, has the following set of beliefs:
(1) His grandmother is honest and has his best interest at heart.
(2) She has told him to never go outside without sun block as his skin will immediately blister and he will become permanently disfigured.
(3) Friends of his do not wear sunscreen and have not immediately blistered or become disfigured.
(4) He does not suffer from any unusual skin condition.
(5) His grandmother is a liar.

Here is a series of beliefs all of which seem true to Tommy. Still, he cannot believe them all without incoherence. After thinking about it, he rejects beliefs (2) and (5) and adds belief (6), that his grandmother exaggerated to make a point and keep him from sunburn. Now he has a coherent set of beliefs.

But how did he go about this decision? Let's say he begins by wondering how (2), (3) and (4) could all be true without (5) also being true which casts doubt on (1). So he runs through various possibilities. Perhaps his grandmother has an evil twin, but if so no one else has heard of her. Perhaps his friends do blister, but still they are not disfigured and he has never seen them blister. Perhaps his friends do wear sunscreen, but he has seen them outside for hours and never apply or reapply it. All of these are possible ways to understand the problem, each arises as an answer to the question "What is going on here?" but none survive the additional question "Does this answer make sense given all the data?" and so Tommy continues to ask until he has a consistent set of beliefs making sense of the data. He finally happens on the possibility that this was all said for exaggeration, that his grandmother loves him but has a sense of humor. This new belief seems to allow him to retain the maximum number of other beliefs which he has no reason to doubt.

The boy attains coherence, but is there any real difference between the activities involved in attaining coherence and those activities which Lonergan believes result in self-transcendence? I think not. He began with data: he has certain beliefs given to him by his own experiences and from the authority of others. The data, however, do not make sense of themselves and in fact appear mutually exclusive. Naturally such incoherence gives rise to cognitive dissonance—*aporia*, wonder—and the boy is motivated to understand how to make sense of it all. He runs through various possibilities, some he rejects out of hand as nonsense, others he entertains for a time, until finally he has an understanding of the problem which survives his critical faculties. The process is exactly as Lonergan predicts and in practice it is quite irrelevant whether we call this the desire for truth or the attempt at coherence—performatively the boy engages in the three-fold structure to attain either.

On the face of it this sounds a bit much, for if anything is certain it is that coherence is conceptually distinct from correspondence. We are inclined, and Rorty accepts it as a given, that coherence and correspondence theories of truth are at odds. It is true that the concepts of correspondence and coherence are at odds, but the project of cognitional theory is prior to those epistemological concerns and once performed exposes the operations that *will* and *must* be performed by any subject engaged in the attempt to know. As argued in the last chapter, it is *impossible* to deny the three-fold aspect of knowing without engaging in the process itself—one rejects the theory because it overlooks some piece of data, misinterprets the data or is unsatisfactory—but such a rejection actually affirms Lonergan's proposal. As such, the structure is normative and universal, *everyone* engages in the process when they try and make sense of things, the young boy and Rorty, too.

The intuitive reaction we have that correspondence and coherence theories are opposed, which they are, is based on the wrong reasons. We often explain these theories in images: coherence is a circle or a web of beliefs contained either in the subject or a particular culture but not isomorphic with reality it-self whereas correspondence is the agreement of the subject and object. Both images, however, assume a by-product of the ocular model, namely, that the subject is over-here and reality is over-there, but in coherence the subject is always incapable of getting over-there whereas in correspondence the over-there of reality somehow gets over- or in-here. This image of correspondence is muddled further when it is a version of naïve realism holding a direct encounter between subject and object unmediated by other beliefs, perspectives, abilities, interests and so forth on the side of the subject. In this image the subject is an empty head, an eye unaffected by any distortion, and the subject merely opens its eyes and some mysterious faculty slips into gear to crank out knowledge. The theory of Aristotle, Aquinas and Lonergan, better termed as the identity, perfection or self-transcendence model, does not naively assume that the subject knows or becomes isomorphic with reality without any mediation, it does not accept the 'principle of the empty head' whereby knowledge is more objective the less the subject contributes and the more they simply 'receive' reality (M 204-205). On the contrary, knowing is not immediate or intuitive but involves the subject in its entirety—history, prior beliefs, cares, community and so on—and attains isomorphic union with reality only *after* the process of experience, understanding and judging. But since Lonergan includes so many more factors on the side of the subject, his understanding of knowing is in many respects performatively similar to the traditional picture of the correspondence theory of truth, *so long as it is recognized that the subjects transcend themselves and know reality as it is*:

> It is repugnant to me to place astrology and astronomy, alchemy and chemistry, legend and history, hypothesis and fact, on exactly the same footing. I am not content with theories, however brilliantly coherent, but insist on raising the further question, Are they true? (I 348)

My point, simply put, is that Rorty's objection is irrelevant to the Lonerganian enterprise. Even if we desire simply to justify our beliefs we will of necessity go about that justification according to the three-fold structure. But since Lonergan develops his account of intentionality analysis and the corresponding desire to know not from an abstraction but by analysis of the concrete knower, it follows that the coherentist cannot help but utilize the structure of knowing. But that places them in a unique situation: Since the structure of knowing is an irrefutable fact, the burden of proof would be on Rorty to demonstrate what is wrong with the account. If we must perform the operations Lonergan describes to justify beliefs and attain coherence, what is incorrect with his insistence that the operations intend the truth? Lonergan's second argument, to which I turn, demonstrates that it is performatively impossible for Rorty to argue against Lonergan's account and meet this burden of proof; you cannot use the structure of knowing to attack the desire to know the truth.

4.72 Denying the Desire for Truth is Performatively Impossible

Lonergan argues that introspective reflection guarantees the existence of the desire to know, or that if one knows oneself one will be forced to accept the facticity of the desire for truth (Morelli 1990, 58). This argument has two aspects: (1) that one will discover such a desire operative in oneself, and (2) that the denial of such a desire cannot take place without performative contradiction. Lonergan writes:

> ... no one, unless some of his organs are deficient, is going to say that never in his life did he have the experience of seeing or of hearing, of touching or of tasting ... Again, how rare is the man that will preface his lectures by repeating his conviction that never did he have even a fleeting experience of intellectual curiosity, of inquiry, of striving and coming to understand, of expressing what he has grasped by understanding. Rare too is the man that begins his contributions to periodical literature by reminding his potential readers that never in his life did he experience anything that might be called critical reflection, that he never paused about the truth or falsity of any statement .... (M 16-17)

I see no reason to think that Rorty would admit himself to be inattentive, unintelligent or irrational. He would merely insist on his alternative explanation, and he has never claimed that one cannot rationally defend a position. Still, given the contingency of justification, inquiry does not intend truth:

> There is no activity called 'knowing' which has a nature to be discovered ... There is simply the process of justifying beliefs to audiences. None of these audiences is closer to nature, or a better representative of some ahistorical ideal of rationality, then any other.

> ... Inquiry and justification have lots of mutual aims, but they do not have an overarching aim called truth. Inquiry and justification are activities we language-users cannot help engaging in; we do not need a goal called 'truth' to help us do so ... There would only be a 'higher' aim of inquiry called truth if there were such a thing as *ultimate* justification—justification before God, or before the tribunal of reason, as opposed to any merely finite human audience. (PSH 36-38)

Here we see the very strong claim that while there is inquiry it does not intend the truth. We see also Rorty's commitment to Cartesian Anxiety; knowledge is possible only given perfect, god-like vision. Lonergan would insist this reductionistic account is possible only if one neglects the program of self-appropriation (LR 421-435). If one is willing to forgo the study of the subject then one will very well develop distorted notions of what the subject is capable of and most concerned with. In Rorty's case, the neglect of the subject results in *general bias*, which is to say that Rorty, although in an incredibly clever and literate fashion, is as adamant as the person of common sense in rejecting the "egg-headed intellectualists" who insist on the validity of the pure, disinterested desire to know (Flanagan 1997, 85; cf. Lamb 1998, 255-284). Since we are incapable of a god's-eye view, Rorty does not accept that Philosophy has ever, or will ever, contribute to the ordering of society, solve political problems or develop normative standards of social ordering, and as such he rejects the knowing proper to the intellectual pattern in favor of common sense (CIS xiv). Since common sense is local, tied to a time and place, and since common sense differs from community to community, it accepts its own standards of justification so long as they allow "more intelligent and successful ways of living," just as with Rorty's ethnocentrism (Flanagan 1997, 70). But while common sense is a very valuable and concrete means to live well, it is incapable of justifying a rejection of the intellectual pattern of experience which is not interested, as is common sense, but disinterested in its benefits for me and my community. (This is not to say that the intellectual pattern of experience has no benefits, it does, and the rejection of the intellectual pattern of experience results in the longer cycle of decline.)

General bias most frequently occurs when the person of common sense scoffs at the theoretical world with its demands for systematic accounts, warranted rigor, universality and so on in favor of concrete know-how and problem solving (UB 84-88). In short, it values the everyday practical skills of a community over abstraction. Now it is fairly obvious that Rorty is a master of technical language and the other trappings of the theoretical realm, so he is not guilty of general bias in the usual sense. But still his thoroughgoing Darwinism results in a commitment to our animality and the reduction of the pure, disinterested desire to the service of practical concerns. The intellect is reduced to the biological pattern of experience. He explicitly claims that theoretical pursuits matter only as they allow us to achieve solidarity, comfort, hope and self-creation. And so, like all victims of general bias, he is "easily led to rationalize [reason's] limitations by engendering a conviction that other forms of human knowledge are useless or doubtfully valid" (I 251). He takes the legitimate endeavor of commonsense and makes it master over all forms of knowledge.

Of course, Rorty would argue that he has justified a rejection of the intellectual pattern of experience with its disinterested desire to know—there is nothing to know and no unmediated access to knowing. Be that as it may, Lonergan responds that given self-appropriation and the rediscovery of the subject we recognize:

> ...however much the egoist may appreciate the efforts of philosophers to assure him that intelligence is instrumental, he will be aware that, in his cool calculations, intelligence is boss and that, in his refusal to consider further questions, intelligence is not made a servant but merely ruled out of court. Again, however much he may reassure himself by praising the pragmatists, still he suffers from the realization that the pragmatic success of his scheming falls short of justification; for prior to the criteria of truth invented by the philosophers, there is the dynamic criterion of the further question immanent in intelligence itself. The egoist's uneasy conscience is his awareness of his sin against the light. Operative within him there is the eros of the mind, the desire and drive to understand ... (I 247).

Rorty's 'sin' is not acknowledging that justification is not equivalent to success, meaning that no matter how well something works it is impossible for us to give whole-hearted assent if we know the belief to be unjustified. Even a bias of the grossest sort leading to ridiculous beliefs is thought true by the person of bias. We cannot believe something we believe to be false. Imagine making the following statement:

> *I will believe x, which I believe to be utter nonsense, but which for some reason is advantageous to believe and which I am capable of justifying to others.*

This is the sort of statement that sophomores believe pragmatists hold. Of course they do not: "we cannot 'will to believe'—believe what we like, regardless of what else we believe" (Rorty 2000, 15). It is impossible to make the above statement because it entails:

> I believe x,
> I do not believe x.

So it is impossible to say we are so little interested in the truth that we could believe what we know to be false, standards of justification cannot be reduced to mere expediency, our intellects will not allow this because always operative is the more basic desire of the mind's proper intention. Rorty acknowledges that we do not believe what is unjustified but localizes the standards of coherence. His argument stands, he would say, because it is impossible to desire Truth, even if one wants truth.

Such a stratagem fails: It is performatively impossible to make the judgment that we do not desire to know Truth *provided that one genuinely exercises intelligence and reasonability in arriving at this conclusion.* This caveat is double-pronged. First, if the judgment that truth is impossible is made without intelligence and reasonability there is no reason to listen to the person making the judgment, it is merely flip. Second, if care was exercised in arriving at the judgment, as with Rorty, then that careful judgment took place according to the norms implicit in the structure of knowing; all that would be necessary is self-appropriation by the skeptic acknowledging those norms: "conscious and intentional operations exist and anyone who cares to deny their existence is merely disqualifying himself as a non-responsible, non-reasonable, non-intelligent somnambulist" (M 17). To deny the operations is to not know one's own self (Kidder 1990, 304). It is possible to not know oneself, it is impossible to consistently deny the fact of the structure of knowing:

> Am I a knower? The answer yes is coherent, for if I am a knower I can know that fact. But the answer no is incoherent, for if I am not a knower *how could the question be raised and answered by me?* No less, the hedging answer 'I do not know' is incoherent. For if I know that I do not know, then I am a knower; and if I do not know that I do not know, then I should not answer. (I 353; italics mine)

Further, if I am not a knower, let alone concerned with knowing, then how could the question even be raised, as Rorty does. To this Lonergan replies:

> For whatever may be true about the cognitional aspirations of others, might not my own be radically limited? Might not my desire to understand correctly suffer from some immanent and hidden restriction and bias, so that there could be real things that lay quite beyond its utmost horizon? Might not that be so? *Yet if I ask the*

question, it is in virtue of my desire to know; and as the question itself reveals, my desire to know concerns itself with what lies quite
beyond a suspected limited horizon. *Even my desire seems unrestricted.* (I 662; italics mine)

To ask a question is to wonder, to care about the question and the answer. How is it possible to ask 'Do I desire to know?' without verifying
that at least in this instance one wants to know. The question would
never arise, otherwise. Further, while it is possible to make the following statement, "we cannot know the truth about the world for various
reasons," it is impossible to make the statement "we cannot know the
truth about knowing for various reasons." To do so is to make a truth
claim about the status of knowing and to claim that one knows something about it. And to say, "I do not care about the truth status of my
claim about knowing," is impossible from the moment one asks. It's
like the old joke where a teacher asks 'Is there really such a thing as a
personal subject?' and the student replies 'Who wants to know?' Do we
desire to know? Why do you ask?

4.73 Instances of the Contradiction

Rorty's denial of the desire for truth is a judgment. It is intelligently
conceived and based on good reasons, but only because of the operations of experience, understanding and judgment. Lonergan's structure cannot be revised or denied without appealing to some data
which were not accounted for, providing an alternative explanation,
defending the alternative explanation and attacking Lonergan's, and
one cannot perform these activities without the condition of possibility behind these operations—the eros of the mind. This works itself
out concretely in Rorty's interest in knowing and in his claim that we
cannot know. Consider the following claims Rorty has made about
knowing, all of which are performatively inconsistent with his theory.

First, Rorty's argument, discussed earlier in this chapter, that it is
impossible to give a non-redundant account if truth assumes a notion
of correspondence. Saying 'x is true because it corresponds to reality'
is no better than saying 'x is true because it is true.' All attempts to
get around this fail because there is to way to explain how knowledge
and reality match up. Instead of such claptrap, we should abandon
the attempt to explain Truth as a definable essence which makes all
true statements true. Rather, we should simply hold the naturalistic

explanation that the world exercises causal influences upon us resulting in certain beliefs (PSH 27). A truth theory, if we had one, is nothing more than "an empirical explanation of the causal relations which hold between the features of the environment and the holding true of sentences," which is to say a physiological explanation (PSH 33). The world causes some of our beliefs and we do not need to add Truth into the mix.

But the reasons behind the denial of the correspondence theory assume that very theory, as John Milbank and Catherine Pickstock argue:

> ... one is saying that the world is such that one can only approach it pragmatically or conventionally or phenomenalistically, and if that claim is made, then this is tantamount to asserting that treating the world in this way in fact corresponds to the way the world is.... One does indeed treat the world and knowledge as two different realms, and then claims that knowledge matches the world. (2001, 3)

To try and clarify the argument: Rorty makes a judgment that there is no way the world really is, thus nothing to correspond to, and no meaningful way to define Truth as correspondence. Implicit in this judgment is a claim about the world, a claim that attempts to explain the way the world is, or more properly, the way the world is not. The world does not have essences, the world is nothing and our description that the world does not have essences is a claim about the world, it is to say 'it is true (in the sense of correspondence) that there are no essences in the world.' Further, since the causal powers of the world are acknowledged one is claiming 'it is true that the world exerts causal powers' and reducing this to 'the world exerts causal powers' misses the point. Finally, acknowledging that the world causes belief is to distinguish the world from belief or knowledge, a sort of out-there versus in-here distinction, but implicit in the distinction is the assumption that if the world causes belief it causes a belief in accordance with those causal powers, somehow matching tongue-in-groove with those causal forces. But that is to say nothing more than that the world causes corresponding beliefs about those causes. This is the correspondence theory, simply giving a different account of the nature of the world in-itself than traditional essentialism.

Second, Rorty makes claims about the nature of knowledge. He claims to have it right when it comes to knowing. The argument that Rorty has made from *Philosophy and the Mirror of Nature* to his later works is fundamentally similar: if true knowledge depends on intuitionism, just as the vast majority of the tradition wrongly supposed, then true knowledge is impossible if intuitionism fails. Since intuitionism is *a priori* impossible, the desire for truth is nonsensical and we should consign it to the dustbin. But Rorty is claiming that his argument is true, that it is impossible to know, and realists of every stripe have misunderstood the way that knowing actually works. He makes this point time and again in his works:

> ... such a tribunal would have to envisage all the alternatives to a given belief, and know everything that was relevant to criticism of every such alternative. Such a tribunal would have to have ... a 'God's eye view'. (PSH 38; ORT 27, 38, 131; 1990, 633-635)

And again:

> To give up the idea of context-free justification is to give up the idea of 'knowledge' as a suitable object of study—the idea which Descartes and Kant inherited from Plato's *Theatetus*. (PSH 34; ORT 30, 98)

And again:

> It is the impossible attempt to step outside our skins—the traditions, linguistic and other, within which we do our thinking and self-criticism—and compare ourselves with something absolute. This Platonic urge to escape from the finitude of one's time and place ... [but] the regress of interpretation cannot be cut off by the sort of "intuition" which Cartesian epistemology took for granted. (COP xx; CIS 3-22)

Intuitionism is necessary for knowledge, intuitionism fails, thus there is no knowledge. This at least is true according to Rorty, but he should not be able to say this.

4.74 Why Rorty Fails to Recognize the Contradictions

The source of the problem is that Rorty has begun with epistemology rather than cognitional theory. He takes the epistemology of the tradition and simply assumes the definition of knowledge provided by the tradition, namely justified true belief, where justification and truth are guaranteed by intuition. Lonergan's genius was the realization that absent the labor of self-appropriation one will remain within a defunct model of knowing based on the ocular metaphor and so not undergo the intellectual conversion which finally overcomes intuitionism. However, it is one thing to achieve self-appropriation and quite another thing to engage in the process of knowing. The process is natural and spontaneous, and everyone, including the skeptical Rorty performs these operations. But when one performs the operations but provides a theoretical account of knowing at odds with the operations one is in what Lonergan calls a *counterposition* rather than a *position*. Positions are propositional accounts of knowing, objectivity and reality which are compatible with the three-fold account of knowing and transcendental method whereas counterpositions are at odds (UB 185-188; M 235-250). Intuitionism is a counterposition because it models objectivity, knowing and reality upon looking rather than rational self-consciousness. Rorty's problem is that he thinks there is either intuitionism or nothing at all and consequently rejects one counterposition without undergoing intellectual conversion and developing a rational account of knowledge. His rejection of the counterposition of intuitionism makes sense *performatively* in that he is attentive, intelligent and reasonable and thus capable of defeating the counterposition, but he merely replaces intuitionism with another counterposition, namely, skepticism.

The notion of Rorty's counterposition is developed at greater length in Chapter 6 where I examine it in light of his conception of reality. What is at issue here is simply the hint that there is a tension between what Rorty is actually doing and what he says he is doing. He says there is no desire for truth, but he cannot help but desire it; he has said there is only a desire for coherence, but the pragmatics of attaining coherence commit him to Lonergan's cognitional structure. In the end, Rorty simply confuses his accounts of knowing and truth with intuitionism. He assumes that one must have intuition in order to make sense of these terms. In fact, his argument depends on a notion of "the Unconditioned—that which escapes the context within which discourse is conducted and inquiry pursued" (PMN 309) which is impossible given the sheer contingency of human rationality and language games (CIS 26). But that is to say that unless there are unconditioned, non-contingent, context-free elements of knowledge that knowledge is impossible. In other worlds: (1) either there are foundational intuitions which ground knowledge or there is no knowledge, but (2) there are no foundational intuitions which ground knowledge, thus

(3) there is no knowledge. Thus "Rorty sees the choice facing us as one between philosophical absolutism and postphilosophical deconstructionism—'ironist theorizing' and is stuck within the early modern and early analytic camps which he critiques" (T. McCarthy 1990a, 644). He is right, of course, to critique them; intuitionism does fail, but by creating such a stark choice between intuitionism and skepticism he has not overcome Cartesian Anxiety and is guilty of a false dichotomy if knowledge is something other than intuition.

4.8 CONCLUSION

I have argued that Lonergan's account depends heavily on the dynamic desire to know to explain both how the cognitional structure works and how we know that we intend to know the truth. Rorty's denial of such a desire would cut the legs out from under Lonergan. Rorty argues, first, that the concept of truth is incoherent, but a minimal correspondence theory is able to explain without tautology what we mean by the truth and thus preserve a meaning for the 'object' of our intending. Second, Rorty argues that since there is no way things actually are, and since we could not know it even if there were, we ought to abandon a desire for truth and replace it with a desire for justified belief according to the rules of our community. To this I have responded that the desire for coherent justification is performatively identical to the desire for truth and that it is performatively impossible to ask and answer Rorty's question without committing oneself to Lonergan's account. Also, we have seen, consistent with the larger claims of this work, that since Rorty has not performed cognitional theory and self-appropriation he does not understand that truth and knowing can be attained without an immediate intuition of the real. He remains trapped in Cartesian Anxiety, holding the false dichotomy that either there is intuition of the real or true belief is impossible. However, since Lonergan's account of knowing is true of all human knowers, Rorty engages in the three-fold process of knowing without acknowledging that such is knowing. This dissonance between his performance and his theory embroils him in a counterposition. These last two claims, that Rorty is guilty of bifurcation and that he is in a counterposition, are developed further in the following chapters.

CHAPTER 5

CONTINGENCY AND THE GIVEN

"He holds a gun to your head and says, 'Is it raining or isn't it? All you have to do is tell the truth...'"

"What good is my truth? My truth means nothing. What if this guy with the gun comes from a planet in a whole different solar system? What we call rain he calls soap. What we call apples he calls rain. So what am I supposed to tell him?"

(Don DeLillo, *White Noise*, 23)

5.1 PREAMBLE

Intuitionism assumes a fundamentally passive knower, the spectator opening the eye of the mind and receiving knowledge of an independently existing world. Consequently, any contribution or activity on behalf of the subject risks interfering with an accurate reception or representation, leaving to epistemology the task of guaranteeing objectivity against the subject's intrusions. And so the tradition distinguishes between nature and convention, reality and appearances, the in-itself and the for-us. Rorty considers such interminable debates tiresome, recommending we simply move on to other, more interesting questions, for there is another tradition rejecting the spectator theory's perfectly-present reality and our accurate reception of such reality—modernity, or at least the Baconian side of modernity. The French Revolutionaries showed that "the whole vocabulary of social relations, and the whole spectrum of social institutions, could be replaced almost overnight" (CIS 3). No longer would the regime model the ideal will of God or human nature—*Fortuna* could be forged into any desired shape free from the constraints of divinity. At roughly the same moment, the "Romantic poets were showing what happens when art is thought of no longer as imitations but, rather, as the artist's self-creation" (CIS 3). No longer is artistic prowess wedded to imitation of a divinely created and ordered world, but is rather a manifestation of genius. The two groups "conspire to slay God the Father, and thence to weed out the vestiges of the divine in political life," a movement still continuing (Hall 1994, 17). But once reality becomes malleable, the idea that "truth was made rather than found began to take hold of the imagination of Europe" (CIS 3). Truth might be contingent, local, relative, dependent on genius or on the rules of a particular local narrative. But, if discourse depends on context rather than a common ground transcending the various contexts of discourse, then no language is isomorphic with the language of creation. Rorty writes:

> We pragmatists must object to, or reinterpret, two traditional methodological questions: "What context is appropriate to this object?" and "What is it that we are putting in context?" For us, all objects are always already contextualized. They all come with contexts attached ... So there is no question of taking an object out of its old context and examining it, all by itself, to see what new context might suit it. (ORT 98)

Now, if all access to the world is contextual, it follows that any cognitional theory depending on intuition is invalid; intuitionism assumes that we speak the language of creation, God's language. The question remains whether Lonergan, without relying on intuitionism, can still defend self-transcendence, since the context-dependence of our knowing implies the end of realism. This chapter investigates whether Lonergan's unique brand of foundationalism is naïve or whether it survives Rorty's challenge to privileged access, i.e., it investigates three important elements of Lonergan's thought which might seem to suffer from a residual intuitionism—(1) the data of sense, (2) the data of consciousness and (3) the transcendental *a priori* operations of the cognitive subject—and argues that Lonergan's understanding of foundationalism is neither naïve nor incapable of accommodating Rorty's demands. Thankfully, we see that Lonergan's understanding of foundations does not depend on the Myth of the Given, privileged representations or a transcendental ego. In fact, Lonergan avoids these plagues of the intuitionist so well that he is able to embrace contingency and the historical mediation of knowledge. Still, care must be exercised when reading Lonergan as his project is susceptible to misrepresentation if terms such as 'given,' 'foundations,' 'data' and 'consciousness' are not understood in their proper context.

I assume that the burden of proof is on Lonergan: if he cannot subsume contingency and historicity his position will likely find itself consigned to the dustbin of interesting but no longer viable possibilities. But if the Transcendental Method survives, it will have its turn to scrutinize the viability of Rorty's irony in the next chapter. This chapter and the next are interdependent, first ensuring that Lonergan does not slip into a naïve foundationalism before demonstrating the failure of Rorty's account of reality and the superiority of critical realism.

5.2 LONERGAN & HISTORICAL CONSCIOUSNESS

It is perhaps a little strange to defend Lonergan against naiveté when his project was to introduce history into Roman Catholic thought and overcome its dependence on a failed classicism. He recognized with great clarity the disillusionment of the twentieth century with its "prolonged cultural crisis and its related disarray and conflict within the domains of philosophical and theological practice" (LR 15). The strong poets of modernity triumphed, collapsing the common framework of meaning and value by which the West understood and guided itself and philosophy and theology lost their footing, replaced first by the so called hard and later by the soft sciences.

Whether modernity was able to deliver on its promises is beyond our concern, but it did succeed in disestablishing the *classicist culture* which for so long provided the common source of meaning:

> On the older [classicist] view culture was conceived normatively. It was the opposite of barbarism. It was a matter of acquiring and assimilating the tastes and skills, the ideals, virtues and ideas that were pressed upon one in a good home and through the curriculum of the liberal arts. It stressed not facts but values. It could not but claim to be universalist. Its classics were immortal works of art, its philosophy was the perennial philosophy, its laws and structures were the deposit of the prudence and wisdom of mankind.... The classicist was not a pluralist. He knows that circumstances alter cases but he is far more deeply convinced that circumstances are accidental and that, beyond them, there is some substance or kernel or root that fits in the classicist assumptions .... (LR 436-437)

Classically oriented culture concentrated on the essential rather than the accidental, the universal rather than the particular and the necessary rather than the contingent (LR 396). Its science assumed true, certain knowledge of causal necessity while writing off the probable and contingent as merely accidental, perhaps unknowable.

Modern culture and science values the probable, contingent and particular: "modern science aims at the complete explanation of all phenomena" (LR 396). Deduction gives way to observation, logic gives way to method, certainty gives way to interpretation. The results of such expanded study dazzle the mind, filling libraries with more data than any one person cares to read, let alone comprehend. In short, empirical culture increased our tools for acquiring data and perhaps our methods for understanding that data, but has not increased the human capacity to judge data or attain a grand universal synthesis to make sense of it all (LR 400). Modern culture has not yet reached its maturity, and so we find ourselves adrift, no longer able to comprehend and manage all the sources of meaning.

Lonergan attempts to "mount to the level of one's time" by pushing philosophy and theology out of classicist culture and into the contemporary milieu—an *aggiornamento* (Crowe 1992, 58). Replacing the extremes of classicism or historicism is "an adequate, up-to-date answer to the question, What is man? ... a strategy by which the pursuit of self-knowledge might be revived" as discovered in *Insight* (LR 17). *Insight* replaces those theories of rationality and knowledge which were not at all rational with a theory that is rational, verifiable and non-falsifiable, thus providing a path between the Scylla of classicism and the Charybdis of modern despair with the extraordinary claim to provide "a rock upon which one can build" (M 19):

> *Thoroughly understand what it is to understand, and not only will you understand the broad lines of all there is to be understood, but you will possess a fixed base, an invariant pattern, opening upon all further developments of understanding.* (I 22)

The new foundation of Transcendental Method excites students of Lonergan but is a stumbling block to their opponents. Foundationalism is dead, the opponents say, agreeing in principle with Rorty, a Cartesian dream, and the project of understanding understanding sounds suspiciously Cartesian. Furthering the problem, Lonergan unabashedly uses the terms method, foundations, introspection and the given; his project, after all, completes the turn to the subject and through introspection discovers the foundations of human knowing. But how can such a project receive serious consideration after Wittgenstein, Foucault and Habermas? The subject is dead, we have turned from subject-centered rationality to intersubjective rationality, from private mental acts to linguistic communities and from introspection to hermeneutics and epistemological behaviorism:

> The appeal of [Lonergan's] generalized empirical method to mental acts and processes, as opposed to language, would generally be taken by contemporary philosophers to be a retrograde step. Is not language, it may be asked, a public, verifiable, and objective matter, as opposed to mental acts and processes, which are the very epitome of what is subjective and so unverifiable? (Meynell 1993, 149; cf. LR 13)

Lonergan's obscurity and background compounds the problem. Relatively unknown, those wishing to learn him confront the massive and complicated *Insight* which resists categorization into any school. Far easier is the assumption that a Catholic theologian—much of whose work takes place before Vatican II—a student of Aquinas, toiling away at the Gregorian, lecturing and writing much of his work in Latin, and claiming to provide introspective foundations must have classicist leanings.

His opponents, as Fergus Kerr notes, recognize that Lonergan's move to the subject advances beyond the cosmological and metaphysical starting points of the neo-Scholastics but fails to take into account the developments of the later Wittgenstein and the phenomenologists (Kerr 1975, 308-309). At the time of *Insight*, in 1957, the influence of Wittgenstein's *Philosophical Investigations* of 1953 would not have established a place in Rome, where Lonergan was teaching, and Lonergan's project was antiquated from the outset (Kerr 1975, 309). By the publication of *Method* in 1972 it is no longer forgivable to proceed with the briefest of nods to linguistic philosophy while continuing to rely on private mental acts to ground meaning. Thus, the papers of the Maynooth Conference in 1973, published as *Looking at Lonergan's Method* (1975), arrive at the general consensus that "however radical Lonergan may seem he is not radical enough to give us a theology that is viable today" (10). The turn to the subject is too Cartesian, too like Husserl, and no matter how many nods are given to historicity the centrality of the subject cannot be retained.

Patrick McGrath argues that Lonergan's failure to take linguistic analysis seriously results in an absurd level of incoherence in his works (1975, 28). His use of the terms 'knowing,' 'understanding,' 'known,' and 'insight' borders on the unintelligible since he fails to provide a rigorous and concise formulation of the meaning and status of these terms. Are these meanings analytic, synthetic *a priori*, or inductive? What is meant by using the term *knowing* rather than speaking of *knowledge?* If understanding is an act then does the mathematician not understand math when they are fishing rather than acting mathematically? Lonergan hopes to evade the laborious work of such analysis through introspection: If we can simply look within and immediately discover the workings of our intellect, then we would automatically know what the various terms mean. However, since introspection is a private affair, Lonergan cannot know "that understanding has an invariant structure which is the same for all" since each individual is "dependent on introspection" (41). Analysis of words operates according to the public rules of a linguistic community while introspection is private and thus unverifiable; introspection hopes to avoid the effort of analysis but is too subjective to be meaningful.

The noted theologian Wolfhart Pannenberg criticizes Lonergan for remaining trapped in the discourse of subjectivity while ignoring the developments of the later Wittgenstein and hermeneutic thought (1975, 89). Such evasion leaves Lonergan in the framework of Husserl where meaning is determined by private intentions rather than the contextual and public realm of linguistic communities and the horizon of discourse (90). Consequently, like Husserl, Lonergan has difficulty dealing with history and context but reduces all meaning to that of the individual subject.

Nicholas Lash draws the conclusion that the normative subjectivity Lonergan claims is so abstract and transcendental that it cannot possibly deal with contemporary pluralism. Diversity exists not only in the functions of communications, which Lonergan admits, and Lonergan cannot cope with the fact of historical and cultural pluralism at the level of thought. Again, the structures of the subject ignore difference and threaten to do violence against historical and linguistic variability (1975, 127-143).

One could provide a point-by-point response to these charges. For instance, Lonergan is clearly aware of developments in Anglo-American philosophy, covering much of this in the 1957 Boston College lectures on Mathematical Logic, frequently discussing logical positivism in *Insight* and *Understanding and Being* before developing a cogent, if pithy, critique in the section on Dialectic in *Method* (M 253-257). Further, as William Ryan has shown, Lonergan's work differs in important respects from Husserl's, whom Lonergan critiques for remaining within the naïve realist framework whereby intuition replaces rational judgment (Ryan 1973, 173-190). Again, Lonergan is not unfamiliar with later developments in phenomenology, as evidenced by his Boston College lectures of 1957 on phenomenology and existentialism and by his frequent approval of Gadamer in *Method* (cf. Lawrence 1972; Lawrence 1980). Finally, while *Insight*, and those students of Lonergan focusing too exclusively on that work, can *appear* classicist in insisting on normative, *a priori* structures of subjectivity, a reading of *Method* with its many discussions on history, language, pluralism and the development of subjectivity should dispel such notions. (It is natural that *Insight* would appear more static as it is the exploration and development of the position, but once developed it expands into more concrete and historical concerns in *Method*. But even that would be unjust, since the motive behind *Insight* is to deal with the crisis of our time, and its discussions on bias and the flight from understanding clearly take account of the contingent aspects of subjectivity.)

But as William Matthews argues, tackling each objection in turn misses the point of the enterprise (1976, 11-21). Perhaps Lonergan could be more precise in his use of terms, perhaps his accounts of language and culture are not complete enough, but such criticisms are red herrings to the central project of knowing oneself. Once the self is known, great care is needed to express the structures, operations and context of the self, but until the self is known the particular criticisms are like mosquito bites on an elephant—mildly disturbing but unlikely to bring the animal to its knees. Still, while Matthews wants to bypass these particular criticisms, we cannot ignore a sticking point behind the particular criticisms, a sticking point in fundamental agreement with Rorty's position. Namely, can Lonergan, "the philosopher of human subjectivity" (Sala 1994, xii) fulfill his project or does it fall prey to the same problems as previous philosophies of subjectivity, i.e., does it ignore the historical, contextual, encultured, linguistic elements of the subject? In another context, Paul Ricoeur argues that "the philosophy of subjectivity had utterly disregarded the mediating factor of language in the argumentation of the 'I am' and the 'I think' … Nietzsche brings to light the rhetorical strategies that have been buried, forgotten, and even hypocritically repressed and denied, in the name of the immediacy of reflection" (1992, 11). Is this true of Lonergan? Richard Topping thinks so, complaining:

The ... foundation or "rock" upon which Lonergan wants to ground objectivity is both pre-propositional and pre-conceptual and thus cannot be strictly identified with any of its concrete, determinate linguistic instantiations.

There is at least one strand of the anti-foundational critique stemming from the philosophy of language that would seem to encompass and deny the foundational option which Lonergan proposes. Simply put, many linguistic philosophers deny that there is such a thing as a pre-linguistic (pre-propositional, pre-conceptual) experience which (1) gives us objective purchase on reality as it is, and/or (2) provides a norm to which language seeks to be adequate. Instead language, particularly as it is embodied in texts, is the objective idiom or paradigm by which human experiences are normed. (1993, 16-17)

It is hardly accidental that so many critics focus on Lonergan's inability to deal with language, context and history. These Rortyish objections, if true, *do* threaten the viability of Lonergan's project, even if the various particular criticisms miss the point. As I see it, the debate rests on two primary issues. First, Lonergan's claim, a claim upon which his project follows and depends, that *"there are the data of sense and the data of consciousness. Common to both is that they are or may be given"* (M 201-202; italics mine). The givenness of this data is used by Lonerganians for a surety of knowledge, as evidenced by Meynell who claims that "short of some data, it looks as though there are no foundations for knowledge; and short of foundations of knowledge, it looks as though 'anything goes...'" (Meynell 1998, 43). But if context goes all the way down, if there are no givens, then Lonergan's surety vanishes. Consequently, it is his burden to prove that the givenness of (a) data of sense and (b) data of consciousness is not naively held. Second, if Transcendental Method is to provide the *a priori* foundations of cognitional structure, the burden is Lonergan's to demonstrate the viability of his project given the presumption against introspective subjectivity. I begin by defending the data of sense, turning in the following section to the data of consciousness before concluding with a good 'look' at the subject.

5.3 DATA OF SENSE

Classical foundationalism held that sense data were basic and incorrigible. As such they both *caused* our basic beliefs about the world and immediately and indefeasibly *justified* those beliefs while providing a foundation for all other knowledge:

> The classical foundationalist divides our beliefs into two groups: those which need support from others and those which can support others and need no support themselves.... our basic beliefs are beliefs which concern the nature of our own sensory states, our own immediate experience. Such beliefs are able to stand on their own feet, without support from others.... a belief which is not about our own sensory states (immediate experience) must, if it is to be *justified*, be *justified* by appeal to beliefs which are about our own sensory states. (Dancy 1985, 53; italics mine)

Rorty, however, argues that this language is nonsense: experience cannot *justify* beliefs as the empiricist claims.

He begins by distinguishing awareness into two sorts: awareness as discriminative behavior and awareness as being in the logical space of reasons (PMN 182). Amoebas and photoelectric cells have awareness in the first sense, for they react with some sort of discriminative behavior to stimuli. But amoebas, photoelectric cells and even pre-linguistic children do not operate in the logical space of reasons. Given this distinction, awareness in the first sense is a *causal* condition of the second but cannot ground or justify knowledge since there is no such thing as a nonpropositional justified belief. Beliefs are justified by reasons, and pre-linguistic awareness, as nonpropositional, cannot serve this function:

> So to speak of acquaintance with redness or with an instantiation of redness as "grounding" (as opposed to being a causal condition of) our knowledge that "this is a red object" or that "redness is a color" is always a mistake. (PMN 183)

While infants react to stimuli, and thus are aware of what the experience of redness *is like*, infants do not know *what sort of thing redness is*. The ability to know what sort of thing redness is depends on concept use—"red is this sort of thing"—and there are no concepts outside of linguistic usage. Further, such concepts are learned in the public sphere—a parent teaches the child how to use a term and to what sorts of things the term applies. So a child experiences redness and knows what it feels like—the raw feel of red is different than green—but the ability to know what sort of thing red is depends on language.

But if justification occurs in the logical space of reasons and arguments, then justification is essentially a public act depending on the norms and rules of the public realm. In that case, private pre-linguistic awareness cannot ground knowledge. We cannot appeal to private experience to justify beliefs or convince others of our pain, or even to know ourselves what sort of thing is "pain." Rather, our belief is justified when our use of language remains unquestioned. One hears the death knell of classical empiricism in these arguments, for while sensation can cause us to have certain beliefs the distinction between basic experiential beliefs and those justified by appealing to basic beliefs collapses.

Garret Barden and Hugo Meynell, both Lonerganians, disagree on the implications of Rorty's statements for Lonergan. For Barden, Rorty claims only that experiences are themselves not instances of knowledge immediately given. Knowledge involves more than just sensing, and so while sensations are given, knowledge is not: "the thesis is simply that there is no given knowledge ... if I judge I do so for reasons, and if I am asked about my judgment I appeal to reasons" rather than some sort of inchoate experience the other cannot possibly enjoy themselves (Barden 1986, 88). Meynell has a much stronger reading. No one in the recent past, he says, maintains that knowledge is immediately given in sensation, as if we merely opened our eyes to the inflow of knowledge (1986, 106). Instead, Rorty attacks "the characteristic empiricist notion that there is a given *component* in knowledge, against which knowledge-claims are to be checked," or that experience is irrelevant to the truth status of statements (Meynell 1986, 106). This stronger interpretation is tantamount to saying that there are no raw feels, no awareness in the first sense, unless the linguistic community says so:

> Whether organisms feel pain depends, according to Rorty, on whether the linguistic community deems them to do so ... on Rorty's view, an organism on a newly-discovered planet would be "capable of feeling pain" just as soon as it suited the human visitors to that planet to say that it did. (Meynell 1985, 45; cf. Meynell 1998, 46)

If Meynell is correct, Rorty's position is absurd and horrific. First, it allows abuse since one group could simply deny that another group felt pain and then torture at will (Meynell 1985, 45). Second, it implies that words create experience, that a person does not have an experience of red or of pain until the linguistic community (a) comes up with a word for this experience and (b) allows the person to use that word with respect to their own experience. Quite literally, I would not see this page unless someone said I was. Third, judgments would have absolutely nothing to check them other than majority opinion, for they would be under no obligation to gel with experience. Supernovas would emit radiation if and only if scientists say they do; Moses existed if biblical scholars say he did, but not otherwise (Meynell 1985, 32). On this reading, Rorty is an idealist of the grossest and most indefensible sort.

I believe Meynell wrong on this issue. Rorty clearly acknowledges sensory experiences, even granting them causal status, and the distinction between awareness as discriminative behavior and logical reasoning actually requires that individuals have perceptions of their own (PMN 183, 189). Meynell conflates Rorty's epistemic claim that knowledge does not represent the world with the ontological claim that the status of the world depends on what we say of it. But if the world exercises causal power, it must exist largely independent of us, as Rorty thinks:

> We need to make a distinction between the claim that the world is out there and the claim that truth is out there. To say that the world is out there, that it is not our creation, is to say, with common sense, that most things in space and time are the effects of causes which do not include human mental states. To say that truth is not out there is simply to say that where there are no sentences there is no truth, that sentences are elements of human languages, and that human languages are human creations. (CIS 4-5; ORT 101)

In fact, Rorty's Darwinism demands a prior world and experiences in touch with the material causality of the world: "our minds and our language could not ... be 'out of touch with the reality' any more than our bodies could," but still language is not *about* the world as much as *a tool to control* the world (ORT 5).

Even if avoiding the idealism charged by Meynell, this last claim is a bit difficult to swallow: How can our language be in touch with the world but not be about, or represent, the world? Rorty responds that beliefs and words are not little pictures of the world, and certainly not little pictures in any privileged way—such was the mistake of empiricism. But the heroes of Rorty's Pantheon—Sellars, Wittgenstein, Davidson—demand rather that our beliefs relate only to other beliefs, not to the world:

> One way of formulating the pragmatist position is to say that the pragmatist recognizes relations of *justification* holding between beliefs and desires, and relations of *causation* holding between these beliefs and desires and other items in the universe, but no relations of *representation*. Beliefs do not represent nonbeliefs. There are, to be sure, relations of *aboutness* ... for aboutness is not a matter of pointing outside the web [of beliefs]. Rather, we use the term "about" as a way of directing attention to the beliefs which are relevant to the justification of other beliefs, not as a way of directing attention to nonbeliefs. (ORT 97; cf. 148-149)

Beliefs have meaning only within the context of other beliefs: "explanation is ... always under a description, and alternative descriptions of the same causal process are useful for different purposes. There is no description which is somehow 'closer' to the causal transactions" (ORT 60). In other words, we have and are aware of experiences, but we are not aware of their cause or able to get outside of ourselves to see the world in its causal primacy (Beards 1997, 57):

> The essentialist philosopher ... says that the "it" which inquiry puts in context *has* to be something precontextual. The antiessentialist rejoins by insisting that it is contexts all the way down. She does so by saying that we can only inquire after things under a description, that describing something is a matter of relating it to other things, and that "grasping the thing itself" is not something that preceded contextualization.... (ORT 99-100)

Rorty's argumentation is consistent from his earlier to later works: the foundationalist uses sensation as the touchstone of knowledge, but this works only if sensation grounds rather than causes beliefs. Because sensation does not provide us with given knowledge, it must be described, explained or contextualized within a previous web of beliefs, but since sensation is unable to ground beliefs it is impossible for sensation to determine which of those descriptions is best or most natural. Consequently, we use, or accept descriptions insofar as they serve our purposes and are consistent in the chain of other beliefs we wish to hold, but beliefs are then *about* other *beliefs*, they fit in a chain of description and explanation, rather than *representing* or being about the *world* (ORT 96). Thus, statements like "truth is what our peers will let us get away with saying" (so grating to the ears of realists like myself) are not literally saying that we make up truth arbitrarily but rather that we have no resource better than the community's web of beliefs.

Now, Lonergan's language—the given, foundations, the subject—makes it sound as though he were part of the tradition opposed by Rorty. Not so. Lonergan largely accepts these arguments, agreeing with the attack on empiricist foundations but finding the attack irrelevant to his own claims. I now turn from Rorty's attack on the given, properly understood, to Lonergan's response.

First, knowledge is not a given, and certainly not given in sensation. Transcendental Method discovers knowing to always include the three-fold process of experience, understanding and judgment—experience is necessary but insufficient:

> No one of these activities, alone and by itself, may be named human knowing. An act of ocular vision may be perfect as ocular vision; yet if it occurs without any accompanying glimmer of understanding, it is mere gaping: and mere gaping, so far from being the beau ideal of human knowing, is just stupidity. As merely seeing is not human knowing, so for the same reason merely hearing, merely smelling, merely touching, merely tasting may be parts, potential components of human knowing, but they are not human knowing itself. (C 222)

Lonergan is not an empiricist, for while sensation provides data about which we inquire, and absent that data there would be nothing about which to inquire, the fact of inquiry about the data implies an unknown: "knowledge of fact rests on a grasp of the unconditioned and ... a grasp of the unconditioned is not the starting point but the end of inquiry" (I 440). Now, if Barden's reading of Rorty is correct, then Lonergan substantially agrees: knowledge is not given in experience, nor does sense data immediately justify beliefs.

Second, Lonergan is a foundationalist, but not of the classical variety depending on the Given. A classical foundationalist divides beliefs into those needing support and those "which can support others and need no support themselves" (Dancy 1985, 53). One would be hard-pressed to discover a passage in Lonergan classifying any particular belief or set of beliefs as an incorrigible foundation for all others since not basic beliefs but basic operations allow knowing, and even then the operations tend to converge on knowledge only insofar as the pure, disinterested dynamism of the intellect follows its natural exigencies of attentiveness, intelligence and reasonability. Foundations in the empiricist sense, as "truths which are certain because of their causes rather than because of arguments given for them" (PMN 157) are suspect; but Lonergan holds rather that

> the real presuppositions are operations, not propositions about operations. The first principles of knowing are the dynamic structure of the mind, not a set of statements purporting to express such first principles. Thus, the foundations which Lonergan affirms are not at all like those sought by Descartes, Russell or Husserl. They were correct to look for ultimates, but they looked in the wrong place and for the wrong kind of thing. Rorty is right to reject foundations of this kind. (Barden 1986, 99)

Again, we discover no illicit appeal to privileged, foundational representations in Lonergan's critical realism.

Third, Lonergan does not naively assume that data spontaneously give rise to significance in a fundamentally passive mind. To recall one of the basic elements of insight, it is caused by internal rather than external conditions (I 29). Reality does not somehow force its way into consciousness and turn itself into knowledge, as Hobbes or Locke would have it, rather "significance is not in data but accrues to them from the occurrence of insights … the data alone are never the sole determinants of the insights that arise in any but an infantile mind" (I 440). Absent the dynamic desire to know, data are just data without significance. In that case, while a datum of sense is defined as "the content of an act of seeing, hearing, touching, tasting, smelling," such contents "do not occur in a cognitional vacuum" but emerge within a pattern of interests and concerns (I 96). Lonergan tells the story of Thales, so intent on the stars he fell down the well, to the milkmaid's amusement (I 96). The data are available to both—Thales could have seen the well, the milkmaid could have looked up and seen the stars, for we do not create data but we do overlook data irrelevant to our interests. So I look at a computer graph and see only a squiggle while the mathematician understands the correlation of two factors. Now, even the mathematician does not *see* the correlation, she understands it, but the data may have meaning for her where I find none. Thus, the "perceptual flow" in one person can differ from that of another (I 406). In that case, what is perceived is fit into a pattern of interests, but that pattern is not unlike a contextual web of beliefs. We advert to or perceive data as is relevant to our purpose, to some desired end. So we do not shed our previous beliefs in order to have unmediated perception; perceptions are not *given* to us in brute facticity ready for our passive absorption. But this too rejects a naïve empiricist account.

Fourth, to further emphasize that meaning is not given immediately in the data and that the condition of the knower influences the grasp of the known, Lonergan distinguishes between the world of immediacy and the world mediated by meaning. The world of immediacy is the world without language, the world of the infant in the crib: "it is the world of what is felt, touched, grabbed, sucked, seen, heard. It is a world of immediate experience..." (M 76). There are two types of knowing—the knowing of extroversion, proper to animals and pre-linguistic children, and properly human knowing. The knowing of extroversion operates completely within the biological pattern of experience and the real reduces to the immediately sensed—bodies rather than things (I 276). Properly human knowing, on the other hand, rises above the limited world of the 'already out there now real' to include the world of form discovered by intelligence and the world of the real discovered by judgment. In this world of things, of unity-identity-wholes, the sensed does not define the real of properly human knowing; knowing occurs when a virtually unconditioned judgment is reached (I 277-278). In fact, extroversion limits our notion of reality to that which is experienced or at best imagined, but the great advance of science in our time is the acknowledgement that some realities are unimaginable. In a similar vein, just as we transcend animal knowing to proper human knowing, the world of immediacy is transcended to the world mediated by meaning: "as the command and use of language develop, one's world expands enormously. For words denote not only what is present but what is absent or past or future, not only what is factual but also the possible ... meaning is an act that does not merely repeat but goes beyond experiencing" (M 76-77). The real, what is known and remains to be known, goes far beyond the world of sensation, and that world cannot be deduced from mere experience. Nor does the world of meaning passively represent or mirror the world of extroversion; while we begin with experience and inquire about the data of sensation, the world of meaning (of form and judgment) is not discovered anywhere *in* the world of sensation, but through it. Take the Pythagorean Theorem, for instance, or the periodic table; these occurred because of reflection on experience but they do not represent or mirror the world like little photographs. Consequently, Lonergan as much as Rorty rejects the notion that animal knowing (awareness in the first sense) is synonymous with fully human knowing (awareness in the second sense). Lonergan also demands judgment on the level of reasonability and not on sight.

The preceding four arguments demonstrated the irrelevance of the Myth of the Given since Lonergan is not a classical foundationalist. Even more, Lonergan also derides the "bundle of blunders" which is empiricism (I 437). Knowledge is not given in sensation, for human knowing and human reality demands the work of the intellect. On the other hand, I agree with Hugo Meynell that "short of some data ... it looks as though 'anything goes'" and that Lonergan is keenly aware of the necessity of *given* data (1998, 42). So, even if the preceding arguments reveal Lonergan's rejection of the given as knowledge, he still insists on the givenness of data, but rightly, for if data were created then idealism ensues.

Thus, fifth, even though knowledge is not given in sensation, and even though not everyone will attend or advert to the same data, i.e., will have the same conscious perception, it is still the case that data of sensation are *simply given* without screening; our screening or "editing" of data occurs only once inquiry and interest demand attentiveness only to relevant data, but all data are simply given. Even though data have significance only once inquiry occurs, and individuals pay attention to radically different data, the data are just there waiting to be noticed; we do not make the data by noticing:

> the given is unquestionable and indubitable. What is constituted by answering questions can be upset by other questions. But the given is constituted apart from questioning; it remains the same no matter what the result of questioning may be; it is unquestionable in the sense that it lies outside the cognitional levels constituted by questioning and answering. In the same fashion the given is indubitable. What can be doubted is the answer to a question for reflection; it is a yes or no. But the given is not the answer to any question; it is prior to questioning and independent of any answers. (I 406)

That to which we actually advert differs given our interest, but that to which it is possible to advert is given. Rorty acknowledges this as well, for he does not deny that we have experiences without the mediation of language, even providing a category—knowing what experience *x* is like—for these given experiences. Perhaps sensible data, then, are best defined as *the given contents of the five senses about which we inquire* (I 406). Data allow us to ask "What is It?"

Sixth, since we inquire as fully human knowers, the standards of objectivity relevant to animal knowing apply only to animal knowing. As fully human knowers, we are, to be sure, empirical, but also intelligent and rational, not just biological but also aesthetic, artistic, dramatic, practical, intellectual and mystical (I 410). Given such a polymorphic consciousness, objectivity cannot be reduced simply to the lowest level of consciousness, since the objectivity proper to this level is quite improper for other levels. It makes good sense to demand to see, clearly and without distortion, if someone claims to perceive a ghost, but it does not follow that sight becomes the standard for all knowing. In fact, Lonergan characteristically reverses such a conception, arguing that since data of sensation are *given* but our advertence or perception varies, objectivity in sensation, or *experiential objectivity*, is guaranteed not by looking clearly but by the pure disinterested desire to know whereby our percepts match up to the given (again, the importance of the previous chapter):

> For there is an intellectual desire, an eros of the mind. Without it there would arise no questioning, no inquiry, no wonder. Without it there would be no real meaning for such phrases as scientific disinterestedness, scientific detachment, scientific impartiality. Inasmuch as this intellectual drive is dominant, inasmuch as the reinforcing or inhibiting tendencies of other drives are successfully excluded, in that measure the scientific observer becomes an incarnation of inquiring intelligence, *and his percepts move into coincidence with what are named the data of sense.* (I 97; italics mine; cf. I 407)

Of course, this is not to say that the disinterested desire to know helps us see what is out there—as if we could not sense without the desire to know. Rather, the data are given in sensation but we screen the data of sense and *perceive* within a pattern of experience. If we are to perceive the data not merely as they serve some purpose but as they are in fact given to sensation, then our percepts—sensations as edited and perceived by consciousness—must be those of the intellectual pattern. Again, objectivity occurs insofar as the subject follows the exigencies of their intellect, and not as we are animals within an environment.

It is not my concern here to defend Lonergan's account against all possible criticisms, but rather to demonstrate that Rorty's objections against the given and in favor of contextuality and contingency do not apply to Lonergan. His understanding of the given and foundations does not commit him to an indefensible foundationalism derived from intuitionism. Now, if these six arguments are considered in totality we arrive at the Thomist position explained in contemporary language, for Thomism holds that all knowledge depends on, but is not equivalent to, sensation. The intellect must have sense data on which to exercise its intelligence to arrive at insights and concepts. Since Thomism does not accept the subject/object split and acknowledges our animality, there is no special problem accepting that in normal circumstances sense data are given to us through the biological functioning of the human body (even if ultimately dependent on the sensitive powers of the soul, the metaphysics of which Lonergan does not speak). So sense data are given, but knowledge is not, although knowledge is (a) verified if and only if concepts can point back to experience as their cause, i.e., can convert back to phantasms. A hypothesis which cannot point back to data is unverifiable; a hypothesis which accounts for only some data is incomplete; a hypothesis which both points back to data and accounts for all relevant data is reasonable. There is a way, then, for sense data to both cause and justify belief: data *cause* belief in the animal realm of presenting to us raw feels, data *cause* belief in the fully human realm by giving to us contents of sensation about which we inquire to arrive at insights (a material cause). Sense data *justify* beliefs in that we must be able to point back to them to demonstrate that our hypotheses have grounds, *but data do not justify* beliefs by their mere presence or givenness—brute sensations are without meaning in the fully human realm. So the justification of belief within human discourse does take place according to reasons and arguments, within the realm of judgment rather than experience, but does so by ensuring that concepts and possible explanations of the data are reasonable accounts of the data. But the givenness of data does not concomitantly justify any particular belief; knowledge occurs at the end of inquiry rather than at the beginning.

Further, since data are given, we do not find ourselves with the Cartesian worry that what we sense is itself suspect. Of course, it is possible for sensations to be disordered, but there is no reason to assume that each and every datum of sense is in this condition, and since

Rorty's self-proclaimed Darwinism implies that generally we are in contact with the world, Lonergan does not bear the burden with any greater responsibility. If Rorty can presume that sensations are caused by the world, so too can Lonergan, and we need not respond here to every possible epistemological worry. But, if sensations are given, and if perceptions coincide with sensations insofar as the intellectual pattern of experience is followed, then the process of justifying hypotheses by ensuring they make sense of the data allows the possibility of experiential objectivity rather than an attitude of "anything goes" (Meynell 1998, 43). Lonergan attains a balance between requiring knowledge to begin with sensation while simultaneously ensuring that sensation has objectivity, but without forcing sense data to perform an epistemic function rather beyond their means. Classic foundationalism demands more of sense data than they can bear; Lonergan does not. His account of givenness recognizes both the limits and necessity of the given.

5.4 DATA OF CONSCIOUSNESS

Perhaps even more troublesome are the data of consciousness. Lonergan is *the* philosopher of subjectivity and quite remarkably creates a project based on "heightening one's consciousness by objectifying it" (M 14). Now, if one has not succeeded at intellectual conversion, one's notion of objectifying likely follows an ocular or intuitionist model. As such, objectifying resembles a sort of absurd introspection whereby one looks inward and rather statically points out items in one's consciousness, the sort of aviary model Plato provides in the *Theatetus*. Lonergan himself suggests many will interpret his project in such a manner:

> People are apt to think of knowing by imagining a man taking a look at something, and further, they are apt to think of consciousness by imagining themselves taking a look into themselves. Not merely do they indulge in such imaginative opinions but also they are likely to justify them by argument. Knowing, they will say, is knowing something; it is being confronted by an object; it is the strange, mysterious, irreducible presence of one thing to another. Hence, though knowing is not exclusively a matter of ocular vision, still it is radically that sort of thing. (I 344)

If one is laboring under naïve realist assumptions, one will assume that Transcendental Method is a means by which one becomes present to oneself in the same manner as something looked at becomes present. Lonergan's rather unfortunate use of the terms 'introspection' and 'objectification' will simply confirm these suspicions.

Such is the case for Fergus Kerr, who assumes that Lonergan's turn to subjectivity commits him, even if unintentionally, to the tradition of Descartes—one cannot escape that fly-bottle once in. Even an explicit rejection of Cartesian dualism "harbour[s] the myth in more subtle and recondite forms" once a commitment is made to introspection and private mental acts (Kerr 1986, 55). The "mentalist-individualist" image of the self with its disembodied subjectivity, epistemological solitude and ignorance of "social and historical surroundings" results (56). Meaning collapses to the intentions of the individual in their private world and solipsism, grossly autonomous individualism and other trappings of Gnosticism are inevitable.

Along with Kerr, many essays in *Looking at Lonergan's Method* assume that Lonergan has not come to terms with Wittgenstein's critique of private languages and mental acts. In the *Philosophical Investigations*, Wittgenstein is "dead set against any explanation of the meaning of language that depends on an appeal to some hidden or occult entity that is said to lie beneath language"(Fitzpatrick 1992, 28-29). In response to the dilemma of the source of meaning, Wittgenstein rejects understanding, or inner mental processes, as conferring meaning on words and instead accepts the use of words within social contexts. Mental processes are too obscure or queer, too difficult to make coherent, and additionally provide no criteria by which they are verifiable. Just as with private languages, there exist no rules to judge the use of mental acts and any criteria appealed to would illicitly sneak in rules from the public realm (Fitzpatrick 1992, 33). Further, since language is not acquired through ostention, as his foil Augustine would have it, Wittgenstein argues that words do not mean by corresponding to or representing some object in the world; they mean only by reference to other words within a form of life (Topping 1993, 17-18). Consequently, meaning cannot derive from the mind's operations which understand or render intelligible the experienced world of sensation, for words refer neither to inner operations or objects of experience but to uses.

Rorty agrees, arguing strongly that the subsequent historical options of (a) the mind and (b) language serving as representations of the real are now defunct. The failure of the turn to the subject raised the possibility that language was the *tertium quid* between the mind and reality and that understanding the structures of language, in a perverse Kantian reversal, could explain the structures of knowing and the known (EHO 50; CIS 10-11). This failed as well, merely substituting language for ideas in the problem of the bridge. Rorty rejects an account of language as either representational or expressive—it neither expresses the meanings and intentions of the mind nor represents the essence of the world (CIS 11). Consequently, he is willing to jettison both the study of the conscious subject and the study of linguistic structures: "this Wittgensteinian attitude, developed by Ryle and Dennett for minds and by Davidson for languages, naturalizes mind and language by making all questions about the relation of either to the rest of the universe *causal* questions, as opposed to questions about adequacy of representation or expression (CIS 15).

Since Lonergan accepts the expressive account of language and an adequation account of intellectual operations, he falls afoul of Rorty's criticism. Lonergan accepts the expressive function of language, first, because he accepts the Augustinian distinction between an inner word or idea and the spoken or written word referring back to the inner word (V vii). The outer word is "grounded on the inner word or idea, which in turn is totally dependent on the operations of the mind," or, in the language of *Insight*, the concept expresses the content of the insight (Fitzpatrick 1992, 30; cf. Flanagan 1972, 66). He accepts the adequation model, second, since through the operations of the mind we attain cognitive self-transcendence. In the end, then, "meaning ... has its source in knowing, knowing has its source in acts of feeling, understanding, judging and deciding, and these acts have their sources in the respective questions that initiate the intelligent, transforming movement that generates ... knowing and deciding" (Flanagan, 1972, 67-68).

So Lonergan rests his case on private mental acts: the dynamic desire to know leads to experience, understanding and judgment—in other words, to knowledge—and our words derive meaning from these operations of knowing. But such a move risks becoming Cartesian, with a secret, disembodied self peeking out from its isolation towards a world out-there. Of course, nothing could be further from

Lonergan's position: As soon as intellectual conversion is effected and self-appropriation attained, it is apparent that Lonergan could not drag along the baggage of naïve extroversion in his use of the terms and must mean something radically different. If knowledge of the real does not entail confrontation with the already out there now, it is highly problematic to assume that introspection and the concomitant presence to self confronts an already in here now. So, if we examine what Lonergan means by introspection and the objectification of consciousness, we understand that he radically reinterprets the terms to his own purposes. Further, he provides a fundamentally new method to go about knowing ourselves and to give ourselves as data to our own inquiry.

Thankfully, the process or method of introspection need not reinvent the wheel as the method is consistent with his cognitional theory. We begin with the now-familiar operations of experience, understanding and judgment: The operations are transitive "in the psychological sense that by the operation one becomes aware of the object" (M 7). In sensation the data of experience are brought to our awareness, in imagination we become aware of what is imagined, in understanding we become aware of what is understood. Thus, by the operations the intended "objects" become present to consciousness, for before sensing there were no data present to consciousness, before judging there was no judgment present to our consciousness. Further, the operations require a conscious operator, the subject, for their performance, as we do not perform them while asleep or unconscious. But since the subject is conscious when performing these operations and unconscious when not, we can conclude that the operations are not merely the actions of a conscious subject but also disclose the conscious subject to himself: "whenever any of the operations are performed, the subject is aware of himself operating, present to himself operating, experiencing himself operating" (M 8). Usually we do not reflect upon these operations and thus objectify our own consciousness, but still we would not be aware of ourselves without the operations and, so, self-consciousness is entailed, no matter how little attention we might pay to this awareness of self, whenever the operations are performed. As Walter Conn puts it, the operations are "occurring consciously, and thereby render the operating subject conscious" (Conn 1977, 218).

Care must be exercised here, for the term presence is not univocal (C 226; cf. M 8). There is, first, material presence, or the place of a physical object, the presence of the cup on top of the desk, for example. In addition to this non-cognitive presence is the intentional presence of the object to the subject in sensation, imagination, understanding, conceiving, formulating, judging. Here the object is present as that which is intended. But the subject is present to themselves in a third sense, for "the presence of the subject resides in the gazing, the attending, the intending," or as a result of the operations (M 8; cf. C 226). Presence in the third sense is not the presence of an object to consciousness but rather the concomitant self-awareness of consciousness, the flow of being awake and alive, which is not necessarily or frequently reflective or introspective:

> as the parade of objects marches by, spectators do not have to slip into the parade to become present to themselves; they have to be present to themselves for anything to be present to them; and they are present to themselves by the same watching that, as it were, at its other pole makes the parade present to them. (C 226)

Consequently, self-presence does not require for its attainment any additional operation over and above the already familiar and frequent operations of experience, understanding and judgment. We need not have recourse to any super-intuition or vantage point, no privileged representation by which to observe ourselves at work, no inner look at ourselves. We work at intending the world and so concomitantly and necessarily reveal ourselves to ourselves (Conn 1977, 219). As such, if Lonergan's cognitional theory is sound, then so too is his account of introspection. We introspect or objectify consciousness not with an inner look or special faculty but by paying attention to what we are doing when we know. Performing the Transcendental Method and arriving at cognitional theory is to objectify consciousness; but by this point in the investigation the process is so familiar as to become dull—hardly a recondite notion:

> introspection ... is misleading inasmuch as it suggests an inward inspection. Inward inspection is just myth. Its origin lies in the mistaken analogy that all cognitional events are to be conceived on the analogy of ocular vision; consciousness is some sort of cognitional event; therefore consciousness is to be conceived on the analogy of ocular vision; and since it does not inspect outwardly, it must be an inward inspection. (M 8)

Lonergan is adamant that there is no knowledge attained through intuition, neither of the real or of ourselves, for "what is asserted is not
that you can uncover intelligence by introspection, as you can point to
Calcutta on a map" (I 347).

Instead of looking inward, introspection, in a self-referentially consistent fashion, "applies the operations as intentional to the operations
as conscious," which is to say that since all knowing involves the three-
fold structure the same three operations are performed when we intend knowledge of ourselves as when we know the world:

> to apply the operations as intentional to the operations as conscious
> is a ... matter of (1) experiencing one's experiencing, understand-
> ing, judging ... (2) understanding the unity and relations of one's
> experienced experiencing, understanding, judging ... (3) affirming
> the reality of one's experienced and understood experiencing, un-
> derstanding, judging.... (M14-15)

What matters, then, is to complete the task of self-appropriation and
perform the operation of knowing in order to know the structure of
knowing. Since knowing involves three operations, self-knowing involves three operations.

First, the operations are experienced as *given* in consciousness (M
15). If the performance of the three operations discloses and constitutes consciousness, if it is "the awareness immanent in cognitional
acts" (I 346), then data of consciousness are experienced precisely
whenever we are "seeing, hearing, tasting, smelling, touching perceiving,
imagining, inquiring, understanding, formulating, reflecting, judging
and so forth" (I 299). In other words, we have the data of consciousness whenever we are conscious, for the operations listed constitute
consciousness and also make present consciousness to the agent. As
such, the data of consciousness are simply given, not as knowledge but
as experience.

Second, whereas cognitional acts are experienced as data of consciousness, as mere experience "they are not described, distinguished,
compared, related, defined, for all such activities are the work of inquiry, insight and formulation" (I 298). To enjoy consciousness is not
to immediately understand the data of consciousness. Nonetheless,
introspection allows us to experience and identify the operations
whereby we stop gaping and begin to inquire about the data, when we
grasp some intelligibility in the data and when we reject or affirm our

account of intelligibility. Since we can identify these moments, and since experience does not itself distinguish them, it must be the case that to identify them we exercised understanding—the fact that we distinguish them demands positing understanding as the condition of possibility for this act. The long efforts of *Insight* were dedicated to distinguishing, understanding, conceiving and formulating these experiences and resulted in the explanation of the three-fold cognitional structure.

Third, understanding only results in hypothesis, and we may understand our experience in a manner identical to Lonergan but still not commit ourselves to his interpretation: "such formulations are, of themselves, just hypotheses" (I 299). The final task, then, just as with all knowing, is to recognize that the terms and relations of cognitional structure may be accurate or inaccurate, but this requires judgment, the third and final cognitional operation (M 16). Judgment occurs in exactly the same manner as with direct, or non-introspective knowledge, namely, we judge whether a set of conditions has been met in a virtually unconditioned judgment.

Allow me to synthesize the preceding arguments: If Lonergan's position is taken seriously, we discover that he escapes the Cartesian fly-bottle, contrary to Kerr's contention. Introspection, objectification and the data of consciousness do not mean what we expect, for there is no occult entity underlying those terms and no privileged epistemic access to stretch our credulity. Rather, the position consistently uses the same cognitional theory for self-knowledge as for all other knowledge—there is no special pleading with respect to introspection. Knowledge begins with experience, moves through understanding and culminates in judgment. In self-knowledge, the data experienced are the data of consciousness; the data of consciousness are given to us whenever we perform the cognitive operations necessary to know the world. We experience, understand and judge the world and thereby constitute consciousness as empirical, intelligent and reasonable, i.e., as we subject data to questions of intelligence and reasonability we become present to ourselves as intelligent and reasonable. At this point all relevant data for self-appropriation are present, although not understood, and the question "What am I doing when I am knowing?" allows us to turn from actually knowing to reflexive self-understanding of our performance. Thus, since Lonergan's cognitional theory is irrefutable, we are necessarily led to his conclusions regarding intro-spection.

Further, since self-knowledge is not immediately given in experi-ence, it follows that the very reasons presented in the previous sec-tion as to why data of sense do not commit the Myth of the Given also apply to data of consciousness—all data are known at the end of inquiry, not the beginning. Lonergan is not a classical foundationalist; in fact, his critical realism, since he applies it consistently, demands a rejection of the Myth of the Given with even greater insistence than Rorty musters. Self-knowing, self-appropriation and self-affirmation are indeed foundational, a rock upon which to build, but they simply are not given in experience, are not given in an intuition, and are not given at the outset of inquiry but only at the end of a very long and tax-ing process of appropriation. As I see it, it is impossible to understand what Lonergan is up to and still think he need concern himself with the Myth of the Given. He simply does not commit or assume the myth and indeed his motivation to overcome intuitionism roots out any last vestiges of the myth and converts the myth to critical realism.

Still, the turn to the subject drags behind it so much baggage about the ahistorical, transcendental ego, that it is likely insufficient to show that Lonergan does not assume any sort of immediate, intuitive vision of the self. Kerr, Lash, McGrath and Pannenberg are not unsophisti-cated thinkers. Presumably they understand that introspection is not an easy inner look. I suspect the itch they feel compelled to scratch is about contingency, a worry that the turn to the subject, even if not guilty of assuming immediately given knowledge, still ignores the me-diation of history and context. In short, can the turn to subject avoid the Transcendental Ego? To this I turn.

5.5 THE SUBJECT BEFORE ALL

Kerr, Lash and Rorty should be concerned when encountering the *transcendental method*. If Michael Vertin is correct in defining philoso-phy as "the effort to discover what in some important sense is most basic and to give a global account of everything in terms of it" and correct in defining transcendental philosophy as pursuing the goals of philosophy by "investigating the elements of human consciousness and seeking to elucidate their apriori structure," then Rorty will in-deed cringe (Vertin 2001, 253). To the skeptic, such a project appears totalizing, universalizing, *a priori*; it assumes a static structure of the self and begins in consciousness, all of which flies in the face of ironic historicism:

> Ever since Hegel, however, historicist thinkers ... have denied that there is such a thing as "human nature" or the "deepest level of the self." Their strategy has been to insist that socialization and thus historical circumstance, goes all the way down—that there is nothing "beneath" socialization or prior to history which is definatory of the human. (CIS xiii)

Clearly, then, the two camps—transcendentalist and historicist—seem at loggerheads.

That would overstate the case. True, Lonergan certainly refers to the unchanging and *a priori* foundations of human intellect, but he speaks just as often of the contingent, mutable, localized, historical situatedness of the human, and not in a dualistic Platonic fashion either. It is not as though the historical is an unfortunate fact which we luckily escape given our really real transcendental selves. As we have already seen in the preceding sections of this chapter, Lonergan is not at all afraid of mediation in our knowledge and gives good reasons against immediate knowledge of our world or ourselves. Since he does not begin with a model of intuition, he does not worry that history, language, culture, background and perspectives somehow impair our vision. He is a foundationalist who is unafraid of the contingent and the mediation of contingency. How does he pull this off?

In the span of two pages, the essay "Pluralism, Classicism, and Relativism" asserts "classicism ... is not mistaken in its assumption that there is something substantial and common to human nature and human activity" but also that "the meaning of any statement is relative to its context" and "it is true that contexts change" (LR 438-439). Such statements are often considered mutually exclusive, for the classicist accepts the universality of concepts and thus refuses the contextual dependence of meanings while the pluralist or relativist rejects anything substantial or common to human nature. Lonergan argues that both the classicist and the relativist make the same mistake: they do not understand Transcendental Method. The classicist thinks of the self as metaphysical soul and so neglects the *openness* and variability supported by the Transcendental Precepts whereas the relativist neglects the *invariant* intentions of the Precepts (LR 438-439). What is required is a firm grasp of cognitional structure, for the structure is invariant but the operations are not static or merely conceptual. One must understand the distinction between the categorical and the transcendental. The transcendentals are the heuristic intentions of cognitive operations. Transcendental *notions* "constitute the very dynamism of our conscious intending, promoting us from mere experiencing towards understanding, from mere understanding towards truth and reality" (M 12). The notions are exhibited in dynamism, for the movement from one operation to the next occurs simply because of desire, because we want what remains explicitly unknown but implicitly grasped for. Upon intentionality analysis, the known-unknown notions are expressed as transcendental *concepts*—the *intelligible*, the *true* and the *real* (M 11-12). Since the transcendental notions and concepts are invariant and operational in all humans, and since they are the condition of possibility for all insights, conceptions, reflections, and judgments, they are transcendental in a two-fold sense. First, they are transcendental rather than categorical or predicable (M 14). Second, they are transcendental in the Kantian sense of *a priori* conditions of possibility for knowledge—without the desire to know none of the operations of knowing would occur. But because the transcendentals are *a priori* and non-predicates, it follows that (a) they are not confined to any particular field or subject, as categories of mathematics are distinct from categories of rhetoric, but operate in both these fields (M 14) and (b) are constant despite cultural and historical differences (M 11, 282, 283). Consequently, since the notions are invariant and context transcendent, it is possible to prescribe them as normative for the knowing subject, i.e., to make them transcendental *precepts*:

> ...our conclusion will not rest on classicist assumptions. Again, we are not relativists, and so we acknowledge something substantial and common to human nature and human activity; but that we place not in eternally valid propositions but in the quite open structure of the human spirit—in the ever immanent and operative through unexpressed transcendental precepts: Be attentive, Be intelligent, Be reasonable.... (M 302)

But if the transcendental is invariant, it is also indeterminate. Reflecting Kant's distinction between the emptiness of categories and the blindness of intuitions (although without relying on the Kantian architectonic), Lonergan argues that transcendental notions make questions and answers possible while categories make both questions and answers determinate (M282). Notions allow desire, the drive to know, but they are empty; even transcendental concepts derived from the objectification of notions do not contain real content, thus the disputes on fleshing out the meaning of 'truth' and 'being'. So while notions are operatively absolute, they need expression and content, and such expression and content is supplied through the categorical, through a particular language, concept, or meaning. Meaning, then, can be said to have two sources: first, the transcendental which as the condition of possibility *for* cognitive operations is the ultimate source of meaning, and, second, the categorical which provides actual content *through* the cognitive operations of experience, understanding and judgment actual content (M 73-74).

For a classicist, categories are themselves universal. In certain interpretations of Aquinas, for instance, concepts in the mind are universal because concepts are the means through which reality is primarily known, and since substances are composed of form and matter the universal concept corresponds to a real distinction between the universal and the particularizing matter in the substance. Thus, concepts are universals because substances in the world possess universal forms and the concept is the universal form with intentional existence (M 301). For Kant, on the other hand, universality derives not from the substance but from the categories of the mind imposing necessity on contingent sense data, and because human nature is a constant we are able to share categories and judgments. So despite the obvious differences in their thought and opposed understandings of the source of concepts, both Aquinas and Kant agree on the universality of the categorical.

For the tradition with which Lonergan is usually associated—the tradition of Blondel, Maréchal, Rousselot—the importance of the universal concept is lessened while the importance of the judgment increased. Consequently, there is a certain relativism of the concept but not a relativism of knowledge, for knowledge is not attained in universal and natural concepts guaranteed by a metaphysics of the human soul but in judgments made by the human subject (McCamy 1998, 12-18). As such, Lonergan is not threatened, and in fact supports, the contextualization and relativity of conceptual frameworks: "human understanding develops over time, such development is cumulative, and each cumulative development responds to the human and environmental conditions of its place and time" (M 302). His cognitional theory would demand this, for it is not static but dynamic, and various understandings are judged false or incomplete. Cultures operate as the individual writ large, and various contexts and understandings may survive or fall, just as the classical understanding rose and fell.

In addition to historical change, there are three additional sources of categorical pluralism: (1) the various differentiations of consciousness, (2) the different brands of common sense and (3) the presence or absence of conversion, religious, moral or intellectual (M 326).

First, although the structure of cognition is invariant, the resulting consciousness may attain varying levels of differentiation. Since every normal adult operates within common sense we may refer to this as *undifferentiated* consciousness. However, consciousness operating both within common sense and another realm of meaning—theory, interiority, transcendence, art, scholarship—is differentiated according to the realm(s) in which it operates (M 272). A realm "becomes differentiated from the others when it develops its own language, its own distinct mode of apprehension, and its own cultural, social, or professional group speaking in that fashion and apprehending in that manner" (M 272).

Common sense, for instance apprehends data as they relate to the subject, to us, whereas in the theoretical realm data are considered as they relate to each other. Eddington's two tables captures the distinction, for the table of appearance and the table of science are apprehended differently in the realm of common sense and the realm of theory. But just as radical a difference exists between the religiously differentiated consciousness of the mystic and the theoretical differentiation of the scientist: the mystic apprehends God through a silent self-surrender to God's gift rather than relating data to other data (M 273). Interiorly differentiated consciousness adverts to conscious operations rather than external data of sense, let alone the texts and artifacts of another as with the scholarly differentiation. And similar differences exist between other realms as well.

It is quite natural, given the varying modes of apprehension, for the realms to develop their own languages, vocabularies, rules of discourse and set of speakers. A scientific lecture alternates between the language of theory and the language of common sense but will not often bring in the vocabulary of mysticism or art. And an observer would be surprised to attend a conference of art historians and find much discussion of the atomic structure of various pigments used in painting, although it is possible. The realms are so unique in their languages that a large component of success within a realm is simply mastering a new language and new vocabulary. But given the differences in apprehension and linguistic expression of that apprehension, it follows that the words of a particular vocabulary will have meaning, or at least a publically understandable meaning, only when used within a particular realm and will seem virtually meaningless within another realm. Thus, as Eddington highlights, there are two apprehensible tables and two means of expressing this apprehension—it feels smooth and it is comprised of elements with certain atomic structures.

Second, although every normal adult exists within the undifferentiated consciousness of common sense, there are many common senses: "as a content, as a determinate understanding of man and his world, common sense is common not to mankind but to the members of each village, so that strangers appear strange, and the more distant their native land, the more strangely they appear to speak and act" (M 273). So appealing to common sense as a source of unity in the face of the plurality of differentiation fails since there are as many brands of common sense as "there are languages, social or cultural differences, almost differences of time and place" (M 276). As a result, the most basic and primary realm of meaning, the realm in which every adult operates and from which even differentiation does not entirely transcend, reveals an irreducible pluralism in basic meanings and expressions. What is of obvious good sense to a person at one place and time is obvious nonsense to another.

Further, as participating in a community of common sense, individuals are provided with a source of common meaning united by common experiences, understanding, judgments and decisions (M 79). But the individual is initially acculturated within such community and does not initially appropriate or reject such common meanings for themselves; it is simply provided to them and is the source of their education before they are capable of accepting or rejecting such common meaning for themselves:

> Within the "we" of the family emerges the "I" of the child. In other words, the person is not a primordial fact. What is primordial is the community. It is within the community through the intersubjective relations that are the life of community that there arises the differentiation of the individual person ... The person is the resultant of

the relationships he has had with others and of the capacities that
have developed in him to relate to others. (in Fitzpatrick 1992, 38)

In addition to exposing Kerr's charges of mentalist-individualism as
specious, Lonergan's placement of the subject always within a prior
community of meaning implies pluralism in the most basic sources of
meaning to an individual. Such common meaning can very well turn
into group bias, and common sense always risks general bias, but common meaning also provides individuals with their basic determinate
categories and is the first content on the bones of the *a priori* notions.

Third, varieties of common sense, differentiations of consciousness
and the unique history and experience of every individual creates a
horizon in which a person operates:

> As our field of vision, so too the scope of our knowledge, and the
> range of our interests are bounded. As fields of vision vary with
> one's standpoint, so too the scope of one's knowledge and the range
> of one's interests vary with the period in which one lives, one's social
> background and milieu, one's education and personal development.
> (M 236)

Since fields of interest and knowledge vary, there are different horizons, and differences in horizons may be complementary, genetic or
dialectical (M 236-237). Complementary differences are the different
worlds of the worker and the foreman, the engineer and the manager,
the artist and the lawyer—for each, according to their differentiation
and concern, lives in his own world. But, of course, they also share a
common world and are, at least to some extent, aware of the world of
the other. Horizons differ genetically insofar as they occupy different
stages of a cumulative development. Later stages surpass but still pre-
suppose early stages, and early stages perhaps anticipate the later; neither stage is simultaneous. Horizons also differ dialectically, in which
case subjects within a horizon are aware of other horizons but find
them unintelligible, false or evil (M 236). They are diametrically opposed, or at least consider themselves in such opposition.

The difference of horizons is exacerbated by the process of conversion—intellectual, moral or religious (M 237-244). I have previously discussed intellectual conversion, or the movement from naïve
extroversion to critical realism, and while it is not to our purposes to
discuss in any detail moral or religious conversion, the fact remains
that conversions occur by which we do not simply exercise choice from

within a horizon but move to another horizon altogether (M 237). Conversion is not simply an organic development from within which brings along prior contexts and meanings but "an about face; it comes out of the old by repudiating characteristic features ..." (M 237). Intellectual conversion, for example repudiates naïve extroversion and the myth that knowing is somehow like seeing, but in so doing creates an entirely new meaning for the language of truth, reality and knowing. For someone who has not yet converted these terms have meaning only within another context—the context of extroversion—and the meanings are in tension to their meanings for critical realism. Thus, since "all our intentions, statements, deeds stand within contexts" and "within such contexts must be fitted each new item of knowledge" (M 237), the presence or absence of conversion results in a pluralism of expression and communication, i.e., of vocabularies. But this language is fundamentally similar to Rorty's. Contexts do go all the way down, or at least all the way down for the categorical.

There is, then, an *a priori* and universal element in Lonergan's thought—the transcendental—as well as a contingent, historical, relative element—the categorical. The balance between these allows Lonergan to be a foundationalist without falling prey to Rorty's objections, for Rorty objects to knowledge immediately given in experience and to privileged representations in his insistence that language and context go all the way down. Lonergan can agree, language and context do go all the way down, but still insist that the human being always operates through certain cognitive operations and by virtue of a transcendental condition of possibility. We operate both in the realm of contingent historicity and in the realm of invariant human nature:

> the shape and form of human knowledge, work, social organization, cultural achievement, communication, community, personal development, are involved in meaning. Meaning has its invariant structures and elements but the contents in the structures are subject to cumulative development and cumulative decline. So it is that man stands outside the rest of nature, that he is a historical being, that each man shapes his own life but does so only in interaction with the traditions of the communities in which he happens to have been born and, in turn, those traditions themselves are but the deposit left him by the lives of his predecessors. (M 81)

Most emphatically, this is not a Kantian division even though using Kantian terms. Lonergan does not posit atemporal categories and he never accepts the noumenal/phenomenal distinction. There are not two selves, no noumenal self free from time while a phenomenal self is trapped in mechanistic determinism; there is only the one self, an incarnate spirit, and one unified consciousness which is animated and cognitively operative given the pure desire to know but always located and substantively filled out by the concrete categories of a specific time and place, differentiation and horizon.

5.6 CONCLUSION

As I understand him, then, there is very little danger that Lonergan's reliance on the given and his dedication to the turn to the subject commits him to the Myth of the Given, privileged representations gained through an inner look, or a mentalist Transcendental Ego—all illicit trappings of a decadent intuitionism. He does not rely on any noumenal, ahistorical, mentalist self free from the contingencies and changes of time and place. Indeed, history would show that it is the intuitionists like Plato, Augustine, Descartes, Kant and Husserl who ignore or abhor the historical. Kerr, Topping, Lash, McGrath and Pannenberg are simply incorrect in their claims that Lonergan is ignorant of the role of context. In fact, classicists fear that Lonergan has given in too much to the historical and the contingent by relativizing concepts; the *a priori* intendings of the subject are insufficient for them and they demand a return to the unchanging faculties of the metaphysical soul. One camp finds Lonergan too classicist, the other finds him too pluralist—one wonders if a man described by some as too tall and thin but too short and stout by others might not be just about average. Perhaps Lonergan is just about right. In any event, he cannot be charged with leaping out of the contingent realm of the everyday.

In this chapter I have emphasized the contingent and relative aspects of Lonergan's thought and his facility to cope with Rorty's or Rorty-like insistence that context and language go all the way down. Since Lonergan need not depend on (a) knowledge immediately given in experience, (b) immediate and privileged access to the contents of consciousness or (c) universally known propositions or categories, he does not regress to an illicit foundationalism. In fact, at this point one might even doubt his ability to transcend the contingent at all. Nonetheless, he is a foundationalist, for it is impossible to deny the desire for truth, and the undeniable search for truth allows intentionality analysis and its resulting cognitional theory. The only foundation necessary is the desire for truth and the operations of cognitions revealed when the desire is reflexively understood. (Thus the importance of the previous chapter.) In the next chapter we turn from Lonergan's acceptance of contingency to the import of the transcendental. For Lonergan, as much as Rorty, accepts the contingent, but Rorty's counterpositions and Cartesian Anxiety force him to reject realism while Lonergan's rational account of knowing allows self-transcendence.

CHAPTER 6

CRITICAL REALISM AND CONVERSATION

The real community of man, in the midst of all the self-contradic-
tory simulacra of community, is the community of those who seek
the truth, of the potential knowers, that is, in principle, of all men to
the extent they desire to know. But in fact this includes only a few,
the true friends, as Plato was to Aristotle at the very moment they
were disagreeing about the nature of the good. This according to
Plato, is the only real friendship, the only real common good.

Allan Bloom, *Closing of the American Mind*, 381)

6.1 PREAMBLE

In the previous chapter we demonstrated how little Lonergan relies
upon the foundations of privileged representation, given knowledge or classicist assumptions of natural vocabularies. Still, and to
the surprise of those who have not attained intellectual conversion, he
affirms the self-transcendence of critical realism. Natural realities exist independent of human ideas and we can know these realities even
though all access is mediated. Clearly, Lonergan transcends the normal dichotomies of realism and antirealism.

But if Lonergan is without Cartesian Anxiety in his acceptance of
mediation, Rorty is not. We now investigate more fully why Rorty assumes that the mediation of contexts inhibits realism, discovering the
counterpositional interplay between his cognitional theory, epistemology and metaphysics. In the end, Rorty has not escaped the hold of
intuitionism, still reducing fully human knowing to the extroversion
proper only to animal knowing. Consequently, he retains the commonsense understanding of genuine knowledge immediately grasping
a world of bodies out-there. Further, since he remains in this counterposition, he inherits the false dichotomy of intuitionism—either
intuition or antirealism—with its concomitant Cartesian Anxiety that
any mediation between subject and object threatens realism. In exposing the counterpositional status of Rorty's argument, we complete the
intellectual conversion of Lonergan's position. Additionally, we learn

how Lonergan's account allows more genuine conversation and mutual investigation than Rorty provides.

6.2 CONTEXTUALITY & CONVERSATION

Philosophy-as-epistemology attempts to discover a neutral framework or ground by which to judge the rationality of each and every discourse, although "sometimes this common ground has been imagined to lie outside us ... sometimes it has been imagined to lie within us..." (PMN 316). In either event, our ability to bring commensurability to the broad variety of discourses is threatened without a universal and natural arbiter of rationality:

> By "commensurable" I mean able to be brought under a set of rules which will tell us how rational agreement can be reached on what would settle the issue on every point where statements seem to conflict. These rules tell us how to construct an *ideal situation*, in which all residual disagreements will be seen to be "noncognitive" or merely verbal, or else merely temporary—capable of being resolved by doing something further. What matters is that there should be agreement about what would have to be done if a resolution were to be achieved. (PMN 316; italics mine)

Rorty does not consider resolution necessary and replaces epistemology with hermeneutics. Hermeneutics embraces the incommensurate and thereby is not a new method but "is an expression of hope that the cultural space left by the demise of epistemology will not be filled— that our culture should become one in which the demand for constraint and confrontation is no longer felt" (PMN 315). Without a viable cultural overseer directing conversation and discovering common ground in various discourses, all that remains is the hope of agreement. No longer, however, will the interaction between discourses be thought of as inquiry, but merely conversation.

Even though discourses are incommensurable, lacking a scientific "algorithm" by which to make them commensurable or by which to choose between discourses, hermeneutics does view the parties of discourse as united by "*societas*—persons whose paths through life have fallen together, united by civility rather than by a common goal, much less by a common ground" (PMN 318). Whereas epistemology sought common ground in *the* criteria of rationality, hermeneutics accepts that standards of rationality are merely internal to discourses;

whereas epistemology hoped for a common goal of Truth, hermeneutics, or the new pragmatism, hopes only for "an appropriate amount of
unforced agreement with tolerant disagreement" (ORT 41). Objectivity is replaced by solidarity.

Despite our hopes for solidarity, we unavoidably value our own context over that of others', even while recognizing the lack of any good
reason for our ethnocentrism (ORT 29). It just simply is our group,
and with our group we share "enough of one's beliefs to make fruitful conversation possible" (ORT 30). But just as two Newtonians
have difficulty conversing with someone from another paradigm, so
the members of our *ethnos* discover no perfect method to make the
discourse of another *ethnos* commensurate. This is not to say that we
cannot attempt to expand our conversation:

> ... we must work by our own lights. Beliefs suggested by another
> culture must be tested by trying to weave them together with be-
> liefs we already have. On the other hand, we can always enlarge the
> scope of "us" by regarding other people, or cultures, as members of
> the same community of inquiry as ourselves—by treating them as
> part of the group among whom unforced agreement is to be sought.
> What we cannot do is to rise above all human communities, actual
> and possible. We cannot find a skyhook which lifts us out of mere
> coherence—mere agreement—to something like "correspondence
> with reality as it is in itself." (ORT 38; cf. COP 80)

There is, of course, no guarantee we will seek unforced agreement
with others, for there are no noncircular reasons why the Nazis should
include Jews in their group (COP xv). But even if we wish to include
others, we cannot simply escape our own group; rather, we become
a conversationalist, a sort of "informed dilettante, the polypragmatic,
Socratic intermediary between various discourses" (PMN 317). The
culture of inquiry is replaced by the culture of the salon, where no one
interlocutor plays the role of cultural overseer but where differences
between discourses are "transcended in the course of the conversation"
(PMN 317) and we "pick up the jargon of the interlocutor rather than
translating it into one's own" (PMN 318).

Accommodating new jargon involves reweaving the web of our
beliefs. If the degree of reweaving is high, we begin to speak of the
process as "recontextualization" (ORT 94) whereby normal discourse
attempts to make abnormal jargon coherent. Such recontextualization
falls into one of two classes: (a) a new attitude towards a previously

held belief, or (b) acquiring an attitude about a belief towards which one previously held no attitude (ORT 94). Recontextualization of the first sort involves *inference*, for the "logical space remains fixed" since "no new candidates for belief are introduced" (ORT 94). The second sort of reweaving is more like *imagination*, as a new possible belief is put forward for examination and possible inclusion in the web. Prior to Kuhn, all inquiry modeled itself after inference with epistemology providing common logical space, but since the pragmatist rejects the notion of a privileged or natural context rapprochement with abnormal discourse occurs through the imaginative reweaving of contexts (ORT 95-96). Such is the practice of hermeneutics, but such conversation leads, at best, to agreement among the interlocutors on which web of beliefs is most desirable to have and not to a context-free grasp of the way things really are.

Such a position is defined by Rorty as *ironism*. An ironist holds the following:

> (1) She has radical and continuing doubts about the final vocabulary she currently uses, because she has been impressed by other vocabularies, vocabularies taken as final by people or books she has encountered; (2) she realizes that argument phrased in her present vocabulary can neither underwrite nor dissolve these doubts; (3) insofar as she philosophizes about her situation, she does not think that her vocabulary is closer to reality than others, that it is in touch with a power not herself. (CIS 73)

We certainly understand why, given his previous arguments, Rorty concludes with the ironist. At the point where humans enjoy no god's-eye view, we enjoy little confidence that our own discourse happens to hit upon the nature of the real. Of course, we begin from within our own ethnos, but once the contingency and arbitrariness of one's own vocabulary are recognized we move into the line of thought which Rorty calls "liberal utopia" (CIS 61), "solidarity" (ORT 21) or "conversation" (PMN 389). Instead of seeking an ideal terminus of conversation, we struggle to ensure that each of us has "hope[s] of becoming a different sort of person" and that "the moral consciousness of each new generation is slightly different from that of the previous generation" (PSH 127). What is to be avoided is stopping the conversation or killing the discourses before they bloom into thousands more. But the point remains simply to allow the greatest amount of unforced agreement and tolerant disagreement while pursuing continual and unending conversation.

With ironism, we see the clearest example of how a small mistake made at the beginning of reasoning results in a large error in the end. Rorty argues, rightly, that all knowledge is contextual, mediated and linguistic, but again he bifurcates by presenting two, and only two, possibilities—epistemology or hermeneutics, as he construes them. Epistemology assumes privileged access and is thus defeated by linguistic mediation while hermeneutics allows only ironism with its commitment to hyper-corrigibility and anti-representationalism. So we have only two options: a non-realizable and naïve realism or a realizable ironism.

Perhaps the greatest difficulty in refuting an argument is constructing an alternative without simply mirroring the presuppositions and premises of the prior argument, if only implicitly. As much as anyone, Rorty demolishes the pretensions of epistemology with its false hopes of intuition and god's-eye views, but consider this possibility: Is Rorty's rejection of epistemology simply the mirror image of intuitionism? Does he begin with the same account of what it is to know?

In Chapter 1, we defined intuitionism as the following: *universal and necessary knowledge of the world as it actually is without any mediating factors that skew or slant the perception of reality.* We could rework this position as the following: Either humans are intuitionists or truth as correspondence is impossible, but we are intuitionists and thus truth as correspondence is possible. Now, Rorty quite clearly judges this disjunction differently, arguing coherently and persuasively that humans do not enjoy intuitions of reality, but he accepts the syllogism itself. His account of knowing is identical to that of the most naïve realist, namely, knowing is somehow like seeing.

His commitment to intuitionism as the model of correspondence has several implications. First, it raises the possibility, if we can provide an alternative, that he is guilty of a false dichotomy, and Lonergan certainly raises such an alternative. Second, thinking that knowing is somehow like seeing is possible only prior to intellectual conversion and the program of cognitional theory with its demand to ask "What is knowing?" before answering whether we know or not. Consequently, since Rorty has not undergone the intellectual conversion proper to an accurate cognitional theory, he is in a counterposition whereby his explicit statements about knowing contradict his performance—this we saw in Chapter 4. Third, counterpositions in cognitional theory do not operate in isolation but have implications for epistemology—as we have already seen in Rorty's denial of any correspondence theory of truth, assuming as he does that correspondence is based on intuition—as well as metaphysics. In what follows we see just how much Rorty's metaphysics and cognitional theory relate.

6.3 EXTROVERSION, NOMINALISM & IRONISM

Intuitionism arises when the extroversion of animal knowing is illicitly smuggled into an account of fully human knowing. In sensation, particularly in sight, the object sensed certainly appears over-there in opposition to the perceiver over-here. The cup is on the table, we see it and walk across the room to pick it up; the kitten perceives the bowl of milk and moves to enjoy it; we see the baseball leave the pitcher's hand and time our swing as the ball approaches. Animal knowing concerns itself with what Lonergan calls *bodies* or the *already-out-there-now-real* (UB 106-107). Certainly senses can deceive or misrepresent bodies—the fish in water is not quite where we perceive it, the familiar face across the street turns out to be a stranger, the car fender was a bit closer than we thought—but both Lonergan and Rorty agree that such mistakes are not all that philosophically interesting, and in fact as animals we do pretty well getting along in the world (UB 107; cf. ORT 5). Thus extroversion presents a cognitional theory, epistemology and metaphysics which cohere: we are concerned with objects out-there, we sense or perceive these objects as they relate to us over-here and objects are knowable insofar as they are bodies.

Extroversion is the model for intuitionism: the real world exists independently of our perceptions and we accurately know this world insofar as we directly confront the world. But Lonergan insists that extroversion is proper only in its own place, whereas fully human knowledge is gained only at the completion of the threefold process, and the real, i.e., what is known, is that which is intelligently conceived and reasonably affirmed. We thus know *things* or *unity-identity-wholes*. However, if extroversion is illicitly smuggled into fully human knowing, one will operate in the world mediated by meaning but judge according to the rules of immediacy (M 238). This is not to say that one is in fact remaining in the world of immediacy, for the operations of understanding and judgment are occurring insofar as one is ask-

ing the questions "What is it?" and "Is it?" rather than dumbly staring and groping about; but one will force cognitive operations to meet
standards quite improper for them. This is precisely what is meant by
counterposition. A counterposition is defined negatively as that which
contradicts a position, and a position is held:

> (1) if the real is the concrete universe of being and not a subdi-
> vision of the 'already out there now'; (2) if the subject becomes
> known when it affirms itself intelligently and reasonably and so is
> not known yet in any prior 'existential' state; and (3) if objectivity is
> conceived as a consequence of intelligent inquiry and critical reflec-
> tion, and not as a property of vital anticipation, extroversion, and
> satisfaction. (I 413)

Smuggling extroversion into fully human knowing is counterpositional in that it (1) does not define the real as that which is intelligently
conceived and reasonably affirmed but as a version of the already-out-
there-now-real; (2) thinks of the self not as subject to be known in
self-appropriation but as substance or an object, often known through
an inner-looking; and (3) models objectivity on extroversion or other
similarly uncritical accounts.

Now, I have claimed throughout the essay that Rorty violates the
third standard, modeling objectivity after intuition and that upon
finding intuition impossible abandons any objectivity proper to realism entirely. The second standard is not our concern here, but the first
certainly is, for we will see that Rorty's image of reality and his conception of objectivity are correlated. If I am right, and Rorty assumes
a relatively traditional account of extroversion in his understanding of
how correspondence must work, and if Lonergan is right that counterpositions tend to influence both cognitional theory and metaphysics, we should find a mirroring of extroversion in Rorty's metaphysics.
This would be surprising given the non-ocular elements of Rorty's
thought, although, to be sure, counterpositions tend to incoherence.
We find such incoherence in Rorty's nominalism, as introduced previously in Chapter 4.

Rorty realizes that, given our tradition, it seems natural for us to
distinguish appearance from reality, but such distinctions result from
contingent choices made in the Western tradition (COP xxx). Rorty
rejects the distinction by undermining the possibility that reality is a
certain way—if reality possesses no fixed essence, then it makes no

sense to distinguish reality from appearance. The metaphysical tradition holds "that there are, out there in the world, real essences which it is our duty to discover and which are disposed to assist in their own discovery" (CIS 75); the antimetaphysical tradition, on the other hand, rejects the dualisms of essence/accident, substance/property and reality/appearance and holds instead that since all awareness is in a context, and since all contexts result from human needs for security and predictability, then essence, substance and reality are meaningless and unknowable (PSH 47-49). There is no way that reality is in itself, and thus no representation, accurate or not, of reality:

> Pragmatists insist on nonocular, nonrepresentational ways of describing sensory perception, thought and language because they would like to break down the distinction between knowing things and using them. Starting from Bacon's claim that knowledge is power, they proceed to the claim that power is all there is to knowledge—that a claim to know X is a claim to be able to do something with or to X, to put X into relation with something else. To make this claim plausible, however, they have to attack the notion that knowing X is a matter of being related to something *intrinsic* to X, whereas using X is a matter of standing in an *extrinsic*, accidental, relation to X.
>
> In order to attack that notion, they need to break down the distinction between intrinsic and extrinsic—between the inner core of X and a peripheral area of X which is constituted by the fact that X stands in certain relations to the other items which make up the universe.... For pragmatists, there is no such thing as a non-relational feature of X, any more than there is such a thing as the intrinsic nature, the essence, of X. So there can be no such thing as a description which matches the way X really is.... (PSH 50)

In this passage, Rorty explicitly states the relation between cognitional theory and metaphysics: nonocular, nonrepresentational accounts are plausible only on the acceptance of nominalism—in fact, it could be suggested that his nominalism is primary and "fuels his desire to eradicate the image of mirroring" (Harrison 1986, 177). But surely the opposite is implied as well, that for Rorty real essences would necessitate ocular-based forms of knowing (PMN 38-43). Later, we will see the falsity of this view and its counterpositional status.

In the meantime, however, consider just how Rorty supports his nominalism: there are no real essences to things because all features of a substance are relational. An essence, then, would be nonrelational, the subsistent *ding an sich* underlying what merely appears to us:

> ... there is nothing to be known about anything save what is stated in sentences describing it. For every sentence about an object is an explicit or implicit description of its relation to one or more objects. So if there is no knowledge by acquaintance, no knowledge which does not take the form of a sentential attitude, then there is nothing to be known about anything save its relations to other things. To insist that there is a difference between a nonrelational *ordo essendi* and a relational *ordo cognoscendi* is, inevitably, to recreate the Kantian Thing-in-itself. (PSH 54)

We discussed in an earlier chapter Rorty's claim that numbers serve the best model of his meaning: the number 17, for instance, is impossible to describe in essentialist language. Just what is 17 apart from its relationships to other numbers? It is more than 12, less than 458, the root of 289 and so on, but none of these descriptions give any intrinsic explanation of 17. And for Rorty, "it also does not pay to be essentialist about tables, stars, electrons, human beings ... or anything else ... there is nothing to be known about them except an initially large, and forever expandable, web of relations to other objects" (PSH 53).

Of a table, for example, we can say certain sentences which are true: "it is rectangular, it is brown, it is ugly, made of a tree, smaller than a house, larger than a mouse, less luminous than a star, and so on and on" (PSH 55). But language, and only language, provides "cognitive access to objects" and language provides only descriptions of relations (PSH 55). Hitting the table, examining its function, determining its atomic composition—none of these activities do more than reveal yet more relationships the table has in an indeterminately large web of relations. There are simply descriptions, some more useful than others, some more easily leading to consensus, but none which Truthfully reveal the real essence of a thing.

Now, Rorty has already admitted the interdependence of cognitional theory and metaphysics in his assertion that a non-ocular account demands nominalism, and he does not shirk from this claim:

> The essentialist's picture of the relation between language and the world drives him back on the claim that the world is identifiable independently of language. This is why he has to insist that the world is initially known to us through a kind of nonlinguistic [read intuitionist] encounter—through banging into it, or letting it bounce

some photons off our retinas. This initial encounter is an encounter with the very world itself—the world as it intrinsically is. (PSH 58)

We notice the dichotomy between linguistic description and barging into the world itself: barging into the world itself is a direct encounter, an immediate touch, a context-free acquaintance with essences. He says as much when discussing the history of form: knowledge of the universal was modeled entirely on sight, and the Eye of the Mind or the human ability to grasp the universal gave the human their special dignity (PMN 38-41). He argues, making reference to *Measure for Measure*:

> There are few believers in Platonic Ideas today ... But the image of our Glassy Essence remains with us, as does Isabella's lament that we cannot grasp it.... To suggest that there are no universals—that they are *flatus voci*—is to endanger our uniqueness. (PMN 43)

And so the "metaphysician" can take at "face value" the question of intrinsic nature, because, as opposed to the "ironism," the metaphysician believes that reality will give us a "final vocabulary" which is "a transparent medium" capable of accurately grasping the real essence of a thing (CIS 74-75).

Lonergan, it seems to me, would be quite willing to agree with Rorty's analysis: the tradition has linked its ocular-based cognitional theory and its metaphysics of essence. But the model of extroversion reduces *things* to *bodies* and so treats form as merely another instance of an already-out-there-now-real, albeit of a special kind. In a pithy but powerful section of *Insight* on "the bundle of blunders" which is empiricism, the false objectivity of extroversion and its root in intuitionism is traced (I 437 ff.). Of Plato, he says: "the objective universals of Platonist thought seem to owe their origin to the notion that, as the eye of the body looks upon colors and shapes, so there is a spiritual eye of the soul that looks at universals" (I 438). The empiricists too easily distinguished between the appearances of secondary properties and the objective presence of the substance, unknown to us as Locke notes, but which has presence in the same manner of a body. Kant realized that we did not have a super-look, but was unable to break from the supposition that real knowledge would be an intuition, and Husserl does the same (I 439-440). So Lonergan is not at all unfriendly to Rorty's argument here.

But Rorty does not replace extroversion with a better cognitional theory; instead, he rightly recognizes the impossibility of modeling fully human knowing on extroversion and declares that since the knowledge of essence requires an ocular model of knowing we do not know essences. He reasons, rightly, that if an essence is a non-relational nature, then knowledge of essences will require a description-free god's-eye view, but that since all knowledge occurs in a descriptive context the notion of a nonrelational nature is impossible and hence unhelpful. But such ironism is counterpositional, possible only if intellectual conversion and the long process of self-appropriation has not been undergone. Counterpositions tend to reverse themselves because they are irrational, and the Rortyian project can be thought of as an incisive and accurate performative demonstration of the counterposition of extroversion reversing itself. But because Rorty's fundamental dichotomy—god's-eye view or ironism—is a working out *within* the counterposition of extroversion, he misses entirely the chance to escape extroversion through a critical realism. Of course, it is one thing to say this and quite another to offer a viable alternative. Lonergan does so, but his solution needs explanation.

6.4 A REASONABLE ACCOUNT OF FORM

We will attempt to explain an alternative notion of a knowable reality consistent with the cognitional theory developed so far. In doing so, we come to terms with the fruits of intellectual conversion, understanding just how the overcoming of extroversion allows the possibility of knowledge and, later, the hope of genuine conversation. In true Aristotelian fashion, *form* is our goal and intentionality analysis our means.

In *Insight*, Lonergan provides a careful definition of form that presupposes a completed cognitional theory based in self-appropriation:

> Form denotes the component of proportionate being to be known, not by understanding the names of things, nor by understanding their relations to us, but by understanding them fully in their relations to one another. (I 457)

The definition includes four elements: form is (1) a component of proportionate being to be known, (2) not by understanding the names of things, (3) not by understanding the relations of things to us but (4) known by understanding things fully in their relations to other things. Each is examined in turn.

6.41 Form is a Component of Proportionate Being

Proportionate being is the being proper to natural human knowledge or, in other words, being known through the threefold process of knowing:

> … being is whatever is to be known by intelligent grasp and reasonable affirmation. But being that is proportionate to human knowing not only is to be understood and affirmed but also to be experienced. So proportionate being may be defined as whatever is to be known by human experience, intelligent grasp, and reasonable affirmation. (I 416)

Form, then, is a *component* (not the entirety) of what is known of proportionate being, but since proportionate being is not defined in the abstract a proper grasp of form is possible only in reference to the results of cognitional theory: "One must have correctly understood what it is to understand before one can properly understand and utilize the concept of form …" (Byrne 2002, 373).

Lonergan discerned this already in the *Verbum* articles where, realizing that metaphysics begins with cognitional theory, he linked the problem of form to a particular question, namely, the question "What is it?" (V 24). Aristotle begins the second book of *Posterior Analytics* by highlighting the sorts of questions that can be asked in demonstrations, and asks, among other questions, "What is X?" and "Why is X a Y?" Lonergan works out the technicalities of *to ti esti* and *to ti en einai* with a specificity that need not concern us here, distinguishing between form and essence, which is form plus the common matter (V 16). But whatever the specifics of Aristotle's grammar, the question of form arises precisely with questions of understanding—when we ask "What is it?" we are asking a question of intelligence and thus intending an answer of intelligibility.

Immediately form is distinguished from the extroversion of experience, for experience can occur absent a question. The sensible is given to us, and the level of experience does not rise to the question of form. Further, since the question "Is it?" is on the level of judgment and not of intelligence, we can distinguish existence, or act, from form; form correlates to the intentionality of questions of intelligence but existence to questions of reason. Form, consequently, is a component of known proportionate being, for knowledge of proportionate being entails experience, understanding and judgment, with form the component of understanding (UB 154).

We know that questions of intelligence give rise to insights, and insights are conceptualized or defined. We know also that insights occur about data which are experienced. Consequently, we know that form is a grasp of intelligibility in the data and that this intelligibility may be expressed (UB 40). For instance, when we ask why the cartwheel is round we begin to grasp the necessary relation between the length of the spokes and the even curvature of the wheel, and eventually we realize that a circle must have equal radii from a center point. This must be so, not only of this particular circle but of every circle. We thus begin to understand not only what must be so in the data but what must be so universally in the data—each and every circle must have equal radii. Further, this necessity and universality is capable of being expressed in a definition, and the definition expresses that which is essential to having the insight; if we are to grasp the intelligibility of a circle we must express the essence of that insight, namely, that a circle is a set of coplanar points equidistant from a center.

Beginning with cognitional theory does lead us both to form and to the expression of the essential, although Lonergan is careful to note that we do not yet claim to know the essence of a circle (for we have not yet judged our insight and conception to be the case) but only what is essential for us or others to repeat our insight (UB 42). But form and essence have their meanings only in relation to the performance of our own intellects, and if our final definition of form is to escape counterpositional status it must continue to be grounded in performance. In the end, Rorty will not have done so, but we cannot make this judgment until the other three elements of the definition are examined.

6.42 Form is not an Understanding of the Names of Things

So form arises from understanding, but of what? Not merely the use of words, or of the correct grasp of names. A nominal definition is an insight without an *explanation* of the cause of intelligibility (UB 45). For instance, a circle may be defined as a "perfectly round plane curve" (UB 45), which clearly exhibits some intelligence as it serves as a decent enough description of how a circle looks and also allows communication with others. Two children will be able to point to circles instead of triangles and call them by their proper names in a way a baby cannot. Still, Aristotle makes a distinction between the person of experience and the person of science in that the person of science knows the causes of things, knows what makes a circle a circle, in a way that neither the baby nor the child can. This is because the child, supposing they can actually define a circle as a perfectly round plane curve, does not understand just what makes the plane curve perfectly round, and perfectly round not just in appearance but in actuality—they have insight only into the use of the word "circle" and to which object the word applies, but they do not have insight into the cause of circularity. The questions "What is X?" and "Why is X a Y?" demand explanation.

Rorty quite obviously recognizes the distinction between merely conventional terminology and definitions which purport to be explanatory. But because he does not grant real essences he reduces objectivity to "the relative ease of attaining consensus among inquirers" (PSH 51). As a result, he is forced to conclude that *all* definitions and explanations are merely nominal, for none actually explain the nature of the thing itself, although some conventional usages are more easily intertwined with the web of beliefs than others, and some usages are more useful for prediction and control. Thus the history of physics from Aristotle to Newton to Einstein did not occur because any one of the systems more perfectly captured the nature of things—the conventional and nominal usage of words just changed, and all the better for us. So there is progress, in the sense of usefulness, but modern physics is no more or less genuinely explanatory, in the sense of realism, than the early cosmological myths, even though the cosmological myths are no longer live options for us and our current web of beliefs.

But for Rorty to fail to distinguish nominal from explanatory definitions (and I am not saying he fails to understand the intended difference, just that he fails in the end to accept any real difference between the nominal and the explanatory), is possible only because he rejects the notion of form or essence. And as we shall soon see, he rejects form for poor reasons.

6.43 *Form is not an Understanding of Things as They Relate to Us*

Just as there was a distinction between a nominal and explanatory definition, so too is there a distinction between an explanatory definition and a description, although both arise from experience. A description, or experiential conjugate, is an expression of things as they relate to us or as how they appear to us:

> Experiential conjugates are correlatives whose meaning is expressed, at least in the last analysis, by appealing to the content of some human experience.
>
> Thus, 'colors' will be experiential conjugates when defined by appealing to visual experience; 'sounds' when defined by appealing to auditory experiences; 'heat' when defined by appealing to tactile experience; 'force' when defined by appealing to an experience of effort, resistance, or pressure. (I 102; cf. UB 308)

So we can describe a lemon as "sour" or a table as "a smooth surface" or the sun as "bright" or a circle as "round," but such descriptions are certainly not explanations and certainly not a grasp of what is necessary, essential and universal in the data.

Because sensible contents are indispensable for descriptions, and because descriptions never rise to the explanatory level expressing what is known only to understanding, descriptions are not understandings of form (Byrne 2002, 375). For instance, the explanation of a mathematical point transcends the sensible content of a dot, and while we might always return to the image of a dot we will not understand the point until we grasp that it is not a dot and cannot, strictly speaking, be imagined or sensibly represented in any way. Form, then, is understood only when we understand an intelligibility incapable of direct experience. We experience data which give rise to insights, and insights express what is intelligible in the data, but the intelligibility is not itself experienced or capable of being experienced. So while we always relate our understanding of form back to the experiential conjugate, conversion to the phantasm in an older terminology, the experiential conjugate does not exhaust what is understood as form.

For the pattern of common sense, things as they relate to us—our needs, desires, purposes—is the limit of concern (UB 87-88). But Lonergan is careful to note that this pattern does not exhaust all that is knowable about the thing, and his nuance guarantees that he will not fall prey to the Myth of the Given; experience is necessary but not sufficient for the complete range of fully human knowing. Further, he is not naïve in accepting the possibility of various conversations and perspectives, as the last chapter demonstrated. Common sense varies in place, time and interest and the thing may very well relate to me quite differently than to another. So understanding things as they relate to me in the pattern of common sense is relative and dependent on my vantage point.

Rorty is thus right to link the ocular model of knowing and the metaphysician who demands the intrinsic, non-relational essence of a thing; such a metaphysician has not distinguished between the world of common sense immediacy and the world mediated by meaning, they believe they know the world just by describing bodies:

> Against the objectivity that is based on intelligent inquiry and critical reflection, there stands the unquestioning orientation of extroverted biological consciousness and its uncritical survival not only in dramatic and practical living but also in much of philosophic thought. Against the concrete universe of being, of all that can be intelligently grasped and reasonably affirmed, there stands in a prior completeness the world of sense, in which the 'real' and the 'apparent' are subdivisions within a vitally anticipated 'already out there now.' (I 410)

On such a common sense model, knowing the real is confused with knowing bodies, and when transposed into fully human knowing such a model results in what Rorty calls metaphysics. Such metaphysics are, in Lonergan's terms, counterpositional, since it reduces form to the common sense level of bodies as they relate to us. A metaphysics which uses only permanent presence as its standard of the real might be partially correct, but it would overlook those things known in judgment which, though known quite well, are simply not out-there in the manner of extroversion. Such counterpositions tend to break down or reverse themselves:

> For any lack of coherence prompts the intelligent and reasonable inquirer to introduce coherence. But counterpositions, though coherent with one another, though the insertion of their symbolic equivalents into an electronic computer would not lead to a breakdown, nonetheless are incoherent with the activities of grasping them intelligently and affirming them reasonably. For these activities contain the basic positions; and the basic positions are incoherent with

any counterposition. One can grasp and accept, propose and defend
a counterposition; but that activity commits one to grasping and accepting one's grasping and accepting; and that commitment involves
a grasp and acceptance of the basic positions. (I 413)

In order to escape the counterposition, then, we need an account of
form consistent with the cognitional acts of our own intellects. Perhaps as adroitly as any, Rorty discerns that intuitionism does not gel
with what we are actually doing when we know—he knows that we
simply do not stare at reality and just see it as it exists. He knows that
we never look into some secret perfectly present essence but that our
language or vantage point always plays a part and cannot be escaped in
privileged representation. He succeeds admirably in derailing the intuitionist, but, like Nietzsche, is better at tearing down than constructing. Consequently, his most basic conclusions—that there is no way
things really are and no way to know reality—are themselves counterpositional, for the strongest conclusion to follow from positional cognitional theory is that "I am a knower!" So why the confusion between
what Rorty does and what he says?

The most likely explanation is simply that Rorty himself has not
escaped the clutches of intuitionism; the very fact that he defines himself in opposition to intuitionism traps him into accepting its most
basic premises, namely, that knowing is like looking and that reality is
the already-out-there-now-real waiting to be looked upon, although
he declares humanity blind. He grasps that "animal knowing is not human knowing" but he "fail[s] to see what human knowing is" (I 439).
Such a mistake is hardly novel: Augustine relates in the *Confessions*
his struggle to conquer dependence on corporeality and an imaginable God but always remains a sublime empiricist by insisting that
through the immutable light we look above to reality (I 437). Plato
denies materiality to the forms but posits an intellectual intuition in a
moment of immediate confrontation. Kant denies the power of intellectual intuition but grants reality only to those sorts of things given
in intuition (Sala 1994, 45-49). Intuition is so familiar to us, so basic
to our animal knowing, and the empirical conjugate always a part in
every known, that even when intuitionism is explicitly rejected it too
frequently worms itself back into the implicit framework of a philosophy, and Rorty's is no exception.

This is precisely why Lonergan uses the language of *conversion* to
describe the process of freeing ourselves from extroversion—this is

not simply another judgment to be made, not simply a proposition for our assent—but the "severing [of] the umbilical cord that tie[s us] to the maternal imagination of man" (I 15). We never leave behind the biological pattern of experience, nor should we, but to distinguish properly the interplay between our animal knowing and our fully human knowing takes a dexterity won only through painstaking and time consuming effort. Becoming adroit at this distinction and winning intellectual conversion requires self-appropriation and cognitional theory, exactly what Rorty fails to do.

Now, while I think it quite clear that Rorty is at least within the domain of a false dichotomy—he leaves only two options, intuitionism or epistemological behaviorism—my claim that he is within a counterposition remains conclusive. To more adequately demonstrate that both his epistemology and metaphysics are counterpositional we need to examine more closely his claims of nominalism, for here he reveals his imprisonment to extroversion by reducing form to that which relates to us in descriptions.

6.44 Form is Understanding Things Fully in Their Relations to Each Other

Rorty suggests we ought to think of everything as we do about the number 17: there is no special non-relational attribute of 17, its essence, which when known lets us know 17 as it is in itself. Assume that Rorty is correct in his understanding of number and that 17 has no non-relational attributes—it is more than 16, equals 9 plus 8, is the root of 289 and so on. Consequently, since there is no non-relational essence to 17, or anything else, X, "there can be no such thing as a description which matches the way X really is, apart from human needs or consciousness or language" (PSH 50). Notice the two intertwined elements of Rorty's thought here: first, all descriptions are inescapably contextual and non-intuitive, and second, thus there is no way X really is: "...we shall never be able to step outside of language, never be able to grasp reality unmediated by a linguistic description ... we should be suspicious of the Greek distinction between appearance and reality..." (PSH 48).

This is problematic, for Rorty slips into extroversion by linking the reality of essence to "prelinguistic knowledge of objects" (PSH 55). For common sense, the world of bodies out-there-now-real is *given* to the observer in experience, and any mediation between the body and the knowing subject threatens the objectivity of the observation. Of course, as we noted previously, common sense is not explanatory but only descriptive; still, experiential conjugates are given of bodies directly. Now that we move to the intellectual pattern of experience, Lonergan suggests a model other than extroversion, but a counterposition merely transfers extroversion into fully human knowing. As a result, form is considered a body out-there and knowledge of the form must be given or intuited without mediation to be objective. Rorty captures the assumptions of extroversion perfectly when explaining why common sense (here his description closely matches Lonergan's use of the term) refuses to model, as Rorty thinks we should, all objects after number: "common sense—or at least Western common sense—has trouble with the claim that numbers are good models for objects in general because it seems counterintuitive to say that physical, spatiotemporal objects dissolve into webs of relations in the way that numbers do ... there is, common sense insists, a difference between relations and the things that get related" (PSH 55). Common sense wishes to insist that a table has substantiality, that it is something over and above our descriptions. The problem, however, is that all we can know of the table, either by banging or describing, is that the table is rectangular, brown, made of wood, smaller than a house but larger than a mouse, good for our use in writing, of a certain height, giving a certain feel and sound when banged upon and so on. There is nothing to be known except certain sentences about the table, and each sentence "attribute[s] a relational property to it" (PSH 55). The table looks a certain shape and shade and size to our view, it sounds and feels a certain way, it looks and sounds and feels differently than other objects, but none of these properties allow us to see the table apart from all relations, which is what the essentialist demands. Further, even more advanced and less obviously commonsensical descriptions about the table's atomic composition merely expands the web of possible relations rather than escaping into a non-relational intrinsic essence.

Common sense essentialism, then, holds that form must, like a body, be substantially present in itself and not dissolve into a throng of mere descriptions and that this substantial presence, to be known, must be known immediately—knowledge requires a non-relational form and the ability to intuit that form. Or in other words, the form must be non-relational in essence but known in an unmediated relation to us. Rorty, however, shares these identical assumptions:

> Unless one believes, with Aristotle, that there is a difference between knowing and using, that there is a purpose called 'knowing the truth' distinct from all other purposes, one will not think of one description of A as 'more accurate' than another *sans phrase*. For accuracy, like utility, is a matter of adjusting the relation between an object and other objects, a matter of putting an object in a profitable context. It is not a matter of getting the object right, in the Aristotelian sense of *seeing it as it is apart from all relations*. (PSH 65; italics mine)

Despite this questionable reading of Aristotle, Rorty does us the favor of spelling out his position with painful clarity: *there is no knowing the truth because the object is not seen apart from its relations*. In fact, objects, like numbers, are always put in "relation between [the] object and other objects" and always described linguistically, not for truth but for utility or profitability.

The two claims—no essence apart from relations and no knowing of truth—are related: "there is nothing to be known about [objects] except an initially large and ever expandable web of relations to other objects ... There are, so to speak, relations all the way down, all the way up, and all the way out in every direction: you never reach something which is not just one more nexus of relations" (PSH 53-54). Consequently, no description of the object is any more real and less apparent than any other; no description is of "the object's relation to itself—of its identity with its own essence" (PSH 54). This "panrelationism ... helps us put aside the correspondence theory of truth" (PSH 47).

We now possess the data to compare the essentialist and Rorty. The essentialist believes that form is non-relational but intuited directly and thus known. Rorty believes form is inherently relational and non-intuitable and thus not known. But Rorty and the essentialist then concur that knowledge requires a non-relational form and the ability to intuit the form. Consequently, since the essentialist arrives at this conclusion because they assume extroversion, and thus a form of intuitionism, Rorty too assumed extroversion and intuitionism as the standard of knowing.

This is unexpected, to say the least. Intuitionism of various stripes has been Rorty's target from *Philosophy and the Mirror of Nature* onwards, and here we see his basic argument assumes intuition as a premise: the subject/object split patterns the spectator theory of knowledge whereby the essence of reality is grasped without mediation, but there is always mediation and thus essence is not grasped and is useless as a notion. Rorty remains trapped by Cartesian Anxiety, the intuitionist's fear that either we have unmediated intuitive access to the real or we cannot know it at all; but Cartesian Anxiety thereby delineates the philosophical possibilities in advance, provided one accepts its premises, and Rorty quite meekly accepts these as the only possibilities, thus explaining his false dichotomy. Essence is non-relational both for the intuitionist and for Rorty. Correspondence depends on context free objectivity, a god's-eye view, for both the intuitionist and for Rorty. Objectivity is defined as seeing what is actually there for both the intuitionist and for Rorty. But then Rorty is merely a heretical intuitionist, for the heretic accepts just enough of orthodoxy to be a deviant rather than the purveyor of a quite distinct religion. Rorty has not transcended intuitionism, he just denies its viability by claiming that all alleged intuitions dissolve into descriptions without remainder.

But this fails to adequately grasp the distinction between *description* and *explanation*. If one models objectivity on extroverted animal knowing, then it certainly is the case that if all knowledge is *descriptive*, i.e., relates to us within some context, vocabulary or perspective, then all descriptions are merely for us and not of the thing itself. Protagoras is correct: man is the measure of all things. Just as lemon might be painfully sour to one but pleasantly tart to another or a room too cold to one but too warm for another, so all descriptions are relative to the vantage point of the perceiver. There are no privileged representations, no natural or final vocabularies of descriptions so long as we concern ourselves with descriptions. But Lonergan agrees; in fact, the point of the preceding chapter was to demonstrate just how much Lonergan agrees, there are a bewildering variety of common senses, horizons, languages and descriptions, and the death of classical culture ends privileging any one vantage point. But if we understand form insofar as we understand things fully in their relation to other things—data relating to data—we move from relative descriptions to causal explanations and transcend extroversion. So Rorty is right to say that we never grasp the non-relational form of an object in a super-intuition, but genuine explanations do not depend on such a non-relational grasp.

Let us take the example of a tree as it relates to us: we point to a fir and a poplar and ask about their characteristics. A fir has needles, it remains green the year round, has a pyramidal shape and cones. A poplar has ovate leaves which it loses in the fall, a spreading shape and fuzzy seeds. Despite these differences, we recognize both as trees because they both have woody perennial trunks of the requisite height and diameter and have foliage. Here we have given *descriptions* based solely on what is experienced or sensed. This is quite useful and allows us to determine genus and species and to distinguish a tree from a shrub and recognize that the fir and the poplar are both trees, albeit of different species. Once these descriptions are agreed upon and disseminated we are able to correctly distinguish the fir from the poplar and both from a bush. But we have limited our knowledge to immediate properties capable of being sensed (Flanagan 1997, 112). Such descriptions allow us to talk about trees and provide names or nominal definitions, but since the descriptions are only as the tree appears or relates to us they do not provide explanatory accounts of a *thing's* form, they describe only a *body*:

> In descriptions, then, sensible components are indispensable, and so they do not appropriately express what is known solely and precisely by understanding. Moreover, the sensible components of descriptive meanings tend to dominate the ways we think about them … We tend, instead, to think about things as having our experiential elements, rather than as being related to them. When this happens, not only do the descriptive terms fail to clearly distinguish the sensible from the intelligible components, they tend to suggest that the pictured shape, etc. exhausts the meaning. How often has some sort of visualizable shape been offered as the primary illustration of something's "form"? (Byrne 2002, 375-376)

Such a descriptive account has the unfortunate "tendency to think of itself as omniscient, assuming that it knows what things *really are*" (Flanagan 1997, 112-113; italics mine). But form is not exhausted by description and to know why things are what they are we "move into an explanatory context in which things may be known, not only in their sensible relations to me, but also in their explanatory relations to one another" (Flanagan 1997, 114-115), exactly what Rorty and the essentialist deny. Botanists soon move past the descriptive accounts of genus and species based on appearance to the fully explanatory by investigating trees not through the sensible elements of leaves and bark but through biochemical and biophysical properties and organic processes, through general theories predicting the general schemes of recurrence and emergence of various chemical and physical properties giving rise to trees in the first place. Further, a statistician can "investigate the numbers and distributions that condition the emergence and survival rates of such trees ..." (Flanagan 1997, 115). There is more to trees than meets the eye. Together, such accounts reveal trees not simply as woody plants of a minimum height and girth, but as "dynamically unfolding systems of cellular schemes which recur with statistical regularity and which develop through a flexible series of higher organic integrations as they pass from an immature stage through a sequence of more mature stages until the adult stage is achieved" (Flanagan 1997, 115). The science of trees may very well start with the experiential conjugate of particular trees but moves very quickly to general characteristics beyond basic observation. Such science reveals the earlier classification schemes to be only nominal, for while descriptions allow us to distinguish properties of trees they do not allow us to explain trees. Biomolecular studies, on the other hand, explain both what trees do and why they do it, both what they look like and why they look that way. So biomolecular studies, which do not simply relate descriptive properties to us but relate cellular processes to each other, explain what a tree is.

Examples abound: the ear can distinguish a middle C from an E, but Pythagoras was right to move beyond a description of how things sound to us to the relation of notes to each other resulting in mathematical ratios of wavelengths which explain the cause of why a C is not an E. A right angle triangle is easily distinguished from an equilateral, and we can describe the properties of each as they appear to us, but the Pythagorean Theorem can explain the relation of the hypotenuse to the other sides not by descriptive properties relative to us but by relating the various sides to each other, the squares of x, y and z. And then on to the sine and cosine of trigonometry which allows an accuracy in determining angles and lengths completely impossible for the child with protractor and ruler to obtain. Budding middle school physicists understand that there is more to be said about a moving object than fast or slow but understand that the relations between time, distance and gravity allow us to determine velocity at every precise moment as the object falls.

Grasping the form, then, does not simply describe what we sense about the body but explains the *thing* when we understand its data fully in relation to other data. The concrete tree is known when we have understood everything there is to be known about this tree and all trees, from the atomic processes which allow their composition to the biomechanical processes allowing their organic functions to their life-span, habitat distribution and so on. What a tree is—its form—is understood exactly when all this relational data is understood. Botanists still make discoveries even after the varieties of evergreens are catalogued and the study of birds did not end with Audubon. New discoveries are made which explain trees and birds and triangles and numbers, and these discoveries are not simply new and more accurate descriptions, although they may entail better observation:

> For that reason, there is a fundamental difference between the notion of metaphysics we are presenting and what has become fairly common ... We arrive at Aristotle's categories most simply by going into the woods, meeting animals, and asking, What kind of an animal is this? How big is it? What is its color? What relations does it have? And so on. They are categories of descriptive knowledge, and descriptive knowledge is science in a preliminary stage. It is something entirely different from science that has reached its explanatory stage.... there has been a tendency to conceive of metaphysics as knowledge, not through causes, but through predicaments....
> (UB 199)

Lonergan thus defines form as a complete explanatory account of things as they relate to other things; clearly, we do not know the form of trees yet, we merely anticipate a heuristic structure of what the form of trees and all else would entail and constantly continue to expand the known relations, thereby providing yet further generations of botanists and scientists something to do. Still, we know enough in common sense to nominally distinguish between various trees and we understand in the intellectual pattern that trees are *things*, i.e., unity-identity-wholes. While we do not yet completely understand the form of a single tree, we are able to understand that our discoveries of biomechanical processes, statistical distribution and all else are not unrelated. It is not as though the various domains of study fail to recognize that they are investigating the same thing, trees and this tree in particular. Beyond each insight into organic process or population density is a further insight recognizing that all the individual insights are related, that the population density relates to the organic processes and that the biomechanical processes relate to the sprouting of the cone after a forest fire. In short, we recognize intelligibility not just in the various studies but among the various studies; we have an insight that all these relations cohere into a unity-identity-whole, that a tree just is what all of these explanatory relations are about. We can then distinguish *conjugate form* and *central form*: conjugate forms are understood when we understand the various relations while central form is understood when we understand that there is unity-identity-wholeness in these relations subsisting through time and change. A particular tree, then, is understood as a concrete thing with central form, perduring through change and explained through the relation of conjugate form. In short, the intellectual pattern of experience recognizes the concrete tree over there just as much as the biological pattern, but the intellectual pattern of experience is well on its way towards understanding the cause of the tree.

Lonergan's account of form is critically grounded, and thus his account is unique. The history of metaphysics is too often a history of extroversion where the knowing, objectivity and intended reality of the biological pattern of experience is uncritically and illicitly carried into the realm of fully human knowing: "being, on this view, is the opaque and independent other that stands over and against the conscious subject, either as a potential object of direct intuition or as an operating constraint on thoughts and actions" (M. McCarthy 1990, 287). Lonergan then has no qualms about granting the relational attributes of 17 and everything else. *Of course* 17 is not understood by staring at it or by mystically transcending its relational properties to an exoteric non-relational essence. 17 just is its relations to all other numbers, as Rorty claims, and 17 is fully understood just when all is relations to other numbers are understood. We are on our way to knowing 17 when we say it is the root of 289.

Here we grasp the distinction between the Aristotelian-Thomist theory of truth and the confrontational model of correspondence. For the Aristotelian, form is known when the mind takes on the form of the thing, or when the mind becomes identical or adequate to the thing. However, if we think of correspondence not as understanding and rightly judging the thing but as accurately representing the thing, then we have not transcended extroversion, for the representation will be an image or picture which is supposed to mirror the thing as it is.

But to mirror the thing as it is, to see it properly, always retains an implicit extroversion, either reducing the mirroring to an accurate sensation of the sensible qualities of the thing or by forcing the eye of the mind to represent its form, although form would thus be understood only by analogy to bodies.

Rorty fails to grasp that understanding a form is "not a matter of ocular vision, but an insight into the sensible data" (V 14), and thus thinks of realism always on the confrontational rather than adequational model. In *Philosophy and the Mirror of Nature*, Rorty recognizes the distinction between identity and representation (45) but insists that the process of identity is that of "internalizing universals, just as the eye of the body knows particulars by internalizing their individual colors and shapes" (41). Now, whatever Aristotle meant, Lonergan's appropriation of Aristotle does not follow this pattern: insight into the sensible, or the process of understanding things as they relate to other things, is not in-sight or in-ternalization in the same way as the eye knows particulars. Quite the opposite since understanding of form does not concern things as they relate to us in the experiential conjugate of sight. Lonergan transcends the extroversion of animal knowing to fully human knowing whereas Rorty still thinks of form as a description, not an explanation, which grasps some non-relational property of the object.

The counterposition occurs, then, when Rorty models objectivity as seeing what is there to be seen, merely denying our ability to see. His epistemology is merely a negative judgment about extroverted intuitionism. His metaphysics follows: since there is no non-relational essence to a thing there is nothing to be known of it as it really is, since to know it as it really is would be to grasp a static and glassy body in the thing. So Rorty is quite rightly denying intuitionism, but he never escapes its basic form. The intuitionist believes that form is non-relational and intuited, thus known. Rorty believes that form is relational and non-intuited, thus unknown. Lonergan believes that form is relational and non-intuited, but still known. It is only Lonergan, then, and not Rorty who escapes the counterposition of extroverted intuitionism.

6.5 BUT DO WE KNOW?

Prior to intellectual conversion, Lonergan's account might seem specious at worst or an idealism at best. It seems quite convenient to define knowing in a certain way, then say that when we know we know being and thus declare by fiat that since we know being, being has the same structure as knowing. This is a fairly common objection, put well by John Milbank and Catherine Pickstock who claim that Lonergan's realism

> ... appears arbitrary. Since the 'look' of the senses or the imagination is not confirmed for Lonergan by an intellectual gaze, but instead the judgment can only grasp the supplied insight within logical and self-consistent structures of holding together ... the human mind does not grasp anything of 'things in themselves'. (2001, 46)

The residue of extroversion could not be more explicit in this objection. Since we are concerned with the 'things in themselves' only an intellectual gaze ensures knowledge. What is to be known, then, is a pre-existing, perfectly present 'out-there' captured by some special faculty of the intellect, but since Lonergan denies this faculty he cannot hope to defend realism—the structure of the argument is identical to Rorty's claim. Now, if form is a non-relational essence of a thing, then it would be known only in an immediate vision and Lonergan's account of form would appear as an "immanently confined idealism" or a sort of coherence theory (Milbank and Pickstock 2001, 46).

Lonergan will get his defense, but notice just how closely the standard objection to Lonergan meshes with Rorty's denial of realism:

> there is nothing to be known about anything save what is stated in sentences describing it. For every sentence about an object is an explicit or implicit description of its relation to one or more other objects ... there is nothing to be known about anything *save its relations to other things*. (PSH 54; italics mine)

For those in the counterposition of extroversion, such as Rorty, Milbank and Pickstock, it is quite problematic for realism to admit that understanding a thing is not to know only the thing as it is in itself but rather in data as it relates to other data. The intuitionist will conclude, with Rorty, that "there is nothing to be known about anything" while forgetting that the caveat "*save its relations to other things*" is precisely what it means to understand something—but they forget the caveat due to their improper account of knowing. Rorty is almost right here, there is nothing to be known about anything (in fully human knowing) except its relation to other things, but to know these relations *is* to know everything there is to be known about a thing. Rorty has undergone the remarkable insight that when we know an object fully what we know is "an initially large, and forever expandable, web of relations to other objects" (PSH 53), but he denies that fully knowing this web of relations is knowing the object. Why? Well, just because he has all along assumed that objective knowledge is an unmediated vision of the perfectly present non-relational essence of an object. It is to see what is already-out-there-now-real.

But the intuitionist remains convinced that an increasing web of relations cannot be known in virtually unconditioned judgment when all relevant questions are answered. Rorty's objection to Peirce is telling on this point. According to Rorty, Peirce

> thought it enough to say that 'reality' means something like 'whatever we shall still be asserting the existence of at the end of inquiry'. This definition of reality bridges the gap the skeptic sees between coherence and correspondence. It reduces coherence to correspondence without the necessity either for metaphysical system-building or for further empirical inquiry. A simple reanalysis of the term 'reality' does the trick. (ORT 130)

The problem with this account, an account somewhat similar to Lonergan's (Potter 1992; Potter 1994), is that the ideal end of inquiry is an impossible notion. How would we ever know that we had reached this point, "as opposed to merely having gotten tired or unimaginative" (ORT 131)? In *Consequences of Pragmatism*, Rorty suggests that "we can make no sense of the notion that the view which can survive all objections might be false" (165), but even then warns that we cannot anticipate all objections or know when all objections are raised and answered (COP 165-166; cf. ORT 130 n. 10).

Such objections are quite disconcerting for the intuitionist assuming that discursivity must end in a moment of clarity, in a moment where contextuality and finitude ends, for the intuitionist thinks that judgment—the answer to the question "Is it?"—takes place with the further insight that all relevant questions are answered but in a moment of certain vision. The intuitionist forces judgment to operate outside of its own cognitional space but according to the rules of common sense. Rorty betrays this tendency by assuming that "knowledge as accurate representation" is naturally linked to a certain class of representation which is "'basic,' 'privileged,' and 'foundational'" (PMN 318) as opposed to the skill of conversation which goes on forever, always seeking yet more discourse and unable to rest. Once again, we meet the distinction between the ironist incapable of considering her vocabulary final and the metaphysician's assurance of attaining a final vocabulary (CIS 75). Now, since Rorty suffers from the false dichotomy of Cartesian Anxiety, he assumes that if it is possible to raise another objection, we are forced into antirealism. Descartes' hyperbolic doubt and demand for indubitability is barely hidden here. Without the absolute certainty that our vocabulary is final we are forced to conclude that every vocabulary is equally likely—none are true.

Lonergan is without this Anxiety because he has undergone intellectual conversion and thus does not demand inquiry to end in a moment of direct and certain vision. He states the problem as strongly as Rorty and Meno: "how can the probable be known to approach the certain when the certain is unknown" (I 325). But, unlike Plato and Rorty, Lonergan has no need to revert to intuition to solve this problem which "is not as acute as it may seem" (I 325). He writes:

> We seek the truth because we do not know it. But though we do not know it, still we can recognize it when we reach it. In like manner we also are able to recognize when we are getting near it. As we have seen, the self-correcting process of learning consists in a sequence of questions, insights, further questions, and further insights that moves towards a limit in which no further pertinent questions arise. When we are well beyond that limit, judgments are obviously certain. When we are well short of that limit, judgments are at best probable. When we are on the borderline, the rash are completely certain and the indecisive full of doubts. (I 325)

At first glance, this appears overly sanguine, for the very question is how one is to know that there are no more pertinent questions to be asked. It may seem that all relevant questions have been asked and answered, that we are in the same situation as classical physics where the future looks simply like "a matter of determining accurately a few more decimal places when along come a Planck and an Einstein with their further questions" (I 327).

But the raising of further questions where it seemed no further problems remained is not, as the Kuhnian Rorty suggests, simply the arbitrary change between an old and new tradition (CIS 6). Rorty would have us believe that we cannot discover something normative in ourselves to explain such shifts; instead, we simply have redescribed reality in a new useful way, a way prompting unending conversation without convergence on reality (CIS 6-7). Lonergan, on the other hand, realizes that an adequate cognitional theory explains the advent of new relevant questions: questions arise when the inquiring mind wishes to understand data that it does not understand. Consequently, a Planck or an Einstein do not simply redescribe reality but have unanswered questions about data. Two possibilities present themselves: either the data differed from the past or the data allowed further questions than was initially thought (I 327). With respect to the first possibility, the data may change or our ability to collect data, say through instrumentation or novel experimentation, may expand. But if the data change or expand we are correct in asking why, although we must be able to demonstrate that the data have in fact changed to justify our inclination to ask further questions and avoid mere indecision (I 326). On the other hand, the data may remain the same but may have the capacity to raise more questions that initially thought. But even here cognitional theory explains that the cause is the dynamic desire to know which does not rest content until the thing is explained fully. Clearly, a nagging doubt, a promising possibility or a fertile imagination prompted someone to withhold assent and to keep asking questions of reflection, but this is to be expected. In fact, it is for exactly this reason that understanding form is not knowing; we know only in a virtually unconditioned judgment, and posing the question "Is It?" of our understanding forces us back to the given data of experience to ensure that our answers are intelligently grasped and reasonably affirmed *of being*.

To deny this account is to ignore the concrete and irreversible facts of cognitional theory, which we know with certainty to be true. Data give rise to questions of understanding; insights and conceptions are in turn challenged by questions of reflection to determine if the understanding is adequate to the data. Rorty's account ignores the fact that new understandings, redescriptions if he prefers, originate from and according to the rules of cognitional acts (M 254-257). The intellect is dynamic, constantly looking for new data, but if and only if the data allows are new questions justified. But this is not unintelligible and is rather accounted for by Lonergan.

For the intuitionist with Cartesian Anxiety this poses an enormous problem. Rorty, in line with such anxiety, declares that because we cannot escape the possibility of further questions, nor our necessarily limiting contexts, we cannot know anything about the way the world really is. Lonergan, on the other hand, declares that our inability to escape further questions is not a source of anxiety but rather the great clue which allows us to start to figure it all out. That we ask questions and cannot remain content with our commonplaces reveals that we are able to transcend the biological pattern of experience and our common sense urging us to cease as soon as the most basic questions are solved. Even more, these very questions allow us to develop and know with certainty the structure of cognition. Rorty, in good Cartesian fashion, finds the possibility of future questions proof that we do not know; Lonergan finds in them proof that we are knowers. Further, because of the isomorphism between the cognitional and metaphysical realms, the basic structure of proportionate being is also known with certainty once we have performed intentionality analysis and examined the trajectory of our questions:

> Metaphysics ... envisages an indefinitely remote future date when the whole domain of proportionate being will be understood. It asks what can be known here and now of that future explanation. It answers that, although full explanation may never be reached, at least the structure of that explanatory knowledge can be known at once.
>
> For proportionate being is whatever is to be known by experience, intelligent grasp, and reasonable affirmation. While there are three components in that knowing, still only one of them is an unknown. The content of intelligible grasp of proportionate being necessarily remains unknown until full explanation is reached. But the content of reasonable affirmation is known already, for it is a virtually unconditioned yes. And the content of experience that survives in fully explanatory knowledge is known already, for it is the fully explanatory knowledge of the empirical residue; and already we know that experience in its intellectual pattern when it is dominated by the detached and disinterested desire to know...." (I 456-457)

Consequently, objectivity does not demand a god's-eye view as Rorty would have it, for Rorty's insistence that realism is impossible unless we know that all further questions are already raised, unless we discover the nonrelational and natural vocabulary of the world and unless we escape the contingency of our contexts and categories, is nothing more than the standard worries of Cartesian Anxiety with its demands for god's knowledge. Instead, Lonergan discovers objectivity in genuine subjectivity, insofar as the dynamism of the intellect is allowed to question in the detached and disinterested manner of the intellectual pattern of experience: "one has to move out of the static, deductivist style—which admits no conclusions that are not implicit in premises—and into the methodical style—which aims at decreasing darkness and keeps adding discovery to discovery" (M 270). Such foundations occur when one moves out of common sense and towards interiorly differentiated consciousness—the self-appropriation of cognitional theory—with foundations resting on the concrete cognitional acts of the subject (M 274). In the end, objectivity is guaranteed insofar as the exigencies of the intellect are allowed to pursue their natural ends, i.e., when the transcendental precepts—be attentive, be intelligent and be reasonable—are followed.

We note, then, that Rorty has confused the supposed objectivity of foundational sensations or concepts with the genuine objectivity of foundational acts. This explains also why he is so worried about the relativity of contexts and vocabularies. Since we can never attain a god's-eye view, he sees only the possibility of ironism, the acceptance that our vocabulary is neither final nor sufficient. But instead of concluding, as he ought, that the present vocabulary may be insufficient either to the data or to the inquiring exigencies of our own intelligence, he despairs that we cannot "step outside of our language in order to compare it with something else," as is demanded by granting objectivity only to a superintuition (CIS 75). As we discovered in the previous chapter, Lonergan admits the contingency and plurality of vocabularies, but since he is not a classicist trying to discover some final vocabulary he distinguishes between the relativity of the categorical and the normativity of the transcendental operations. Admittedly, the intellectual pattern of experience is most likely to use categories adequate to the transcendental drives, but it is not the categorical but the transcendental which both allows and ensures objectivity. There certainly are a plurality of categories and vocabularies, but we need not determine their adequacy by placing them and reality both before our gaze and comparing them, we need not step outside of ourselves as Rorty puts it; instead, we can admit, given the transition from classicist to empirical culture, that there may be a variety of ways to communicate insights and understandings and that more than a single vocabulary is adequate to the task, even if the vocabularies themselves seem exclusive. But we test these vocabularies according to the transcendental precepts: are they attentive to the data, are they intelligently grasped, are they reasonable? If they are, then we have no reason to doubt them and no reason to declare one more natural than another. If they are not, as is likely the case, we do not judge them inadequate because of a direct intuition but because they overlook some data, because they are not intelligently grasped or because they cannot answer all relevant questions of reason. But to do so is to compare the vocabularies to genuine foundations—to the demands of our own intellects—rather than directly with the already-out-there-now-real. This is not mere coherence, however: if reality was merely the already-out-there-now-real, then the satisfaction of our intellects would not be realism but coherence. But because *reality* is also that which is intelligently grasped and reasonably affirmed, then intelligently grasped and reasonably affirmed *judgments* are self-transcending true statements about reality, even if we can only anticipate that complete knowing when there are no further questions.

6.6 SAVING CONVERSATION

These considerations allow us to return full-circle to the initial concern regarding conversation. Since we cannot attain intuition, Rorty concludes that only conversation is left. But such conversation is a touch decadent if it has no hopes of becoming adequate to reality; this is not Socratic dialectic. Rorty declares that there is no inherently rational reason for conversation since it cannot attain reality. At best it hopes for consensus or solidarity, but such solidarity is not "a fact to be recognized by clearing away 'prejudice' or burrowing down to previously hidden depths," but by "increasing our sensitivity to the particular details of the pain and humiliation of other[s]" (CIS xvi). There are no adequate, true answers to the question "Why not be cruel?" but only the hopes for a liberal utopia where everyone is willing to consider the viewpoint of another and continue the conversation. The conversation does not attain consensus because of the rationality of an argument but because of self-transformation (PSH 63). One simply chooses to live a different way and to take account of the needs of others, perhaps to redescribe one's beliefs so they are the most beneficial to all. After all, people do such things, they do undergo conversions: "such conversions are typically as much a surprise to the new person herself as to her friends. The phrase 'she has become a new person—you would not recognize her' typically means 'she no longer sees the point or relevance or interest of the arguments which she once deployed on the other side'" (PSH 63).

But to converse thus is Pollyannaish since it can raise no normative objections to the conversation-stopper or the bigot or the Nazi but hopes only to "wheedle," "haggle," and "with luck, eventually turn into a mutually profitable conversation" (Rorty 2000, 8). The problem, of course, is that not only bigots and Nazi's but also well-intentioned people of good-will often end in impasse, or worse. Alasdair MacIntyre's analysis seems to me much more likely, that without a standard of rationality by which to adjudicate between competing claims

> human relationships are perforce relationships of will and power unmediated by rationality. I do not mean that where there is no resort to such standards, each of the competing parties in such communal relationships will necessarily act unreasonably, that is, unreasonably from its own particular point of view as to what constitutes unreason. But it is just that point of view that in their transactions each community will be trying to impose upon the other. And when it becomes reasonable from the point of view of one of the contending parties to impose their will by force upon the other in the name of their own idiosyncratic conception of reasonableness, that is what they will do. (in Baynes, Bohman and McCarthy 1987, 395-396).

Rorty unapologetically champions that since we must begin with a context, we should be frankly ethnocentric and choose our own, working all the while to make it better—better according to our own standards of liberalism. Of course there is no way to persuade anyone to accept the logic of this position who wishes to reject it (although, to be fair, this is hardly a problem unique to Rorty), nor to critique them adequately. Neither can Lonergan magically convert the bigot, but he provides a means of critique since the transcendental precepts are normative. Any and all systems are subject to the demand to be attentive, intelligent, reasonable and responsible (a precept beyond cognition and thus largely beyond the scope of our discussions).

The difference, then, is for the person of good-will: if someone is of good-will he is likely to engage in conversation, but supposing his basic premises to be different than Rorty's, he can hope only, with luck, that others will convert to his side after some wheedling and rede- scription. They may, but if they remain convinced of the truth of their own logic Rorty is entirely bereft of any means to critique them, or himself for that matter. On the other hand, Lonergan, by appealing to the pure and disinterested desire to know, can critique various logics incompatible with the transcendental precepts. Once this common- ality is established, the other is capable of counter-critique, develop- ment or synthesis. As such, there is no reason to think that Lonergan's account is a conversation-stopper; it is at least as capable as Rorty's to spur conversation. In fact, conversation is more likely since there are standards other than sheer will or the brute facticity of an *ethnos* to which to appeal and discuss. In fact, Rorty skates perilously close to group and general bias—the group bias of ethnocentrism and the general bias of the common sense from which he cannot escape. He does, after all, reduce rationality to the ability to describe and attain the more useful over the less useful (PSH 27) and declare that the disinterested desire to know, wonder, is too linked to realism to be of use (PSH 52).

The group bias of ethnocentrism inevitably quells conversation, per- sons of good-will notwithstanding, just as MacIntyre predicts. What happens in group bias, without context-transcendent criteria to ap- peal to, is that disagreement tends to polarize groups who speak at rather than with each other:

> … social order divides into a reform group and a reactionary group. The reform group may turn rebellious and break away, or it may be- come revolutionary and end up using force to accomplish its goals. Unfortunately, this course of events has two negative results. The reform group becomes the new dominant group and will develop symbolic stories, rituals, slogans, and songs to celebrate and justify its own wisdom and righteousness while denouncing the follies and injustices of the vanquished. The defeated group, on the other hand, has its own hatreds and resentful memories which it will hand on to future generations to motivate and promote revenge whenever op- portunities for retribution emerge. (Flanagan 1997, 86)

Rorty's commitment to this project is explicit; since he longs for in- tuition but cannot find it, he resorts to redescription, amounting to stories, rituals, slogans and songs to further the *ethnos* that he has ar- bitrarily chosen:

Those who hope to persuade a nation to exert itself need to remind their country of what it can take pride in as well as what it should be ashamed of. They must tell inspiring stories about episodes and figures in the nation's past—episodes and figures to which the country should remain true. Nations rely on artists and intellectuals to create images of, and to tell stories about, the national past. (AOC 3-4)

Stories about what a nation has been and should try to be are not attempts at accurate representation, but rather attempts to forge a moral identity. The argument between Left and Right about which episodes in our history we Americans should pride ourselves on will never be a contest between a true and a false account of our country's history and its identity. (AOC 14-15)

Rorty's hopefulness aside, such redescriptions have not resulted in broad consensus or solidarity, as the culture wars and the inner workings of the courts indicate quite clearly, but something more like mutually exclusive visions of the world. The analysis of contemporary moral discourse and emotivism in the first few chapters of MacIntyre's *After Virtue* demonstrates this quite well. What is much more likely is that genuine conversation will decrease so long as the transcendental precepts are not recognized. Even worse, such short term conflicts threaten to become a longer cycle of decline precisely because of positions such as Rorty's which advocate the general bias of common sense toward usefulness rather than the pure desire to know, as evidenced so clearly in Chapter 4. When the norms of questioning and understanding are localized only within communities suffering from group bias, the inevitable result is to stunt the development of new and more intelligent policies and actions. Such a short-term decline of intelligence snowballs into a longer pattern of decline where previous oversights become cumulative and incredibly damaging (Flanagan 1997, 88). Rorty's liberal utopia, so long as he rejects the disinterested desire to know, becomes less likely, and his *salon* of urbane intellectuals ever more willing to consider the suffering of others and engage in discussion with them recedes from possibility. Conversation depends entirely on the interlocutor's virtue, and an authentic subject follows the dynamic desire to know. Cephalus abandoned conversation as soon as he lost interest; it was only Socrates, completely and utterly committed to the transcendental precepts, who continued inquiry until all questions were answered and thereby created the ongoing conversation of all those who desire to know.

6.7 CONCLUSION

I have argued that Rorty is guilty of Cartesian Anxiety and accepts the ocular myth as the best standard for objectivity and knowledge, simply denying our powers to attain such objectivity. He does so because, like any intuitionist, he assumes that the real is reducible to the status of a body known not in its relations to other things but only in a direct relation to the knower. His account of nominalism and his cognitional theory, then, are intertwined in their counterpositional status. Further, the problem of intuition has always been that it is incapable of fostering genuine conversation and discussion. If one has an intuition and another does not, there is no way to argue them to agreement; all one can do is point and say, "See! There it is!" But when the other does not see one can do nothing more than leave them in their "self-evident folly" or merely repeat more loudly "See! See!" This is not to say that dialectic is immune from such outbursts of frustration; it is not, but there the problem is the lack of patience, humility or charity in the arguer rather than a necessary by-product of the mode of cognition. In fact, it is the subject's lack of commitment to the transcendental precepts and the desire to know which is responsible for breakdown in conversation. Lonergan provides a means, self-appropriation, whereby one develops fully rational norms of rationality and another means, dialectic, whereby the critique of positions can develop according to transcendent, objective, normative and irrefutable principles. But these principles are known only when the concrete subject is known. Unfortunately, Rorty does not fully know himself.

CHAPTER 7

EPILOGUE

ARIADNE'S THREAD

In my end is my beginning.

(T. S. Eliot, *Four Quartets*)

7.1 PREAMBLE

Although there are indications of recovery, philosophy has ailed for some time now. Of course, there are many explanations and solutions, but the breakdown of classical culture and the growing pains of modernity have created unease and some confusion in the discipline. At root is a crisis over the nature and efficacy of rationality, and at times the tortuous and rather labyrinthine paths of this discussion seem without end. Like Theseus, we need Ariadne's golden thread by which to orient ourselves and escape confusion. There are some, myself included, who think Lonergan is the new Ariadne and his cognitional theory the new golden thread.

Lonergan does not provide a system of doctrines promising a way out of the impasse of late modernity. Instead, Lonergan discovers a new method of thinking, an organon for our times:

> ... I present Lonergan's contribution as a new organon for our times.... At certain momentous points in history, this Greek word or its equivalent has been used to designate an instrument of mind ... a mentality, a formation of incarnate spirit, a way of structuring our conscious activities, that has been of immense importance for the ongoing work of the human race. Such was the case with the Aristotelian organon, the logic of twenty-three hundred years ago, and such was the case again not quite four hundred years ago with the *novum organum* for experimental science of Francis Bacon. (Crowe 1980, 11)

Hugo Meynell calls this project the New Enlightenment, finding in the transcendental precepts of attentiveness, intelligence and reasonability norms free from the excesses of the Old Enlightenment but capable of replying to the nihilism of postmodernity (1999, xi,19). It

is a new organon for a New Enlightenment that we have been studying in this essay, ultimately concluding its superiority to the claims
of Rorty. Along the way, it has become exceedingly apparent to me
how easily Lonergan is misunderstood, either by turning his method
into a Cartesian recipe anyone can follow (M xi), or by thinking Lonergan provides only a variety of coherentism rather than a genuinely
critical realism. My initial hunch was that Lonergan was right, but in
investigating this claim I very often turned Lonergan into a classicist
or doubted his solution once freed from my classicist assumptions.
But unlike my encounters with other thinkers, I could not correct my
understanding simply by re-reading the texts and then re-writing my
chapters, although I did that many times. Instead, one understands
Lonergan by appropriating one's own consciousness and cognitional
acts. This is not a matter of learning a system but of learning the lab-
yrinths of one's own intellect, which takes a great deal of time and
perseverance. I discovered that each time I turned Lonergan into a
foundationalist I experienced a subsequent bout of despair because
of incomplete intellectual conversion. Extroversion is so natural to us
that arguments alone are insufficient to free us from its recesses.

It is precisely the element of conversion which makes Lonergan's
work so difficult to defend or refute, for many of the positions appear
deceptive unless one realizes they are not arguments as much as spiritual exercises. If one is, as I was before encountering Lonergan, a naïve
realist, then his accounts of knowing and being seem sanguine, almost
verbal tricks, since being is obviously the present out-there and not
the amorphous whatever is known and remains to be known. To the
naïve realist, Lonergan seems like an idealist, or at least that is how I,
in my classicist Gilsonian days, interpreted Lonergan. But even then I
was bothered by the statement made by a former professor of mine, in
an extrapolation from an early page in *Insight*, that idealism was only
a half-way point between naïve realism and critical realism (cf. I 22),
since it seemed so obvious to me that idealism and realism were polar
opposites, exactly why I tended to flirt with Kant whenever his arguments seemed momentarily stronger than those of Gilson. In time,
I came to realize that naïve realism and idealism share the common
genealogy of intuitionism, for both assume that realism depends on an
unmediated gaze. Critical realism, on the other hand, transcends this
either/or dichotomy, but the solution of critical realism was not one
that I took to naturally given my fear of idealism. In fact, it was only

the encounter with Rorty, particularly his linking of nominalism and antirepresentationalism, which allowed me to understand just how critical realism escaped from intuitionism and its children—naïve realism and idealism.

The preceding pages, whatever their flaws, are essentially a recounting of how Rorty pushed me entirely into Lonergan's camp, for it was only Rorty's attack on intuition which allowed me to see that my own worries about mediation depended, as did Rorty's attack, on an intuitionist understanding of knowing. But it was precisely this account which Lonergan found irrational and in need of correction. The rest of the essay fleshes out this basic insight, probably one obvious to anyone already through intellectual conversion. This basic insight is hard-won for most of us, however, since the patterns of extroversion entangle us so deeply—even the gifted Rorty was unable to escape.

In the end, my argument is rather simple: Rorty has not escaped extroversion, extroversion is the basic model for intuition, and thus Rorty remains firmly committed to intuition as the model for knowing even while denying our ability to intuit the real. Once he has denied the ability to intuit the real his extroverted understanding of reality crumbles, nominalism ensues, and we are left only with epistemological behaviorism. Given his firm commitment to modern liberalism, he views the collapse of realism as an opportunity and urges us to ironism and never-ending conversation. The argument is simple, but the persuasiveness of the argument, at least for me, depended on a lengthy conversion to the self-transcendence of critical realism.

7.2 THE FIVE QUESTIONS

Chapter 1 posed five questions as the source of this essay. We have been answering the questions throughout, but a brief review is in order:

1. *Does Rorty suffer from Cartesian Anxiety, and can Lonergan best avoid this fear?* Cartesian Anxiety and its concomitant intuitionism are fruits of extroversion, for it is when the knowing proper to the biological pattern of experience is smuggled into fully human knowing that ocular assumptions about objectivity and the real come into play. Lonergan identifies the objectivity and reality proper to fully human knowing by defining the real as that which is intelligently

conceived and rationally affirmed and by grounding objectivity in the pure desire to know with its corresponding transcendental precepts. Both epistemology and metaphysics are critically grounded in the performance of our own intellects rather than in the metaphorics of sight. Rorty, on the other hand, is convinced that the real, if it were to be known, would exist in a non-relational perfect presence known only by a privileged representation. Of course, his attacks on givenness thus preclude knowledge. Consequently, Rorty is convinced that two and only two options exist, the certainty of intuition or ironism—a form of Cartesian Anxiety.

2. *Do Rorty's statements about knowledge performatively contradict his own intellectual performance, and does he perform exactly as Lonergan predicts?* While we can ignore the transcendental precepts in our judgments, and while we can develop epistemologies and metaphysics inconsistent with cognitional theory, we cannot, as a matter of fact, *operate* in any fashion other than as Lonergan describes. We just simply do perform the cognitional acts of experience, understanding and judgment, and it just is these acts which constitute consciousness. Further, while the cognitional acts might be refined or described with additional clarity, they cannot be fundamentally revised without performative contradiction, as to revise them is to exercise attentiveness, intelligence and reasonability. Consequently, even as Rorty denies that humans are cognitively self-transcendent, he performs the three cognitive acts in developing his own arguments and critiquing others. His explicit statements about knowing, objectivity and reality performatively contradict the exigencies of his own intellect. Since Lonergan's account is invariant, and since Rorty's account contradicts his own performance, I conclude that Rorty's thought is counterpositional.

3. *Can Lonergan's dependence on the pure desire to know survive Rorty's critique of such a desire?* Rorty's critique rests on two flawed assumptions. First, his criticism of the desire for Truth is a criticism only of the intuitionist's version of truth, but since he incorrectly reduces all realisms to versions of intuitionism his arguments do not apply to critical realism. Second, his rejection of Truth assumes a counterpositional version of nominalism easily addressed by Lonergan. Subsequently, a complete turn to the subject in intentionality analysis allows positions based in the empirically verified drives of our own intellects. Again, Rorty's own intellect betrays him here, for his own

activities demonstrate a desire for the real, properly understood. Further, as we noted several times, his refusal to accept the dynamic intentionalities of the three-fold operations places him at risk of the general bias of common sense, which is not only counterpositional but which risks the cycle of longer decline.

4. *Can Lonergan survive the linguistic turn or is he trapped by the Myth of the Given?* The subject of Chapter 5, we learned there how completely Lonergan breaks from the ocular metaphor with its dependence on foundational knowledge given immediately or through privileged representations. Lonergan depends instead on the foundational acts of our own intellects, and while the categorical content of our vantage points, languages, horizons, and common senses are historical, mediated and contextual, the normative precepts founded upon our own performances are transcendental. Not only does fully human knowing exist in the world of mediation, but much of Lonergan's project was assisting in the *aggiornamento* from classicist to empirical culture with its pluralism of the categorical. Only the intuitionist, however, is overly concerned about contributions to knowing made on the side of the subject and his context; the critical realist rejects the demand for the immediate but grounds experiential objectivity as well as epistemological normativity in the transcendental precepts mediated categorically by a situation.

5. *Given the normative standards inherent in the Transcendental Method, can Lonergan (a) provide more adequate notions of epistemic progress, and (b) can Lonergan's solution provide a more adequate motivation for ongoing conversation and thus co-opt Rorty's own position?* Lonergan's account is not a conversation-stopper; in fact, his emphasis on the pure desire to know and the need for questions of intelligence and reasonability guarantees the need for the further question. But the further question is genuine inquiry, not just the gossip of the salon. The inquiry of conversation tends to converge on the truth insofar as it accords with the transcendental precepts and follows the normative exigencies of the pure, disinterested desire to know. Progress is made, then, insofar as more data is attended to, insofar as insights are intelligently conceived and insofar as more relevant critical questions are considered. Rorty's dependence on the *ethnos* risks group bias, which coupled with the general bias of his common sense pragmatism risks the shorter and longer cycles of decline and the end of fruitful inquiry and conversation.

In the end, Rorty, like Nietzsche, assists those too easily tempted by naïve realism but fails in his prescriptions. Lonergan, however, provides an invariant account consistent with our own experience, intelligence and reasonability.

7.3 CONCLUSION

Both Rorty and Lonergan engage in fundamental questions of the nature and efficacy of human rationality. This ensures that their thought is germane to virtually every human endeavor. Both offer versions of an organon, and their methods thus impact matters far beyond the scope of this investigation. In recent years, Rorty has written extensively on politics and education in ways fundamentally deriving from his earlier work on knowing. Lonergan, too, is relevant to education, politics, economics, psychology, ethics, theology and so on, sometimes writing explicitly but just as often creating a *way* to think about these subjects. In a manner somewhat analogous to Aristotle, Lonergan gives us a way to begin investigations already possessing a notion of what a good answer would be like and what sorts of answers ought to prompt our suspicion. Further, since Lonergan gives us a rational and critically grounded realism, he allows realism to pervade every aspect of human activity, although, to be sure, we must remember that such realism is not classicist but admits of a great deal of variety in its categorical determinations.

It is precisely with the distinction between classicist and empirical culture that we ascertain the fundamental disjunct between the two thinkers. Rorty has not abandoned modernity and is still committed to the self-aggrandizing Enlightenment story of public liberty and private perfectibility, but he has stripped it of its epistemological pretensions. But this is a tired story, just as all of modernity is tired, sinking beneath its own weight and increasingly vulnerable to the voices of its opponents. And Rorty's insistent defense of liberalism seems a bit tired, too, especially given its complete and utter inability to normatively defend itself against its critics, just as Rorty admits. Eventually a story incapable of defense is seen as just myth and a crisis of meaning develops.

But Lonergan is no alarmist. We do not see him crying "Vandals at the gate!" or turning to St. Benedict. He knows that modernity has not fully understood itself and that many of its pretensions collapse under their own counterpositional irrationality. The answer was the development of a new organon for a New Enlightenment. Such a new organon would take years to develop, decades to perfect and generations to teach:

> Classical culture cannot be jettisoned without being replaced; and what replaces it cannot but run counter to classical expectations. There is bound to be formed a solid right that is determined to live in a world that no longer exists. There is bound to be formed a scattered left, captivated by now this, now that new development, exploring now this and now that new possibility. But what will count is a perhaps not numerous center, big enough to be at home in both the old and the new, painstaking enough to work out one by one the transitions to be made, strong enough to refuse half-measures and insist on complete solutions even though it has to wait. (LR 400-401)

But this is fundamentally a hopeful endeavor. Icarus and Prometheus, the twin icons of modernity, are fallen and bound. Rorty would have us admit their philosophical failure while struggling to complete their political aspirations. Lonergan's is the longer and harder way; not trying to overcome our place we patiently retrace our steps, all the while grasping firmly to the golden cord of intellectual conversion until we, like both Theseus and the Platonic prisoner, escape the shadows for the really real.

SELECTED BIBLIOGRAPHY

BERNARD LONERGAN

Lonergan, Bernard J. F.. 1966. *Collection: Papers by Bernard Lonergan, SJ.* Edited by Frederick E. Crowe. New York: Herder and Herder.

———. 1972. *Method in Theology.* New York: Seabury Press.

———. 1974. *A Second Collection.* Edited by William F.J. Ryan and Bernard J. Tyrrell. Toronto: University of Toronto Press.

———. 1990. *Collected Works of Bernard Lonergan.* Edited by Elizabeth A. Morelli and Mark D. Morelli. Vol. 5, *Understanding and Being: The Halifax Lectures on INSIGHT.* Toronto: University of Toronto Press.

———. 1997. *Collected Works of Bernard Lonergan.* Edited by Frederick E. Crowe and
Robert M. Doran. Vol. 2, *Verbum: Word and Idea in Aquinas.* Toronto: University of Toronto Press.

———. 1997. *Collected Works of Bernard Lonergan.* Edited by Frederick E. Crowe and Robert M. Doran. Vol. 3, *Insight: A Study of Human Understanding.* Toronto: University of Toronto Press.

———. 1997. *The Lonergan Reader,* Edited by Mark D. Morelli and Elizabeth A. Morelli. Toronto: University of Toronto Press.

———. 2001. *Collected Works of Bernard Lonergan.* Edited by Philip McShane. Vol. 18, *Phenomenology and Logic: The Boston College Lectures on Mathematical Logic and Existentialism.* Toronto: University of Toronto Press.

RICHARD RORTY

Rorty, Richard. 1967. *The Linguistic Turn: Recent Essays in Philosophical Method.* Chicago: University of Chicago Press.

———. 1979. *Philosophy and the Mirror of Nature.* Princeton: Princeton University Press.

———. 1982. *Consequences of Pragmatism.* Minneapolis: University of Minnesota Press.

———. 1984. "The histiography of philosophy: four genres." In *Philosophy in History: Essays on the historiography of philosophy,* ed.

Richard Rorty, J. B. Schneewind and Quentin Skinner, 49-75. New York: Cambridge University Press.

———. 1989. *Contingency, irony and solidarity*. New York: Cambridge University Press.

———. 1990. "Truth and Freedom: A Reply to Thomas McCarthy." *Critical Inquiry* 16: 633-643.

———. 1991. *Philosophical Papers*. Vol. 1, *Objectivism, Relativism, and Truth*. New York: Cambridge University Press.

———. 1991. *Philosophical Papers*. Vol. 2, *Essays on Heidegger and Others*. New York: Cambridge University Press.

———. 1996. "The Ambiguity of Rationality." *Constellations* 3: 73-82.

———. 1997. *Truth, Politics and 'Post-Modernism'*. Amsterdam: Van Gorcum.

———. 1998. *Achieving Our Country*. Cambridge, MA: Harvard University Press.

———. 1998. *Philosophical Papers*. Vol. 3. *Truth and Progress*. New York: Cambridge University Press.

———. 1999. *Philosophy and Social Hope*. New York: Penguin.

———. 2000. "Universality and Truth." In *Rorty and His Critics*. Edited by Robert B. Brandom. Malden, MA: Blackwell.

SECONDARY TEXTS

Allen, Barry. 2000. "What was Epistemology?" In *Rorty and His Critics*. Edited by Robert B. Brandom. Malden, MA: Blackwell.

Augustine. 1958. *City of God*. Edited by Vernon J. Bourke. Translated by Gerald G. Walsh et al. New York: Image Books.

———. 1991. *The Trinity*. Translated by Edmund Hill. Brooklyn, NY: New City Press.

———. 1993. *Confessions*. Translated by F. J. Sheed. Indianapolis, IN: Hackett.

———. 1993. *On Free Choice of the Will*. Translated by Thomas Williams. Indianapolis, IN: Hackett.

———. 1995. *Against the Academicians*. Translated by Peter King. Indianapolis, IN: Hackett.

———. 1995. *The Teacher*. Translated by Peter King. Indianapolis, IN: Hackett.

Barden, Garrett. 1986. "Insight and Mirrors." *Method: Journal of Lonergan Studies* 4: 85-104.

Baynes, Kenneth, James Bohman and Thomas McCarthy, eds. 1987. *After Philosophy: End or Transformation?* Cambridge, MA: MIT Press.

Beards, Andrew. 1987. "Übersicht as Oversight: Problems in Wittgenstein's Later Philosophy." *Method: Journal of Lonergan Studies* 5: 1-17.

————. 1997. *Objectivity and Historical Understanding*. Aldershot, UK: Avebury.

Bernstein, Richard J. 1985. "Philosophy in the Conversation of Mankind." In *Hermeneutics and Praxis*, ed. Robert Hollinger, 54-86. Notre Dame, IN: University of Notre Dame Press.

Bettoni, Efrem. 1961. *Duns Scotus: The Basic Principles of His Philosophy*. Washington, D.C.: The Catholic University of America Press.

Bloom, Allan. 1987. *The Closing of the American Mind: How Higher Education Has Failed Democracy and Impoverished the Souls of Today's Students*. New York: Simon and Schuster.

Blumenberg, Hans. 1983. *The Legitimacy of the Modern Age*. Translated by Robert H. Wallace. Cambridge, MA: MIT Press.

————. 1993. "Light as a Metaphor for Truth: Preliminary Stage of Philosophical Concept Formation." In *Modernity and the Hegemony of Vision*. Edited by David Michael Levin. Berkeley, University of California Press.

Bradley, Gerard V. 1994. "Inescapably a Liberal: Richard Rorty as Social Theorist." In *Liberalism at the Crossroads: An Introduction to Contemporary Liberal Political Theory and its Critics*. Lanham, MD: Rowman & Littlefield.

Brandom, Robert B., ed. 2000. *Rorty and His Critics*. Malden, MA: Blackwell.

Byrne, Patrick H. 1986. "The Fabric of Lonergan's Thought." In *Lonergan Workshop*. Volume 6, ed. Frederick G. Lawrence. Atlanta: Scholar's Press, 1986.

————. 2002. "Lonergan's Retrieval of Aristotelian Form." *American Catholic Philosophical Quarterly* 76: 371-392.

Conn, Walter E. 1977. "Transcendental Analysis of Conscious Subjectivity: Bernard Lonergan's Empirical Methodology." *The Modern Schoolman* 54: 215-231.

Corcoran, Patrick, ed. 1975. *Looking at Lonergan's Method.* Dublin: Talbot Press.

Crowe, Frederick. 1980. *Method in Theology: An Organon for Our Time.* Milwaukee: Marquette University Press.

———. 1992. *Lonergan.* London: Geoffrey Chapman.

———. 1993. "Neither Jew nor Greek, but one Human Nature and Operation in All." In *Communication and Lonergan: Common Ground for Forging the New Age,* eds. Thomas J. Farrell and Paul A. Soukup, 89-107. Kansas City, MO: Sheed and Ward.

Dancy, Jonathan. 1985. *Introduction to Contemporary Epistemology.* Oxford: Basil Blackwell.

Day, Sebastian J. 1947. *Intuitive Cognition: A Key to the Significance of the Later Scholastics.* St. Bonaventure, NY: The Franciscan Institute.

DeLillo, Don. 1991. *White Noise.* New York: Penguin.

Descartes, Rene. 1954. *Rules for the Direction of the Mind.* In *Descartes Philosophical Writings.* Translated by Elizabeth Anscombe and Peter Thomas Geach. London: Thomas Nelson and Sons.

———. 1998. *Discourse on Method* and *Meditations on First Philosophy.* Fourth Edition. Translated by Donald A. Cress. Indianapolis, IN: Hackett.

Dewey, John. 1929. *The Quest for Certainty: A Study of the Relation of Knowledge and Action.* New York: Minton, Balch & Company.

Dupré, Louis. 1993. *Passage to Modernity: An Essay in the Hermeneutics of Nature and Culture.* New Haven: Yale University Press.

Edgerton, S. 1976. *The Renaissance Rediscovery of Linear Perspective.* New York: Harper and Row.

Eliot, T. S. 1968. *Four Quartets.* San Diego, CA: Harvest Books.

Hall, David L. 1994. *Richard Rorty: Prophet and Poet of the New Pragmatism.* Albany, NY: SUNY Press.

Farrell, Thomas J. and Paul A. Soukup, eds. 1993. *Communication and Lonergan: Common Ground for Forging the New Age.* Kansas City, MO: Sheed and Ward.

Fitzpatrick, Joseph. 1992. "Lonergan and the Later Wittgenstein." *Method: Journal of Lonergan Studies* 10: 27-50.

———. 1995. "'Town Criers of Inwardness' or Reflections on Rorty." *Method: Journal of Lonergan Studies* 13: 1-33.

Flanagan, Joseph. 1972. "Knowing and language in the thought of Bernard Lonergan." In *Language Truth and Meaning: Papers from* the *International Lonergan Congress 1970*, ed. Philip McShane, 49-78. Notre Dame, IN: University of Notre Dame Press.

————. 1997. *Quest for Self-Knowledge: An Essay in Lonergan's Philosophy*. Toronto: University of Toronto Press.

Gillespie, Michael Allen. 1995. *Nihilism Before Nietzsche*. Chicago: University of Chicago Press.

Gilson, Étienne. 1929. *The Philosophy of St. Thomas Aquinas*. Translated by Edward Bullough. Edited by Rev. G. A. Elrington. New York: Dorset Press.

————. 1937. *The Unity of Philosophical Experience*. New York: Scribner's Sons.

————. 1990. *Methodical Realism*. Front Royal, VA: Christendom Press.

Gregson, Vernon, ed. 1988. *The Desires of the Human Heart: An Introduction to the Theology of Bernard Lonergan*. New York: Paulist Press.

Grieco, Eileen. 1996. "Concupiscence and Benevolence in the Thomistic Epistemology of Maritain, Lonergan and Rahner." *Method: Journal of Lonergan Studies* 14: 155-182.

Habermas, Jürgen. 2000. "Richard Rorty's Pragmatic Turn." In *Rorty and His Critics*, ed. Robert B. Brandom, 31-55. Malden, MA: Blackwell.

Harrison, Stanley. 1986. "Our Glassy Essence: A Peircean Response to Richard Rorty." *International Philosophical Quarterly* 26: 169-181.

Hollinger, Robert, ed. 1985. *Hermeneutics and Praxis*. Notre Dame, IN: University of Notre Dame Press.

Jaeger, Werner. 1971. *Paideia: The Ideals of Greek Culture*. Vol. II, *In Search of the Divine Center*. Translated by Gilbert Highet. New York: Oxford University Press.

Jonas, Hans. 1963. *The Gnostic Religion: The message of the alien God and the beginnings of Christianity*. Second Edition. Boston: Beacon.

————. 2001. *The Phenomenon of Life: Toward a Philosophical Biology*. Evanston, IL: Northwestern University Press, 2001.

John Paul II. 1998. *Encyclical Letter, Fides et Ratio, of the Supreme Pontiff John Paul II: To the Bishops of the Catholic Church on the Relationship Between Faith and Reason*. Washington, DC: United States Catholic Conference.

Judovitz, Dalia. 1993. "Vision, Representation and Technology in Descartes." In *Modernity and the Hegemony of Vision*, ed. David Michael Levin, 63-86. Berkeley, University of California Press.

Kant, Immanuel. 1996. *Critique of Pure Reason*. Translated by Werner S. Pluhar. Indianapolis, IN: Hackett.

Kerr, Fergus. 1975. "Objections to Lonergan's Method." *New Blackfriars* 56: 305-317.

————. 1976. "Beyond Lonergan's Method: A Response to William Matthews." *New Blackfriars* 57: 59-71.

————. 1986. *Theology After Wittgenstein*. New York: Basil Blackwell.

Kidder, Paul. 1990. "Lonergan's Negative Dialectic." *International Philosophical Quarterly* 30: 299-309.

Kitcher, Patricia W.1996. Introduction to *Critique of Pure Reason*, by Immanuel Kant. Translated by Werner S. Pluhar, xxv-lix. Indianapolis, IN: Hackett.

Kulp, Christopher B. 1992. *The End of Epistemology: Dewey and His Current Allies on the Spectator Theory of Knowledge*. Westport, CT: Greenwood Press.

Lamb, Matthew L., ed. 1981. *Creativity and Method: Essays in Honor of Bernard Lonergan, SJ*. Milwaukee, WI: Marquette University Press.

Lash, Nicholas. 1975. "Method and Cultural Discontinuity." In *Looking at Lonergan's Method*, ed. Patrick Corcoran, S.M., 127-143. Dublin: Talbot Press, 1975.

————. 1976. "In Defense of Lonergan's Critics." *New Blackfriars* 57 (1976): 124-126.

Lauer, Quentin. 1958. *Phenomenology: Its Genesis and Prospect*. New York: Harper Torchbooks.

Lawler, Peter Augustine. 2002. *Aliens in America: The Strange Truth About our Souls*. Wilmington, DE: ISI Books.

Lawrence, Frederick G. 1972. "Self-Knowledge in History in Gadamer and Lonergan." In *Language Truth and Meaning: Papers from the International Lonergan Congress 1970*, ed. Philip McShane, 167-217. Notre Dame, IN: University of Notre Dame Press.

————. 1980. "Gadamer and Lonergan: A Dialectical Comparison." *International Philosophical Quarterly* 20: 25-47.

————. 1993. "The Fragility of Consciousness: Lonergan and the Postmodern Concern for the Other." In *Communication and Loner-*

gan: Common Ground for Forging the New Age, eds. Thomas J. Farrell and Paul A. Soukup, 173-211. Kansas City, MO: Sheed and Ward.

―――. 2000. "Lonergan, the Integral Postmodern?" *Method: Journal of Lonergan Studies* 18: 95-122.

―――. 2002. "Lonergan and Aquinas: The Postmodern Problematic of Theology and Ethics." In *The Ethics of Aquinas*, ed. Stephen J. Pope, 437-455. Washington, D.C.: Georgetown University Press.

Levin, David Michael, ed. 1988. *The Opening of Vision: Nihilism and the Postmodern Situation*. New York: Routledge.

―――. 1993. *Modernity and the Hegemony of Vision*. Berkeley, University of California Press.

―――. 1999. *The Philosopher's Gaze: Modernity in the Shadow of Enlightenment*. Berkeley: University of California Press.

Malachowski, Alan. 2002. *Richard Rorty*. Princeton: Princeton University Press.

Marsh, James L. 1975. "Lonergan's Mediation of Subjectivity and Objectivity." *The Modern Schoolman* 52: 249-261.

―――. 1995. "Postmodernism: A Lonerganian Retrieval and Critique." *International Philosophical Quarterly* 35: 159-173.

―――. 2002. "Justice, Difference, and the Possibility of Metaphysics: Towards a North American Philosophy of Liberation." *Proceedings of the American Catholic Philosophical Association: Philosophy at the Boundary of Reason* 76: 57-76.

Matthews, Gareth B. 2001. "Knowledge and illumination." In *The Cambridge Companion to Augustine*, eds. Eleonore Stump and Norman Kretzmann, 171-185. New York: Cambridge University Press.

Matthews, William. 1976. "Lonergan's Awake: A Reply to Fergus Kerr." *New Blackfriars* 57: 11-21.

Matteo, Anthony M. 1992. *Quest for the Absolute: The Philosophical Vision of Joseph Maréchal*. DeKalb, IL: Northern Illinois University Press.

McCamy, Ronald. 1998. *Out of a Kantian Chrysalis? A Maritainian Critique of Fr. Maréchal*. New York: Peter Lang.

McCarthy, Michael H. 1990. *The Crisis of Philosophy*. Albany, NY: SUNY Press.

McCarthy, Thomas. 1990a. "Ironist Theory as a Vocation: A Response to Richard Rorty." *Critical Inquiry* 16: 644-655.

―――. 1990b. "Private Irony and Public Decency: Richard Rorty's New Pragmatism." *Critical Inquiry* 16: 355-370.

————. 1996. "Philosophy and Critical Theory: A Reply to Richard Rorty and Seyla Benhabib." *Constellations* 3: 95-103.

McGrath, Patrick. 1975. "Knowledge, Understanding and Reality: Some Questions Concerning Lonergan's Philosophy." In *Looking at Lonergan's Method*, ed. Patrick Corcoran, S.M., 27-41. Dublin: Talbot Press.

McDowell, John. 2000. "Towards Rehabilitating Objectivity." In *Rorty and His Critics*, ed. Robert B. Brandom. Malden, MA: Blackwell.

McPartland, Thomas J. 2001. *Lonergan and the Philosophy of Historical Existence*. Columbia, MO: University of Missouri Press.

McShane, Philip, ed. 1972. *Language Truth and Meaning: Papers from the International Lonergan Congress 1970*. Notre Dame, IN: University of Notre Dame Press.

Meynell, Hugo A. 1976. *An Introduction to the Philosophy of Bernard Lonergan*. New York: Barnes and Noble.

————. 1985. "Reversing Rorty." *Method: Journal of Lonergan Studies* 3: 31-48.

————. 1986. "Reply to Garrett Barden." *Method: Journal of Lonergan Studies* 4: 105-107.

————. 1993. "Philosophy after Philosophy." In *Communication and Lonergan: Common*
Ground for Forging the New Age, eds. Thomas J. Farrell and Paul A. Soukup, 137-152. Kansas City, MO: Sheed and Ward.

————. 1998. *Redirecting Philosophy: Reflections on the Nature of Knowledge from Plato to Lonergan*. Toronto: University of Toronto Press.

————. 1999. *Postmodernism and the New Enlightenment*. Washington, D.C.: The Catholic University of America Press.

Milbank, John, and Catherine Pickstock. 2001. *Truth in Aquinas*. New York: Routledge.

Morelli, Elizabeth. 1990. "A Reflection on Lonergan's Notion of the Pure Desire to Know. Remarks on F. E. Crowe's Essay Entitled 'Bernard Lonergan's Thought on Ultimate Reality and Meaning, URAM 4: 58-89." *Ultimate Reality and Meaning* 13: 50-60.

Muck, Otto. 1968. *The Transcendental Method*. New York: Herder and Herder.

Nielsen, Kai. 1991. *After the Demise of the Tradition: Rorty, Critical Theory, and the Fate of Philosophy*. Boulder, CO: Westview Press.

O'Daly, Gerard. 2001. "The response to skepticism and the mechanisms of cognition." In *The Cambridge Companion to Augustine*, eds. Eleonore Stump and Norman Kretzmann, 159-170. New York: Cambridge University Press.

Orenstein, Alex. 2002. *W. V. Quine*. Princeton: Princeton University Press.

Pannenberg, Wolfhart. 1975. "History and Meaning in Bernard Lonergan's Approach to Theological Method." In *Looking at Lonergan's Method*, ed. Patrick Corcoran, S.M., 88-100. Dublin: Talbot Press.

Plato. 1989. *The Collected Dialogues of Plato*. Edited by Edith Hamilton and Huntington Cairns. Princeton: Princeton University Press.

Pope, Stephen J., ed. 2002. *The Ethics of Aquinas*. Washington, D.C.: Georgetown University Press.

Potter, Vincent G. 1992. `Peirce on "Substance" and "Foundations". *The Monist* 75: 492-503.

————. 1994. "Objective Chance: Lonergan and Peirce on Scientific Generalization." *Method: Journal of Lonergan Studies* 12: 91-107.

Quine, W. V., and J.S. Ullian. 1970. *The Web of Belief*. New York: Random House.

Rehg, William. 1994. *Insight and Solidarity: A Study in the Discourse Ethics of Jürgen Habermas*. Berkeley: University of California Press.

Ricoeur, Paul. 1967. *The Symbolism of Evil*. Translated by Emerson Buchanan. Boston: Beacon.

————. 1992. *Oneself as Another*. Translated by Kathleen Blamey. Chicago: University of Chicago Press.

Ryan, William F. J. 1973. "Intentionality in Edmund Husserl and Bernard Lonergan." *International Philosophical Quarterly* 23: 173-190.

Sala, Giovanni B. 1994. *Lonergan and Kant: Five Essays on Human Knowledge*. Translated by Joseph Spoerl. Edited by Robert M. Doran. Toronto: University of Toronto Press.

Stump, Eleonore and Norman Kretzmann, eds. 2001. *The Cambridge Companion to Augustine*. New York: Cambridge University Press.

Topping, Richard R. 1993. "Transcendental Method and Private Language." *ARC* 21: 11-26.

Vaden House, D. 1994. *Without God or His Doubles: Realism, Relativism and Rorty*. Leiden: E.J. Brill.

Vertin, Michael. 2001. "Transcendental Philosophy and Linguistic Philosophy." *Method: Journal of Lonergan Studies* 19: 253-280.

Voegelin, Eric. 1990. *Anamnesis*. Translated by Gerhart Niemeyer. Columbia, MO: University of Missouri Press.

Warnke, Georgia. 1987. *Gadamer: Hermeneutics, Tradition and Reason*. Stanford: Stanford University Press.

Williams, Michael. 2000. "Epistemology and the Mirror of Nature." In *Rorty and His Critics*, ed. Robert B. Brandom. Malden, MA: Blackwell.

Wittgenstein, Ludwig. 1958. *Philosophical Investigations*. Third Edition. Translated by G. E. M. Anscombe. New York: Macmillan.

———. 1961. *Tractatus Logico-Philosophicus*. Translated by D.F. Pears and B.F, McGuinness. London: Routledge and Kegan Paul.

Wolter, Allan B.1972."Duns Scotus, John." *Encyclopedia of Philosophy*. Edited by Paul Edwards. Vol. II. New York: Macmillan.